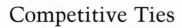

Competitive Ties

Studies of the East Asian Institute,
Columbia University

Competitive Ties

Subcontracting in the Japanese
Automotive Industry

Michael J. Smitka

Columbia University Press
New York

Columbia University Press

New York   Oxford

Copyright © 1991 Columbia University Press
All rights reserved

Library of Congress Cataloging-in-Publication Data

Smitka, Michael.
Competitive ties : subcontracting in the Japanese
automotive industry / Michael J. Smitka.
p. cm.—(Studies of the East Asian Institute, Columbia
University)
Includes bibliographical references and index.
ISBN 0-231-07282-1
1. Automobile industry and trade—Japan—Subcontract-
ing. 2. Motor vehicle industry—Japan—Subcontract-
ing. I. Title. II. Series:
Studies of the East Asian Institute.
HD9710.J32S59 1991
338.4'76292'0952—dc20   91-6713
CIP

Studies of the East Asian Institute, Columbia University

The East Asian Institute is Columbia University's center for research, publication, and teaching on modern East Asia. The Studies of the East Asian Institute were inaugurated in 1962 to bring to a wider public the results of significant new research on modern and contemporary East Asia. A Study of the East Asian Institute.

To Gloria, Mayumi, and John

Contents

Figures

Tables

Acknowledgments

The genesis of this book was the first paper I did as a graduate student at Yale in 1980. In that paper I wanted to see what, if any, role subcontracting had in the rapid technical change in Japanese manufacturing in the 1930s and the early post-WWII era. I continued to study and think about subcontracting for the next ten years. While my theoretical emphasis shifted from economic development to contracting and the theory of the firm, I ultimately concluded that the main benefit of subcontracting was, indeed, its contribution to innovation and the diffusion of technology. I have been unable to visit Japan more than briefly since 1984, and so have not been able to include data on the turbulent period since then, when the yen doubled in value. That many Japanese firms have remained competitive in markets overseas, however, suggests that increases in productivity have continued apace with those of the 1960s. I am eager to see what has changed when an upcoming sabbatical will permit me to again spend a year in Japan.

After ten years of work on this and related topics, I find that much of what I might say has been left out. I am afraid the same is true for these acknowledgments. Many names will be left out, particularly those of individuals whom I interviewed during the course of this research (some explicitly requested anonymity). I apologize to any whose contribution is thus slighted; specific citations are on pages xiii–xiv, below.

First and foremost, I want to thank my wife, who gave up a two-income no-kids life in Manhattan to begin supporting her graduate-student husband and (before long) two children. She also was willing to adapt to life in Japan. I similarly thank my children, who have never known "daddy" without dissertation or book; I pray they have not suffered thereby.

Second, I received financial support from many sources besides my wife. While I was a graduate student, the Committee on Japanese Economic Studies and Yale University provided fellowships. The Committee on Japanese Economic Studies also funded research in Japan in summer 1982. A Fulbright Doctoral Dissertation Research Abroad Fellowship administered by the U.S. Department of Education underwrote my research in Japan during 1983–1984. A Mellon Grant provided release time at Washington and Lee University. W&L also provided secretarial and other assistance, including covering substantial copying and mailing expenses.

I benefited from the input of many individuals. Robert Chapman Wood, Hugh Patrick and Gary Saxonhouse encouraged me to take up economics. Gary Saxonhouse and Mr. Kudo of the Ministry of International Trade and Industry arranged a summer 1982 internship in the Research Department of the Medium and Small Business Agency in Tokyo, while Shintaro Takagi graciously offered my family the use of his house. Konosuke Odaka served as my adviser at Hitotsubashi University during 1983–1984, and I only regret that I did not make a greater effort to learn from him. Takafusa Nakamura permitted me to participate in his University of Tokyo seminar and Akira Goto invited me to the Tokyo-area industrial organization workshop. In addition, Masayoshi Ikeda, Shoichiro Sei, Akira Umeki, Y. Nabejima and others taught me about the auto parts industry, introduced me to firms, and guided me to the published literature. Of course, this research would not have been possible without the active cooperation of individuals in many firms. I thank in particular the staff at Mitsubishi Motors, Kachikachi Corporation, Eagle Wings Industries, Diamond Star Motors, the Soja Industrial Park and Suzuki Bankin. Finally, among other friends, Katsuhiko Adachi, Hitoshi Kobayashi, Tetsuo Machida, Yoshiaki Obara, Koichi Ohtawa, Masaaki Ogasawara, Greg Rubinstein, Michitaka Suzuki, and Caroline Willis and their families contributed immeasurably to my understanding of Japan. I also valued the chance to fellowship in (depending on locus) Baptist, Episcopal, Lutheran and Presbyterian churches, and with "internationals" in the U.S. and Japan.

I benefited from discussions and other assistance from

Masahiko Aoki, Banri Asanuma, Phyllis Genther, Akifumi Goto, Junichi Goto, Kenichi Imai, Anil Khosla, Kazuo Koike, Mark Komaki, Toshihiro Nishiguchi, Yuzo Ohkawa, Thomas Rohlen, Koichi Shimokawa, Steven Nussbaum, Kotaro Suzumura and many others. For many constructive comments I thank participants in the Yale Trade and Development Workshop, the Ph.D. Kenkyu Kai, the Japan Economic Seminar, and seminars or paper presentations at Earlham College, Eastern Michigan University, Washington and Lee University, North Carolina State University, Virginia Polytechnic Institute, the Association of Japanese Business Studies and the Business History Conference. David Flath, Josh Haimson, Koichi Hamada, Susan Helper, Bruce Herrick, Jeff Homan, Carl Kaiser, Toshihiro Nishiguchi, Mari Sako, Lad Sessions, Fred Smith, Robert Chapman Wood and an anonymous referee read and commented on drafts. Bill Nelson proofread an early version, and Donna Hollifield, Lyn Hammet, Flora Day, Mary Bobenia, Anne Zeigler and Anna Claytor provided secretarial assistance.

In closing, the economics faculty at Yale University were crucial to my learning economics. I am glad that they were without exception dedicated to teaching and not just research. I find to my surprise that I cannot single out any one of them as having been "the" most influential intellectually. However, Hugh Patrick merits special mention for serving as a friend and supporter, not only of myself, but also of many others interested in the Japanese economy. He stimulated me to continue with my interest in Japan, and offered encouragement through courses, comprehensive exams, orals, fellowship applications and job hunting. He and my other dissertation advisers, Oliver E. Williamson and Merton (Joe) Peck, were all most helpful. They were willing to read through the roughest of draft material. All have had more impact than they realize. I thank them for wisdom, help and patience.

Those whom I interviewed and cite by name all graciously permitted me to use the information they provided. In addition, I thank the following authors and publishers for granting me permission to cite their works.

Tables 2.1, 2.2, and 2.3: Professor Kikutaro Takizawa, for permission to cite from his 1966 article, "Kozo Hendo Katei ni okeru Chusho Kikai Kogyo no Zonritsu Kiban" (The Economic Base of Small Scale Manufacturing in the Face of Structural Change), *Chosa*

Geppo (Chuso Kigo Kinyu Koko) (March), 7(4):11–45 and his 1963 article, "Jidosha Kogyo ni okeru Shitauke Keiretsu Kozo" (The Changing Structure of Subcontracting in the Automotive Industry), *Shoko Kinyu* (June), 33(6):3–26.

Tables 3.1, 3.2, and 3.3: Nihon Hyoron Sha, for permission to cite Seiji Nakamura, *Nihon no Jidosha Kogyo* (The Japanese Automotive Industry), Tokyo: Nihon Hyoron Sha, 1957.

Table 3.3: Aki Shobo, for permission to cite Shogo Amagai *Nihon Jidosha Kogyo no Shiteki Tenkai* (Historical Perspective on the Japanese Automotive Industry), Tokyo: Aki Shobo, 1982.

Tables 3.4 and 3.6: Aki Shobo, for permission to cite Katsumi Kodaira, *Jidosha* (Automobiles), Tokyo: Aki Shobo, 1968.

Table 3.5: Professor Konosuke Odaka and his colleagues for permission to cite pp. 302–303 of their *The Automotbile Industry in Japan: A Study in Ancillary Firm Development*. Tokyo: Kinokuniya Company and Oxford University Press, 1988.

Tables 3.1 and 3.5: Dr. Phyllis Genther, for permission to cite her "The Changing Government-Business Relationship: Japan's Passenger Car Industry," Ph.D. dissertation, George Washington University, 1986.

Table 5.1: Kato Shatai Kogyo, permission to cite *Michi: Kato Shatai Kogyo 70 Nen no Ayumi* (Paths; The 70–Year Journey of Kato Auto Body), Ebina City, Kanagawa Prefecture: Kato Shatai Kogyo, 1971.

Competitive Ties

ONE

Overview

The Benefits of Subcontracting

In 1950, Nissan and Toyota together assembled a mere 1,300 cars, the entire industry only slightly more. Imports from the U.S. and Europe dominated the Japanese market, despite a 40% tariff and other trade barriers. By the auto makers' own accounts, quality was poor and productivity abysmal. In fact, then-Governor Ichimada of the Bank of Japan felt it was better to rely on imports, and fought against additional protection for the industry. The government overruled him and excluded foreign cars from the Japanese domestic market after 1956. This protection permitted the fledgling auto companies to survive, but it did not guarantee that they would ever come to match their erstwhile foreign competitors.

Forty years later it is the American and European industries that suffer in quality and cost comparisons, and operate behind trade barriers that limit the import of Japanese vehicles. Nevertheless, in 1989 Japanese auto firms supplied 30% of the cars sold in the U.S., including the one million units they assembled in the U.S. and Canada.[1] While the U.S. Big Three—GM, Ford and Chrysler— have significantly improved their productivity and quality during the past ten years, they continue to trail Japanese-operated assembly plants, including the Japanese "transplants" (Krafcik 1988a, 1988b, 1988c). Perhaps more important, in the mid-1980s the Big Three required 50% more time and twice as much money as the Japanese to develop and launch a new car (K. Clark et al. 1987), and the rapidity of recent Japanese new model announcements suggests this gap has since widened. The Japanese auto firms thus continue to gain market share over their less maneuverable U.S. (and European) rivals, as they adapt and expand their product lines for changing markets (Sheriff 1988; Womack et al. 1990).

How did the Japanese auto firms catch up? While government protection allowed the domestic manufacturers to survive, it was stiff competition in the domestic market that kept firms on their toes. The number of small car assemblers expanded from three in 1950 to ten in 1965, in the face of Japanese government efforts to limit new entry. In addition, Nissan, Toyota and their contemporary rivals knew they were backward and could readily enhance productivity and quality. With a growing number of rivals, they had to if they were to survive. The auto firms thus worked hard to improve functional design and lower their own production costs. In their efforts to hold the competition at bay, they adopted many innovative approaches in manufacturing, often borrowing management techniques and licensing technology from the U.S. Not only did they aggressively invest in better production facilities (helped by a rapidly expanding market), but they also worked to improve the skills of their workforce and managers. Firms, in other words, developed their internal resources.

But the Japanese automotive assemblers also mobilized and developed a key external resource, their suppliers. This "strategic alliance," in fact, was a central element of their competitive strategy. Purchasing was not a mere clerical function that sought after low-priced parts; rather, it played a vital role in product development and manufacturing. Historically, suppliers in the automotive industry helped firms:

- o enter the industry. After 1945 would-be auto makers avoided the expense of building parts plants by turning to factories that still had idle capacity.

- o lessen the strength of a radical labor movement. By using suppliers, Toyota increased output five-fold during 1952–1957 while its workforce rose only 15%.

- o lower unit costs. An egalitarian social ethic restricted large firms' ability to make wage distinctions among workers. Outside suppliers, however, could pay rural and other segments of the labor force lower wages.

However, the most important element was that this strategy let firms:

o tap the entrepreneurial vitality of the small firms, which
   employed most of Japan's skilled workers.

Over time suppliers worked harder to improve their product
and cut costs than did the auto firms' own plants. Parts factories
operated directly by an auto company—the standard U.S. Big Three
practice—typically have no direct competitors to keep them on
their toes, nor do managers reap large rewards from improved performance. In contrast, most Japanese suppliers were family businesses, and cutting costs translated directly into better performance: profits for themselves, a better future for employees, or,
when rivalry was strong, survival instead of bankruptcy. Furthermore, since purchases in the Japanese auto industry made up 70%
of total manufacturing costs, continual small improvements in supplier operations were crucial to the success of the Japanese automotive industry. Thus, while during 1958–1965 the Japanese assemblers halved the cost of making a car, 54% of the reduction
stemmed from lower purchased parts prices, 16% from lower steel
and materials prices, and only 32% from their own internal cost
savings (see table 2.7). Subcontracting was thus integral to success
in the domestic market, as well as to the eventual achievement of
international competitiveness: it permitted management to mobilize not only internal but also external resources.

The "How" of Subcontracting

It is how parts are purchased that determines the benefits, not
the mere volume of subcontracting. Purchases make up about 70%
of Chrysler's manufacturing costs, roughly the level of the Japanese
auto firms. Until recently, however, Chrysler did not employ suppliers as a positive resource for change. Instead, it (and the other
U.S. firms) utilized as many as 10,000 suppliers, playing them off
against one another through annual competitive bids. Often, in fact,
the auto companies bought the same part from several firms. Without the assurance of future orders, however, suppliers naturally
limited their investment in modern machinery. Similarly, they were
reluctant to innovate; proprietary designs could hardly be put out
for competitive bids. Thus, by seeking cheap parts, the Big Three
often ended up purchasing problems (Helper 1990a).

In contrast to the U.S. Big Three, the Japanese automotive
firms purchased parts on an ongoing basis from a stable group of

200–300 subcontractors. With a reasonable assurance of orders, these suppliers invested aggressively in better facilities. Furthermore, they were encouraged by the auto firms to undertake development projects, and at present account for half of the engineering of a new model (K. Clark et al. 1987). Subcontractors likewise implemented statistical quality control and just-in-time production systems tailored to their customer's needs. But to function, this system required innovations in subcontracting management.

Firms that depend on outside suppliers encounter two problems. First, the typical auto part is specific to one model of one manufacturer, and often requires expensive tooling or dedicated production lines. A supplier thus has only one customer for a given part; in turn, the need for tooling makes it costly for an auto company to use multiple suppliers. The two firms become interdependent, but managing such an interdependent relationship is very difficult on an ongoing basis, while the real gains from subcontracting are only realized over time. How can the supplier be assured that, after investing, its customer does not use the threat of taking business elsewhere to beat down price? (A supplier could similarly hold out at the last minute for a higher price.) This is related to the second problem: if the supplier is assured of orders, what incentive does it have to provide quality parts or to control costs? In fact, the U.S. automotive industry was generally unsuccessful in managing interdependence with suppliers (Klein et al. 1978; but see Helper 1990c).[2] Instead, the Big Three integrated vertically, relying on their own parts manufacturing operations, or purchased simple parts under short-term competitive contracts.[3]

Auto firms in Japan, however, made two sets of innovations that let them better manage interdependency. These were:

o a conscious reliance on trust as a tool for governing relationships, and

o the pricing of parts using historic costs and comparisons with one or at most two other firms.

This combination created an environment within which the Japanese auto firms (and their suppliers) were willing to invest in formal and informal mechanisms for coordinating design, engineering and production. This stopped far short, however, of integrating suppliers into the hierarchical controls of a firm. At the same time, while the pricing mechanism was standardized and formal contracts were used for actual parts purchases, no contract detailed the overall relationship. The subcontracting relationship was thus governed neither by market nor by hierarchy.[4]

Instead, trust was employed to govern the relationship. One element was personal trust: both parties put themselves at risk of loss, without assurance of long-term gain, out of the belief that the other party would not take unfair advantage of them.[5] Both sides, of course, discussed their expectations for the long run, while seeking sanctions and enticements to lessen the need for trust. But in the end mutual trust remained central. Ultimately neither side had much recourse to outside authority, nor could they structure the relationship so that each side would want automatically to hold up their end. Firms sought to avoid a climate where each action was greeted with suspicion, with the consequent necessity to dot every *i* and cross every *t*. Cooperation in such a case would inevitably break down. They instead sought to create an atmosphere where each other's claims would be taken at face value—at least in the first instance.

Creating trust (and subsequently maintaining it) required investment. The techniques employed by the Japanese auto firms included:

- o the gradual expansion of a purchasing relationship, so that interdependence was limited until trust was established. New business was initiated only after a long period of courtship, socializing and small orders.

- o investments by both sides in the transaction. Commitment was thus made concrete as the relationship developed— which of course lessened the reliance on personal trust.

- o the establishment of clear norms for business behavior. Standards were created for pricing, quality, delivery and ordering, which limited the room for disputes.

- o the creation of reputation. The auto firms routinely brought suppliers together, so that untrustworthy behavior could not be hidden while trusting behavior was advertised.

In practice supplier cooperation associations (*kyoryoku kai*) played a major role. Each Japanese auto company (except Honda) has maintained a cooperation association of which all direct parts suppliers are members. (Some firms also have associations for their suppliers of steel and other materials, and for machine tool builders and other suppliers of capital goods.) The cooperation associations provided a forum in which auto company management discussed future trends and business plans, and served as a nexus for golf games and other social activities. Both enhanced personal trust and the flow of information that undergird reputation. (In addition, technical subcommittees helped diffuse best practice in manufacturing and management.) In short, purchaser and supplier expended resources to demonstrate their trustworthiness, and to foster trust among top managers.

Yet rivalry was maintained, despite such close ties, and even though this would at first glance seem inimical to trust. This was achieved through the careful collection of relevant information from suppliers, backed up by the visible presence of one to three potential rivals. First, suppliers presented cost breakdowns by manufacturing process as part of their bid. To keep suppliers honest, these direct costs were compared with those in previous bids, and with the costs of similar processes at other firms. (Indirect costs were accounted for separately.) In addition, there were potential rivals. While a supplier might produce small metal stampings for the doors of a given model, another firm would be making similar parts for a different model. As long as suppliers could match their rivals' prices and quality levels, they were guaranteed repeat business. Through gradually decreasing orders, firms that ran into short-run problems received a warning that could not be missed, while being given a chance to recover. Firms that betrayed trust and continued to perform poorly would eventually be dropped. Rivalry was thereby made credible without having to be cutthroat; trust was thus maintained. And, of course, both sides were conscious of their investments in the relationship and the consequent losses should it be disrupted.

The "Why" of Subcontracting

Despite the apparent benefits of subcontracting, Toyota, Nissan and Isuzu adopted the opposite policy in the 1930s: they tried to minimize their reliance on suppliers. While small firms did provide some stampings and other simple parts, as in Detroit, the fledgling auto producers made their own brakes, castings, and other subassemblies and critical components, as well as many simple parts. Likewise, both Toyota and Nissan set up captive suppliers of specialty steels. In the period leading up to 1950, therefore, they were vertically integrated.

This changed rapidly in the 1950s. The auto industry went through a series of bitter strikes in the face of layoffs from 1949 to 1954, and when output began to expand, the assemblers avoided rehiring by shifting work out to suppliers. The primary reason for subcontracting was thus to avoid renewed conflict with militant labor unions, and to support more tractable "second" unions (Gould 1984; Halberstam 1986). Hence, as noted above, employment at the automotive assemblers remained relatively stable throughout the 1950s, while that at suppliers rose. This motive continues today, albeit in a slightly different manner. Not only did the labor movement press for permanent employment, but in wage setting it also established an egalitarian ethic, which gradually became the norm for Japanese society as a whole. Under this ethic, firms found it difficult to make distinctions in compensation among their employees except (in the first instance) on the basis of age and gender, and to a lesser extent education. In particular, within a firm it was very difficult to make distinctions in pay between those who did skilled work and those carrying out unskilled tasks. Firms thus directly employed a relatively homogeneous group of individuals— and subcontracted both less-skilled work *and* more specialized tasks to other firms that drew their workers from a different segment of the labor market. While labor unions are no longer as militant today, this egalitarian ethic remains strong.

Other factors, many peculiar to the 1950s, also contributed to the adoption of a subcontracting strategy. In the face of booming demand, the most important of these were financing considerations. The number of small manufacturers expanded rapidly during the late 1930s and early 1940s, but the end of World War II left their facilities idle, and excess capacity remained into the late 1950s. Hence, by subcontracting parts production to such firms, industry output could be increased and yet neither the auto plants nor their new suppliers needed to find funds to finance additional capacity. This was critical, given the limited ability of the auto firms to borrow funds in the underdeveloped capital markets of the time. When in the late 1950s the automotive firms did begin building specialized assembly and engine plants, they continued to rely on outside suppliers, and did not invest in a comparable manner in building parts facilities. Indeed, they continued to shift additional parts production to outside suppliers.

In sum, a militant labor movement, an egalitarian ethic that affected wages, and the difficulty of directly financing new capacity all contributed to the adoption of a subcontracting strategy in the automotive industry. By the mid-1960s, each of the eleven surviving Japanese automotive assemblers had developed a network of 200–300 direct suppliers, on which they relied for the bulk of their parts and subassemblies. Once the auto firms had successfully adopted a subcontracting strategy, they found no necessity to return to older practices even when most of the initial conditions—militant unions, unused capacity among suppliers—had disappeared. If anything, they came to value their suppliers more highly.

The Evolution of Subcontracting Practice

Most current parts makers were originally small firms with little automotive experience, and often meager management and engineering capabilities. As long as they made only simple parts or carried out a single manufacturing process, this mattered little. The auto firms could buy on the basis of short-term price considerations, as in the U.S., from shops run by skilled machinists. But over time the auto firms sought to subcontract more complicated work, while the sheer volume of purchases expanded greatly. They could no longer shift such specialized work among vendors at will, so that short-term contracting proved inadequate. They also needed suppliers capable of running a more complex operation, and so began to educate their more promising subcontractors in modern ("American") manufacturing and management methods. But for suppliers to be willing to invest on behalf of and become dependent on a single customer, that firm had to prove itself trustworthy.

Part of the reason the auto firms had initially turned to suppliers was to be able to guarantee permanent employment to their own workers. By implication, suppliers were then cut during downturns. As the auto firms became more interdependent with their suppliers, however, they could no longer use other firms as a safety valve: they no longer had the relevant production equipment and hence needed their suppliers' factories as well as their workers. The auto firms of course had to personally convince their suppliers' owner/operators of this change in strategy, and foster personal trust. Part of this included taking steps to made commitments credible. The assemblers thus bore visible losses on behalf of their suppliers in downturns by not cutting orders disproportionately. In addition, they made tangible their commitment to outside suppliers by giving up their own internal capacity. (In contrast, the Big Three's parts operations have often been their suppliers' fiercest rivals.) To bolster the impact of their investments in trust, the auto firms advertised their behavior; creating reputation was one motive for establishing supplier cooperation associations.

Pricing rules evolved naturally. Up through the early 1950s, many firms vied to undertake the simple processes subcontracted by the auto firms, and were thus simply paid the going rate for an hour of stamping, welding or machining. As suppliers undertook production of more complicated parts, they continued to be paid in a similar manner, with the price calculated as the sum of the going rates for the relevant sequence of simpler manufacturing steps. (Eventually a margin for overhead and profit was included, as suppliers took over administrative and engineering tasks from the auto firms.) Productivity in Japan improved rapidly, but the lower costs that resulted were automatically reflected in pricing, as the "market" rate for a given process fell. (A firm that adopted new techniques in advance of its rivals, however, could hold costs below the "market" rate and thereby show a handsome profit.) Eventually, these decreases were simplified into standard semiannual price reductions for all suppliers. Furthermore, this meant that over time pricing became more predictable, as the rules and formulae became standardized. Pricing ceased to be a matter of pure bargaining skill, and was thus less of a source of contention and distrust.

In addition, both the pricing mechanism and the supplier cooperation associations accelerated technical change. The pricing system generated valuable information on suppliers' strengths and weaknesses. In particular, the bidding process pinpointed high-cost manufacturing steps, and hence directed efforts to areas where significant improvements seemed likely. The assembler, as purchaser, sometimes sent in their own engineers as consultants, or pointed the way to others who could help. The cooperation associations played a similar role. Technical subcommittees were established in different areas of manufacturing, which again helped best practice to diffuse rapidly, and made the provision of consulting services by the "parent" auto firm more cost-effective. These were crucial in the subsequent adoption of improved production control ("just-in-time" production), statistical process methods for quality control, and value analysis and other engineering and design methodologies. Similarly, they helped in diffusing general management techniques, encouraging the implementation of computer-based management information systems and in pushing the use of quality control (QC) circles as a labor relations tool.

These latter techniques had first been implemented by the auto firms to handle specific internal management tasks. Through the supplier associations their use was extended across firm boundaries. Many of the techniques were invented in the U.S., such as statistical process control (SPC) and value analysis (VA). But they were particularly important in a decentralized system: the purchaser could not readily place inspectors in the factories of its many suppliers (hence SPC), and better methods were needed to facilitate communication on design modifications among purchasers and suppliers (a key contribution of VA). Future demand projections were disseminated through the supplier associations, helping to coordinate investment; the associations also helped diffuse new techniques. In sum, the auto firms were able to capture the benefits of a large corporate organization for coordination and information processing without having to build up a rigid bureaucracy. Furthermore, as noted above, measured rivalry (combined with the detailed comparisons made possible by the bidding format) maintained the discipline of the market. They thus achieved the best of both worlds.

This entire system of governance by trust lowered the costs of subcontracting by solving many of the more intractable problems, and contributed as well to improving the administrative efficiency of purchasing. In postwar Japan, therefore, management in many industries gradually came to operate under the presumption that subcontracting was a desirable strategy. Japanese manufacturers have therefore remained small by Western standards in their direct employment. In contrast, in the U.S. in the 1920s, GM, DuPont, Sears and other firms adopted a strategy of vertical integration (or, at any rate, found themselves with large internal operations). They thus worked to refine bureaucratic management techniques such as the multidivisional corporate structure and the associated system of financial controls (Chandler 1962, 1977). This encouraged American firms to presume that, when possible, operations should be carried out within the firm; they thus chose to integrate rather than to subcontract. In international competition, this vertical integration strategy now appears the weaker of the two.

The remainder of this chapter provides an overview of the structure of the industry, together with basic definitions and a description of data sources, and a summary of the book's theoretical framework. Chapters 2 and 3 delve into the Japanese auto parts industry, through a case study and a brief history of the overall industry. The principal motive for subcontracting is then traced in chapter 4, including the evolution of the egalitarian ethic. After another set of case studies (chapter 5), the structure of contracting and governance by trust is analyzed in chapter 6. Chapter 7 then compares and contrasts automotive practices with those found in other industries in Japan. In conclusion, chapter 8 asks what, if any, lessons this analysis—the benefits of subcontracting, the motives for subcontracting and the ability to manage subcontracting—offers for U.S. industry.

Definitions and Data

Over 10% of output and employment in Japan, as in the U.S., revolves around the automotive industry. It is linked directly or indirectly to most sectors of the economy, from the producers of steel to consumer financing. This study analyzes only the manufacturing end of the industry, and hence arbitrarily excludes the complex organization of marketing and distribution. Within manufacturing, the focus is on the assemblers of regular passenger cars, trucks (both 3–wheel and 4–wheel), and buses, and the firms supplying them with parts. The motorcycle, heavy equipment and specialty vehicle ends of the industry are ignored.

At present there are eleven automotive firms in Japan, two of which produce only buses and large trucks. Total industry output in 1989 was 12.8 million vehicles. The eleven automotive firms are largely designers and assemblers of vehicles, rather than diversified enterprises. While Honda and Suzuki are major motorcycle producers, Nissan has an aerospace venture, and Fuji Heavy Industries makes railroad cars, automobile production remains the predominant business for these and the other auto firms. Furthermore, not all vehicles are assembled by the auto firms proper. Both Toyota and Nissan have subsidiaries or other closely affiliated firms assembling vehicles under contract, while all assemblers have relationships with firms that adapt their regular production vehicles for special purposes—racing cars, ambulances—or, in the case of trucks, add on bodies to bare chassis. Hence applying the term "automotive firm," "vehicle manufacturer" or "assembler" to only the eleven incumbent producers is not totally accurate, but mirrors reality well enough for the purposes of this study.

The automotive firms, of course, do not constitute the whole of the manufacturing end of the industry; using *Census of Manufactures* data, suppliers account for 65% of employment and 42% of value added. Suppliers—to avoid tedium they will be referred to interchangeably as subcontractors, parts firms and vendors—are a heterogeneous lot. No attempt is made here to cover firms supplying capital equipment or office supplies, nor are the suppliers of steel, paint and other materials treated in detail. Instead, the focus is on the firms whose products are incorporated directly in finished vehicles: the suppliers of parts, subassemblies and components. Because of this concentration, firms manufacturing only replacement parts or accessories such as custom leather seats are also ignored. In the U.S. the replacement market is very large, but in Japan the rapid growth of the domestic market meant that the demand for parts by the automotive assemblers for new cars was much more important than that for repairs of existing cars.

An automobile consists of 10,000 to 20,000 individual parts, depending on the complexity of the vehicle and the method of counting. One group of parts is generally referred to as "related items." These include tires, batteries and window glass, and more recently integrated circuits and other specialty electronics. These items are technically very different from other parts, and are typically classified separately in the *Census of Manufactures* and other statistical sources. Contracting patterns for related parts may vary somewhat from that for other parts (there is less interdependency among firms, and a separate section may handle their purchase). Most data used herein only poorly reflect their existence, and by default little detail is included here. The same is true of the materials suppliers that provide paints, steel, and plastics. As with the related parts firms, their presence is poorly reflected in most automotive statistics, while their purchase (as with capital equipment) is generally handled by a section separate from other parts purchases.

Component manufacturers are commonly distinguished as a second group of suppliers. Here an attempt is made to use the term "components" in line with common usage. While in technology there may be little that separates them from other parts makers, most began as producers of parts for which historically there was high replacement demand; they therefore developed independently of the auto firms. These include the makers of radiators and hoses; pistons, piston rings, valves, seals and similar engine parts; brake pads, wheels, shock absorbers, springs and other suspension elements; water and fuel pumps; starters, distributors, coils, wiper motors and other electrical items; seats, meters, cables, and other interior trim; lights and wipers; and complex systems, such as brakes, automatic transmissions and power steering, where the licensing of U.S. and European patents was important. Components in most cases are therefore subassemblies, or in other words comprise many individual parts. The term "subassemblies," however, is used here in a more general sense: door panels and alternators are both subassemblies, but only the latter is typically considered a component.

Automotive parts manufacturing has a number of distinctive traits. First, it is repetitive; parts may be produced in quantities of 100,000 or more. Second, production occurs over a considerable period of time. Until the 1980s, a model was typically in production in Japan for one to two years, chassis parts for four years, and an engine for up to eight years. Third, parts are interdependent with other parts; while the pieces of a component can be designed mainly in relation to each other, the overall parameters are contingent on the design details of other facets of a car. (Thus the design of a part for a fuel injector will depend on the engine for which it is made, and on space and other requirements.) Fourth, parts are for an assembled product, so that a part must be at the requisite place in time for incorporation into a subassembly or vehicle. Fifth, quality is important, because poor quality affects costs both directly (scrap is costly, and bad parts interrupt the assembly process) and indirectly (by affecting performance, safety, market image and warranty claims). Sixth, as noted above, the variety of parts is mind-boggling and their manufacture involves a tremendous range of technologies.

(With 100 models, each having at least 10,000 unique parts, there are over a million different parts in production. The manufacturing processes used include casting, forging, stamping, machining, heat treatment, painting, plating and the production of electric motors, semiconductors, glass, fabrics, petroleum distillates, plastics and papers.) Finally, production quantities cannot be anticipated with accuracy until after a new model is introduced, and even then weekly and monthly output will vary widely.

The organization of parts purchases reflects these factors. An auto is complex, so that teamwork is required in the design process, while the high volume typical of most segments of the industry requires precise coordination among a very large number of individuals and establishments. This necessitates great attention to administrative and other aspects of purchasing management, and for efficient production, mutual adaptation in the design of parts to facilitate manufacturing. All of these require regular interaction with suppliers. These transaction-specific investments make both ongoing (or at least long-term) contracts and small numbers of participants desirable.[6]

Other industries differ from the automotive industry in one or more respects, as analyzed in chapter 7. Thus, as noted above, some industries produce essentially unique units, as in engineering and shipbuilding; in others the product cycle is very short (such as watch cases). Many goods are relatively simple in design, use only a few manufacturing technologies, are not affected by minor quality variation, are made only to order, or have low unit manufacturing cost. In such industries close interaction with suppliers can be immaterial. The automotive industry is nevertheless sufficiently important in and of itself to merit study, even if it is not necessarily representative of industry as a whole.

Another feature of the automotive industry is its vertical structure. As noted above, each of the vehicle manufacturers in Japan has a network of 200–300 direct or "primary" suppliers. For the eleven auto firms combined, there are currently 1,200 primary subcontractors. Of these approximately 300 are component manufacturers that sell to most or all of the automotive firms, and are thus often called "independent" suppliers. Many of these component makers are listed on the stock exchange, and have 1,000 or more employees; some produce a wide variety of items, of which automotive parts are only one (sometimes minor) product line. For the majority of the primary suppliers, however, most of their sales are to only one or two of the assemblers, the "parent" firms with whom they are closely tied. These "first-tier" suppliers typically have a few hundred employees, and are relatively undiversified. Each primary firm in turn has its own network of "second-tier" suppliers. No precise count is available, but there are perhaps 8,000 small, indirect "secondary" subcontractors with 100 or fewer employees. In turn, there are 40,000 or more "tertiary" suppliers, often with 10 or fewer workers. The auto parts industry is thus organized in a pyramid.[7] (See figure 1.1.)

Published Japanese research concentrates on the larger "primary" suppliers. The data presented in this study suggest that these primary suppliers currently resemble the auto firms in their extensive and formally organized supplier networks. This was not the case, however, in the early 1960s. There is thus some difference between "independent" and "tied" primary suppliers, and a more

Figure 1.1. The Structure of Automotive Subcontracting

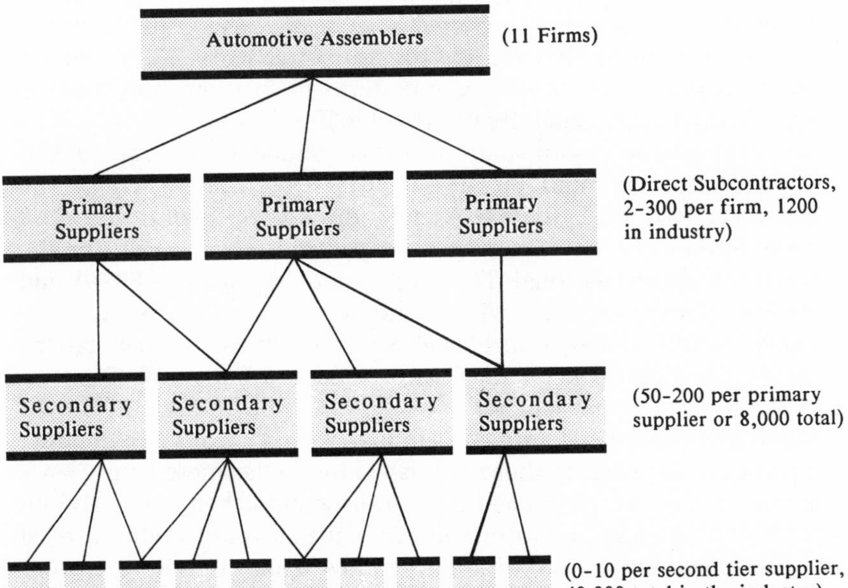

substantial difference between primary and secondary suppliers. In particular, the secondary suppliers of the early 1980s and their relationships with the primary firms resemble those of primary suppliers and the automotive firms in the 1950s. Tertiary suppliers are far more distinctive, and are not central to the analysis of this study. Instead, I focus on smaller direct suppliers (rather than component manufacturers) and on secondary suppliers.

Ironically, data are more readily available on the Japanese auto parts industry than on its U.S. counterpart. There are, of course, the standard statistical sources, such as the *Census of Manufactures*, an annual survey of output, establishments, employment and other items. (Similar sources exist on labor. All suffer from classification problems.) Even more useful, however, is the Japanese literature on small business, which often provides data for which there are no U.S. counterparts. In Japan, small business studies developed as a distinct field within economics in the late 1930s, due in part to the prevalence of small business and in part to a Marxist intellectual heritage that studied small firms as presumptive victims of exploitation (Shinohara 1968).[8] While this literature is not highly theoretical or analytic, it does offer a wealth of survey and case study-based material on subcontracting over the past sixty years, and encompasses many studies specific to automotive parts. These sources routinely provide information on patterns in customer and supplier relationships, data generally unavailable in the U.S.

Official sources on small business include the annual *Chusho Kigyo Hakusho* (Small Business White Paper), published by the Small and Medium Enterprise Agency; the *Kogyo Kihon Jittai Chosa* (Basic Survey of Manufacturing), undertaken every five years by the Ministry of International Trade and Industry and the Small and Medium Enterprise Agency; and the occasional *Shitauke Chusho Kigyo* (Small- and Medium-Scale Subcontractors) surveys carried out by the Central Bank for Commercial and Industrial Cooperatives (Shoko Kumiai Chuo Kinko 1971, 1977). Data are also published by the auto and auto parts industry associations and in directories of firms, such as those published by the Japanese equivalents of Dun & Bradstreet.[9] In addition to these published materials and the small business literature, this study utilizes case studies carried out in Japan during 1983–84. These draw upon interviews, factory visits, company histories and unpublished materials made available by firms. The case studies provide details on labor relations and contracting practices that were otherwise unavailable, and make an important contribution to the literature on the industry.

Perspectives on Subcontracting

The importance of manufacturing is increasingly being recognized in the U.S. (Smitka 1989). The Massachusetts Institute of Technology, for example, recently assembled its first commission on a domestic issue since World War II to examine U.S. industrial competitiveness (Dertouzos et al 1989). One prominent theme there, and in the *Harvard Business Review* and other business and management periodicals, is the need to mobilize not only workers and other internal resources, but also customers and other external resources. The potential benefits of "strategic alliances" with suppliers, customers and near-competitors are therefore receiving much attention. Such "strategic alliances" have long been pervasive in Japan; not only are there the horizontal "corporate groups" of Mitsui's and Mitsubishi's, but there are also vertical groups of manufacturers, such as those of the automotive assemblers described here.

The present volume should of course interest those wanting to know more about Japanese manufacturing, as well as businessmen and academics concerned with broader issues of strategic management. Explanations for and interpretations of interfirm ties, however, vary enormously; while I draw on a broad social-science perspective, the primary analytic tools I use here are those of economics. This study should thus also prove of interest to economists, sociologists and anthropologists. Before turning to economics, I first outline alternative theoretical and policy perspectives. These are then contrasted with the analytic approaches that I employ.

To foreign businessmen and politicians, interfirm ties in Japan are a frustrating and unfair business practice that works to exclude them. (This is reflected in the current U.S.-Japan Structural Impediments Initiative and the earlier MOSS talks.)[10] To culturalists, they mirror an unusually trusting, honest and homogeneous society and a tolerance for hierarchical relationships (Dore 1983). To Japanese Marxists, concerned with the wielding of power, they are a symptom of the domination of the small of society by the large (Shinohara [1968] surveys this literature). To dualists, they are an attempt to reap benefits from the small and flexible (Piore and Sabel 1984). To economists steeped in the antitrust literature, unusual institutional arrangements indicate the presence of monopoly, an attempt to wield market power (Perry 1989; Katz 1989). To other economists interested in transactions costs and the incentive problems of contracting, novel institutions instead reflect a search for efficiency rather than market power (Williamson 1985) or provide solutions to principal/agent problems (Holmstrom and Tirole 1989). To make matters worse, the explanations offered by these theories are not mutually exclusive.

The approach I use here contrasts and contributes to the others in several ways. On the one hand, I explicitly reject the culturalist perspective. While trust is central to interfirm ties in Japan, this trust is primarily economic in nature. Japanese culture provides images for conceiving of and talking about trust, and for casting cooperation in a positive light. In this sense, contracting draws on cultural resources, but contracting may also have helped shape these resources, by drawing out and reinforcing "cooperative" elements in the modern Japanese business ethos. Of course, our own culture is not devoid of such imagery, and in fact trust is central to the survival of firms in the financial services sector. (Witness the virtually instant demise of Drexel Burnham Lambert, once trust was tarnished.) The main distinction, perhaps, is that Americans are less aware of the potential for positively employing and, indeed, manipulating and reinterpreting, culture (Smith 1989).

On the other hand, this study backs up the long-standing assertion of dualists and Marxists that reliance on outside parts suppliers was in part a response to the militant postwar labor movement. (As noted above, however, that was not the only motivation, since subcontracting also let large firms draw upon idle manufacturing capacity at other, often smaller, firms.) However, as more complicated parts and subassemblies were subcontracted, and as output expanded, suppliers adopted modern mass production methods and management systems; the auto firms in fact supported these efforts. The car assemblers could no longer treat suppliers as a mere safety valve; instead, assembler and supplier became interdependent. (This, of course, also limited their contribution to flexibility.) Thus, while the Marxist and dualist perspective is useful for understanding the 1950s, it has limited applicability to contemporary automotive subcontracting. Neither, then, do I fully accept the contention of Japanese Marxists that subcontracting is a means for large business to systematically exploit and squeeze small business.

Instead, I highlight the role of the firm as a social entity rather than an economic or legal entity. For example, the ability to coordinate activities across firm boundaries via subcontracting meant that, for many purposes, the firm was no longer the unit of economic activity in the Japanese auto industry. It remained, however, the largest social unit. At a deeper level, subcontracting was not merely a response to the Japanese labor movement, but reflected the emergence of a societywide acceptance of egalitarian norms as an appropriate foundation for labor relations. Historically, firm boundaries developed in response to social cleavages; societal norms imposed constraints on what was done within the firm. Furthermore, this continues to be a motive for subcontracting today.

My primary concern, however, is with economic analysis. Ironically, economics lacks a widely accepted model of the firm, or of hierarchy as an alternative to contracting. In the model of a pure market economy, institutions have no explicit role: all agents are atomistic, and contracts are straightforward and always honored. This simplification is useful for many purposes, but it provides little insight into why there are firms and what their function is. (The antitrust literature, for example, suggests that in general it is profitable for a monopolist to integrate vertically, but offers little insight into why this process stops short of the point where one firm would encompass the entire economy.)

During the past two decades, two strands of theory arose to address this gap, transaction cost analysis and optimal contract theory. In a 1937 paper, Ronald Coase posited that organizational boundaries will be chosen so as to lower the transaction costs. Recent work, in particular that of Oliver Williamson, has developed Coase's basic insight. Williamson (1985) tries to pin down the costs and benefits of organizing transactions within a firm, and to link these to observable traits. He notes that transactions often require dedicated investments. (Thus, in the auto industry, tools and dies are used which are unique for a given part.) Contracting in such cases is difficult, however, and so firms will instead resort to vertical integration and the use of hierarchy and command rather than the market. As should be obvious, Williamson's insights inform much of the analysis I undertake in this book.

The formal modeling of contracts began in the 1970s with the analysis of "principal/agent" problems. This literature models problems such as that of a "principal" (e.g., a manager) who is unable to directly monitor the effort supplied by an "agent" (e.g., a worker), and then solves for the pay system that will minimize shirking. Contracting models have since been applied to analyze not only work incentives but also risk-sharing and other issues that arise from limited information and related constraints. Similarly, game theory has been used to analyze contracting. In particular, work by Axelrod (1984), Radner (1981) and Telser (1987), among others, suggests that repeated contracting can be used to support cooperation, independent of "trust" or other noncontractual elements. All of the optimal contracting and repeated games models, however, remain highly mathematical. While they suggest rationales for a particular contracting form, they do not offer convincing arguments for why firms exist (Holmstrom and Tirole 1989; Kreps 1990). Furthermore, the "optimal" contracts produced by these models are often either more complex than anything found in the real world or are near-infinite in variety.

Whatever the weaknesses of current theory, it does provide a set of queries that help organize this research. The transaction-cost models focus attention on investments specific to a relationship, and on the inherent difficulties of contracting between separate firms in such situations. The principal/agent literature helps draw attention to risk-sharing, incentives and the information each party has about the other. Game theory provides one explicit model in which an ongoing relationship overcomes the difficulties of short-term contracting, and in general suggests a role for reputation. My emphasis, however, is on describing the rich detail of real-world contracting, as a necessary accoutrement to work in pure theory.

But while this work is primarily empirical, I nevertheless extend existing theory in two directions. First, my analysis of Japanese subcontracting suggests why firms might choose to subcontract, and hence limit their size. (In contrast, most existing work on the "theory of the firm" concentrates on why firms might seek to undertake additional operations.)[11] I argue that in Japan, social and cultural factors make it costly to increase firm size. In other words, the structure of labor and other factor markets affects the "make" versus "buy" decision, and hence the locus of firm boundaries, in a manner that encourages subcontracting. In addition, I contend that in Japan, innovative management methods lowered the costs of running a supplier network. Furthermore, these management methods provided strong incentives to innovate and to reduce costs. The net affect of such innovations is thus to favor more subcontracting, leading to smaller firms.

My second contribution to theory is the analysis of trust and reputation as an alternative method of governing transactions. Economics has concentrated on "market" organization (contracts); comparisons, when made, have been with "hierarchy" (command). While others acknowledge the existence of hybrid forms of organization, there is little discussion of what these might be and how they might function. (The primary exception here is the "exit/voice" paradigm of Hirschman [1986], which Helper [1987, 1990a] applies to the U.S. automotive parts industry.) Yet extending theory to analyze situations which are neither pure "market" nor pure "hierarchy" is necessary if economists are to assess the relative strengths and weaknesses of alternate organizational forms. Such analysis is also necessary if economists are to provide guidance to firms seeking to form strategic alliances. My empirical work on automotive subcontracting demonstrates that transactions can be organized in a manner that relies neither upon market nor upon hierarchy, but instead is based upon trust and reputation. Furthermore, transactions governed by trust appear to combine the best of market and hierarchy, permitting close coordination while continuing to keep the parties on their toes.

In sum, this study highlights subcontracting in Japan as neither a purely contractual relationship nor as a simple extension of hierarchy through which large firms pressure the small. Instead, it stresses the role of trust in forming and maintaining interfirm ties, backed by mechanisms that make longer-term commitments credible. The overall relationship—including trust—remains primarily economic in nature; in the Japanese auto industry, both parts makers and assemblers expend considerable resources in establishing and maintaining reputation. Most important, the resulting cooperative relationship enabled the auto firms to combine the strengths of both market and firm. In sum:

- o The strategic ties among auto firms and parts suppliers depended on trust. Trust, however, had to be earned, and earning it was costly; firms had to invest in trust.

o Trust was never taken for granted: firms sought their own advantage, and had to be restrained by the presence of rivals. Ties had to be kept competitive.

o Trust was worth the investment: building trust paid. Trust permitted the Japanese auto industry to better compete in the rapidly evolving domestic and world markets.

A Case Study: The Soja Industrial Park

The Soja Industrial Park is located in Okayama Prefecture, about halfway between Kobe and Hiroshima.[1] Its sixteen firms sell almost all of their output to the nearby Mizushima Assembly Plant of Mitsubishi Motors—and have done so since the park was founded 25 years ago.[2] This long-standing relationship is typical of the direct suppliers to the Japanese auto makers; in most other ways the evolution of these firms and their relationship with Mitsubishi is also representative. The history of this park thus provides a useful introduction to the development of the Japanese auto parts industry, and the genesis of contemporary contracting practices. The details provided in this case study complement the general overview of the industry provided in chapter 3. Taken together, these two chapters supply background for the analysis of subcontracting motives and methods in subsequent chapters.

The Mizushima Machining and Metalworking Industrial Park Cooperative, as the park is formally known, is in Soja City. It is situated about 40 minutes (20 km) from the heavy industrial complex at Mizushima, facing Japan's Inland Sea, where Mitsubishi's principal passenger car assembly plant is located. The park commenced operations in 1964, though not all the factories were up and running until the following year. But from the time the park began, its factories have concentrated on auto parts production for Mitsubishi; the park thus illustrates the continuity of subcontracting ties. However, several original members exited, so that looking backward exaggerates the extent of continuity. Participants and outside observers alike term the current relationship between Mitsubishi and the park firms cooperative, another typical trait of automotive subcontracting. The motive for establishing the park, however, was to overcome an adversarial attitude between the Mizushima plant of Mitsubishi Motors (MMC) and its local suppliers. This effort was successful, and over time, in part due to Mitsubishi's technical and managerial guidance, this group of firms evolved from suppliers of simple parts made to Mitsubishi's specifications, to manufacturers of subassemblies which they helped design.

The relationship between MMC and its suppliers is still evolving, as Mitsubishi internationalizes its operations. In 1980, MMC exported 65% of its passenger car output,[3] but Asian markets were saturated while "voluntary" export restraints prevented increased sales to the U.S. and Europe. MMC's domestic sales were slipping when I visited the Soja Park in 1984. In addition, Mitsubishi had initiated overseas CKD (completely knocked down) assembly in Malaysia and Thailand in place of direct exports, and had technical and licensing ties to Hyundai in Korea. The next move was to the U.S.: Chrysler and Mitsubishi announced a joint manufacturing venture in April 1985. Production at the Diamond-Star Motors plant in Normal, Illinois commenced in fall 1988, with target production of 240,000 vehicles a year (the production rate had reached 10,000 per month by late 1989). The Soja Park firms followed Mitsubishi to Illinois, establishing a sixteen-firm joint venture, Eagle Wings Industries. Now a few of the firms—none of which previously had operations more than a few miles from Soja—are entering into U.S. ventures on their own. None of the firms could have dreamed of such a future when the Park began.

A case study of a single group of firms offers insights that are lost in a statistical or historical survey of the entire industry, such as that of chapter 3. However, it can never be completely representative of a large industry. Let me indicate here several ways in which Mitsubishi and the Soja Park firms are distinctive. MMC entered the automotive industry late, producing regular passenger cars only from 1960. It also produces the widest range of vehicles of any of the Japanese car makers, ranging from heavy trucks to minivans to subcompact cars. Mitsubishi is one of the middle-tier firms, near Honda and Mazda in size but ranking far behind Toyota and Nissan in the domestic car market. (In 1988 it sold 660,000 cars, one-third of Toyota's volume.) The suppliers of MMC tend therefore to be both younger and smaller than those of Toyota and

Nissan. Because of its wide product range, MMC also has more direct suppliers than the other auto firms. As with other late entrants, Mitsubishi avoided equity ties with its suppliers, though not always successfully (see the Kato Shatai case study in chapter 5), whereas Toyota and Nissan held equity in many of their suppliers. Finally, for geographic reasons the Soja suppliers have been heavily dependent on MMC as a customer, although since the late 1970s the park firms have increased their sales to Mazda, the only other nearby automotive firm, presumably at the expense of Mazda suppliers. Nevertheless, the commonalities are sufficient that the story of the Soja Park firms provides useful insights into the industry as a whole.

The "Parent" Firm: Mitsubishi Motors' Mizushima Plant

The Mizushima plant was built in 1943 as an aircraft factory by Mitsubishi Heavy Industries (MHI), which produced the Zero fighter and the Musashi battleship.[4] It never entered into full production, for while the factory itself survived the war without major damage it was unable to obtain an adequate supply of materials because of the U.S. interdiction of Japanese shipping. When it commenced operations at war's end, it instead turned out pots and pans and other household items. The firm, however, inherited a large engineering staff, who along with their peers at other Mitsubishi plants viewed motor vehicles as the only potential peacetime product that would make use of their accumulated skills. They soon designed the "Mizushima," a small three-wheel truck.

The "Mizushima" never sold well, although subsequent three-wheel vehicles did better in the 1950s. A more salable product was found by Mitsubishi's Nagoya plant in the "Silver Pigeon" motor scooter, which captured a substantial part of the domestic market by 1950. The Nagoya plant also began automotive subcontract work, making car bodies for Toyota and Nissan from 1948. These ventures helped the firm garner experience in automotive design and manufacturing, and thus aided the launch of a miniature four-wheel wagon in 1960, while the success of the scooters helped the firm develop a marketing base. Mitsubishi also entered the subcompact passenger car market with the "Minica" in 1962.[5] But the strength of the firm remained engineering and production technology. MMC had a poor grasp of styling—the initial vehicles had a strictly utilitarian interior more appropriate for a military vehicle—and marketing remained weak. The sales of both models were disappointing.

A further complication was the breakup of Mitsubishi Heavy Industries by the U.S. Occupation. At its peak in World War II, MHI employed 400,000 workers in thiry-one plants. It and the other wartime combines (*zaibatsu*) were a natural focus of the Occupation's democratization efforts. In 1950, Gen. Douglas MacArthur ordered Mitsubishi and the other large zaibatsu dissolved. MHI was broken into three firms. Western Japan Heavy Industries inherited much of MHI's shipbuilding operations, while the Mizushima, Kyoto and Nagoya plants of the old MHI became part of Central Japan Heavy Industries. But the Kawasaki and Tokyo plants, which had ventured into heavy trucks, became part of Eastern Japan Heavy Industries. The fledgling automotive ventures were thus split between two different firms.

The Tokyo plant had produced "Fuso" trucks in the 1930s, and reentered the truck market after the war. But its initial automotive work was the repair of military vehicles for the U.S. Occupation, not manufacturing new vehicles. Foreign licenses also proved important in expanding its automotive skills. From 1951 the firm assembled the "Henry J" subcompact under a short-lived license from Kaiser-Fraser,[6] and from 1953 produced Jeeps under a license from Willys-Overland, which included the "localization" of parts production within Japan. Finally, in 1960, the Tokyo portion of Mitsubishi drew upon this experience to introduce its own car, a two-cylinder rear-engine model. The legacy of the Occupation was not all bad.

Then, in 1964, the three separate Mitsubishi firms merged to reform Mitsubishi Heavy Industries. Along with automobiles, this larger firm was also a major shipbuilder and producer of industrial machinery. Not only was MHI unique in this broad product range, but within the Japanese automotive industry it also manufactured the widest range of vehicles. Scooters and three-wheel vehicles had been dropped by then, but MHI made miniature, subcompact and medium-sized cars; jeeps; and light, medium and heavy trucks. Mitsubishi was also the only automotive firm whose plants initially were not concentrated in a single geographic region.

None of the firm's 1960s passenger car models was particularly successful; its vehicles continued to be styled by engineers, not artists. From a manufacturing standpoint, its plants were very well run, with productivity reportedly second only to Toyota's, despite the many types of vehicles in production. But from a management standpoint, coordination of the disparate and geographically separate parts of the firm proved difficult. It sought a foreign influence to improve its product styling, but its attempt to work with an Italian design house ultimately fell through. Instead, in 1969 it signed an agreement with Chrysler to spin off its automotive operations into a separate firm, forming Mitsubishi Motors Corporation (MMC), with Chrysler as a minority (15%) shareholder.[7] The infusion of capital was timely, as it helped the firm launch a series of what proved to be highly successful models (the Galant and Mirage).

From 400,000 vehicles in 1970, MMC's production increased to 1 million in 1979; expansion thereafter slowed. Output was up only to 1.25 million units in 1989, although revenues doubled in the decade. In the domestic market it is the dominant bus manufacturer and is consistently second in heavy trucks (after Isuzu). It is also strong in minicars, but trails a distant fifth of the regular passenger car market, with a mere 7% (and hence ranks after Toyota, Nissan, Honda and Mazda). Within Japan, Mitsubishi Motors has its headquarters in Tokyo; manufacturing plants in Tokyo, Nagoya, Kyoto and Mizushima; and two engineering centers, one in Nagoya for passenger cars and another in Tokyo for trucks and buses. The firm had 23,341 employees in 1979, and 25,300 in 1989. Kyoto, with about 3,000 workers, was the smallest plant; Mizushima, with 5,000 workers, was the largest.[8]

The Mizushima factory has all along been MMC's principal car assembly plant. In 1955 the plant assembled three-wheeled vehicles and light trucks, but output of three-wheelers fell sharply in 1961 and ceased in 1963. Miniature and later subcompact passenger car assembly then commenced, and gradually increased alongside light truck assembly to comprise two-thirds of production in 1984. While total output rose rapidly through the late 1970s, so did that at Mitsubishi's other plants. Thus, from 67% of MMC's vehicle production in 1960, Mizushima's share fell to 58%-60% after 1970. (Since Mizushima assembles smaller vehicles, its share in terms of value must be smaller.) After two decades of rapid growth, the

Mizushima plant reached a plateau. Table 2.1 summarizes these changes. From 1988 the domestic car market has expanded at a double-digit rate, but future growth for Mitsubishi must come primarily from production overseas. Suppliers, in turn, have gone through a similar transition, scrambling to keep up with demand for the simple vehicles of the 1960s, while facing stagnant domestic production levels of increasingly complex cars in the 1980s. They must now decide whether (and in what form) to follow MMC abroad.

The Soja Industrial Park: Genesis and Startup

In 1980 the Mizushima plant had thirty substantial local suppliers, but its single most important source of parts was the Soja Park (followed by the Mitsubishi Kyoto plant, from which it purchased engines). Of the 8,000 employees at local suppliers, half worked in Soja. Park sales to MMC totaled ¥97 billion ($650 million), which made up 25% of Mizushima production costs,[9] and in turn represented 80% of the total output of the Soja Park firms. They had done well during the previous decade. During the 1970s output of the Mizushima plant doubled, while employment fell 15%. While the increase in output per worker reflected some gain in productivity at MMC, it above all represented a shift of production to suppliers. Sales by park firms more than doubled. This shift continued a strategy that was adopted explicitly about 1959. The

Table 2.1. **MMC Mizushima Production and Employment**
(1,000 units)

Year	Cars	Trucks	Miniature Vehicles	Mizushima Total	Total MMC Production	Total Japanese Production	Mizushima Workforce
1955	—	7[a]	—	7	?	70	1,500
1960	—	11[a]	18[a]	28	42	760	2,000
1965	8	12	93	113	179	1,920	4,200
1970	27	25	220	272	468	5,300	6,900
1975	211	40	64	315	533	6,940	6,200
1980	483	43	193	719	1,206	11,040	6,000

Source: Takizawa (1983:5, 6).
Note: All trucks in 1955 and 3,000 trucks and 7,000 cars in 1960 were three-wheelers; production of three-wheelers ceased after 1962.

ratio of parts purchases to sales was at the 35%-40% level in the years up to 1958, but increased to 47% during 1959–1961 and 60% in 1964.[10] The dependence of Mitsubishi on the Soja Park firms thus increased significantly during the early 1960s, and continued to grow slowly thereafter. Soja suppliers thus became integral to MMC's overall operations.

This had not always been the case; in the late 1950s, MMC had not perceived itself as dependent on cooperation from its suppliers. MMC forecast increased demand for its three-wheel light trucks in 1958, and pushed suppliers in the Mizushima region to invest accordingly. But with the 1958 recession, demand fell; 1959 sales were less than half those of 1957. In response, MMC canceled orders and pulled work in-house (Takeshita 1967:300). With the end of the recession and a recovery in light vehicle sales,[11] Mizushima found itself unable to meet demand due to a lack of parts: local firms were understandably reluctant to increase their capacity on Mitsubishi's behalf.

To help rectify the situation, MMC sought outside help. In response, MITI's Hiroshima Bureau brought in a team, headed by Professor Kikutaro Takizawa of Nagoya University, that was experienced in undertaking evaluations (*shindan*) of small manufacturers. During 1960–1961, they evaluated MMC's purchasing system and of 74 of its suppliers (Takizawa 1966, 1983). Recommendations of these small business and management experts included: (1) avoiding the use of outside suppliers as a buffer against business downturns, (2) setting prices high enough to encourage firms to stick with MMC, (3) purchasing in accordance with a long-term plan, (4) channeling contacts with suppliers through a single office, the purchasing department, to see that the firm spoke with one voice, and (5) organizing suppliers into a formal association and improving communication to take advantage of government funding for cooperatives. These recommendations were based in part on the success of similar recommendations made to Toyota by outside consultants almost a decade earlier, in 1952–1954 (see chapter 7).[12]

MMC heeded their advice, sharing production plans and organizing a supplier association. The Japanese government (through the Ministry of International Trade and Industry and the Small Business Agency) was pushing an industrial park financing program in 1961, and Mitsubishi seized on this as another way to implement the consultants' recommendations. Therefore, in 1962 MMC organized a group of twenty-six local suppliers, and the following year obtained the government's imprimatur for an industrial park.

The main motive for establishing the industrial park was to foster supplier cooperation and development. MMC hoped that gathering suppliers in one place would facilitate technical change. It expected there would be synergies from suppliers trading engineering advice with one another. MMC also could station engineers there, who could then rotate among the firms without spending half of each day commuting among them. For the same reason, purchasing managers strongly favored the Park.

Containing labor costs was another motive. In the early 1960s MMC hired many new workers, so that the average age of employees fell. Because seniority was the largest single component in MMC's compensation system, this might be expected to hold down labor costs. Nevertheless, because starting wages were climbing rapidly at the time, overall labor costs increased.[13] Wages at suppliers rose even faster, but from an average of 42% of the Mizushima level in 1960, labor costs at one small sample of suppliers remained a mere 53%-68% of the MMC level in 1964 (Takeshita 1967:299, table 11). By shifting additional work to suppliers rather than expanding internally, Mitsubishi could alleviate its own rising labor costs.

Next, there were financial considerations. Of ¥1.9 billion ($5 million at ¥360) in startup costs, the Japanese government provided a subsidy of ¥300 million and member firms supplied ¥750 million in capital. MMC guaranteed in full loans from small business banks for the remaining ¥860 million. But neither MMC's nor its suppliers' banks had to be approached for loans, as none of these funds were from traditional sources of outside finance (Takeshita 1967:table 6). It was expected, though, that member firms would invest a further ¥900 million over the first three years. This was a substantial sum for the small firms in the park. As participants phrased it, they would be "rich" on the outside, with expansive lots and buildings, but "poor" on the inside, as investment in machinery would have to be pared to the bone. Meanwhile, Mitsubishi could devote its financing efforts to product development and the expansion of its assembly operation.

Thus the park was begun. The initial 26 firms had formed a

cooperative, which purchased the 64–acre Soja site in 1964. (Local government helped Mitsubishi obtain the acquiescence of landowners to attract the park. In 1984 the Park accounted for half the city's manufacturing employment and 70% of manufacturing shipments.) Site preparation commenced immediately, with two dormitories for single male employees and a few other buildings finished by the summer of 1965. However, four firms dropped out of the original group, while one new firm joined in; the Soja Industrial Park thus began operations with 23 members. The facilities met the immediate needs of many of the firms, and eleven of them consolidated all their operations in the Park.[14] Some needed to expand their plant, and due to zoning restrictions or lack of an adjacent lot had been unable to do so. (Several had leased sites adjacent to the Mizushima plant, which needed that land for its own expansion.) Others were in locations with poor roads or inadequate industrial water supplies or waste disposal. Finally, several firms needed new factory buildings to support increasingly heavy machinery, and found it easier to move than to renovate.

While the greenfield site at Soja thus solved one or another problem for most of the firms, MMC anticipated many additional small savings. The Soja site not only had adequate land, but it had good transport to the Mizushima plant (the one stretch of bad road was soon rebuilt), and was located at a rail and road nexus that facilitated commuting (members hoped publicity about the Park would ease recruitment). In addition, at the new site suppliers could run two shifts, as they were no longer near residential areas that imposed noise constraints. Many of the firms were initially quite specialized, and did not undertake stamping, or surface treatment, or machining. The firms, now adjacent, could subcontract such specialized work to each other more readily. Other firms had received steel and partially finished work from Mizushima (Takeshita 1967:295). (Initially no supplier had large presses. Instead, large stampings such as door panels were shipped from Mizushima to suppliers for further work.) Having most suppliers in one central location relieved this logistical nightmare, as did having suppliers procure raw materials for themselves after 1965. Park firms purchased electricity jointly, at a significant quantity discount, and centralized waste-water treatment. The Park included a gasoline station and truck repair shop, and one initial member was a trucking firm, which arranged for truckload shipments to Mizushima. MMC expected these various small savings, when aggregated, to be substantial.

However, with wages increasing, with repayments of their loans commencing, and with unprecedented current interest expenses, balance sheets deteriorated more than anticipated.[15] To Mitsubishi's disappointment, these higher costs were not offset by productivity increases. MMC had guaranteed the majority of the loans, and for a while feared that it would be called upon to honor its pledge. This induced it to call back the consultant team in 1965, in 1968 and again in 1971. When Mitsubishi's fortunes improved in the 1970s, these fears evaporated. Instead, the park proved a valuable resource.

The Soja Industrial Park: Growth

Before joining the Park, the Soja firms were very small in scale, in part because most were relatively new ventures. In fact, of the 23 original firms, only 11 firms had been founded before 1955, while 7 started up between 1955 and 1960, 4 after 1960, and one commenced operations with the startup of the Park. (This was Sanyo Brake, a joint venture set up by Mitsubishi Motors). During the decade before the park began, however, these firms grew quite rapidly. In 1955, value added was a mere ¥8 million per firm, for the twelve firms then in existence or for which data were available. Value added rose to ¥28 million per firm (19 firms) in 1960 and ¥118 million per firm (22 firms) in 1964. At the then-current exchange rate of $1 to ¥360, firms thus averaged $22,000 in value added in 1955, and $328,000 in 1964, a fourteen-fold increase. (In contrast, sales averaged $48,000 in 1955 and $1.0 million in 1964.)[16] During the next decade, however, sales grew only five-fold. (Tables 2.2 and 2.3 summarize this growth.)

Part of this growth reflected the rapid rise of the automotive industry, but it also reflected an increase in the range of orders they received from Mizushima. For the park firms, in other words, Mitsubishi grew in importance as a customer, even while they tried to maintain outside business. For example, only 38% of OM Kogyo's sales were to Mizushima in 1960, but this had already risen to 81% in 1964, after the decision to enter the park. By that date the park firms averaged 87% of sales to Mitsubishi, and most anticipated that more than 90% of sales would be to MMC by 1968. That suppliers would countenance such dependence demonstrates that Mitsubishi had reversed the adversarial atmosphere that motivated the formation of the Park. The growth record, in turn, suggests they were amply rewarded for their trust.

The move to the Soja Park, however, was not a success story for all of the firms; some failed or exited. As noted above, even before the Soja Industrial Park commenced operations four firms quit the cooperative. A merger of two members in 1966 further decreased the number of firms to 22. Just before the first oil crisis in 1973, three more firms merged, and two merged soon thereafter.[17] (Another firm ceased to have a business relationship with Mitsubishi and closed its Soja plant in 1983. And in at least one case, it appears MMC was forced to step in and help reorganize a firm.[18]) Thus, of the initial 26 firms, only 16 now remain; in other words, over time 40% of the original participants exited for one or another reason. (Table 2.4 details current park members.)

While the number of firms declined over time, total employment increased rapidly. Employment at the eventual park members totaled 489 workers in 1955; there were 1,280 workers by 1960 and 3,362 by 1964. While none of the firms were large, workers at seventeen of them had been unionized before the opening of the park in 1965. For the remainder, the MMC union saw to it that their workers were organized. However, while average wages rose, this did not mean an immediate end to the disparity in pay between the small park firms and the Mizushima plant.[19] One consequence of this differential was that in their first year 44% of new hires in the park quit, and on average 30% of the remaining workers

Table 2.2. Growth of the Soja Park Firms, 1955-1964

Year	Firms	Employees	Sales (¥ million)	Value Added (¥ million)	Investment (¥ million)	Annual Wages (¥1,000)
1955	14	489	226	98	9	121
1960	18	1,276	1,552	529	224	183
1962	21	2,480	4,125	1,295	614	222
1964	22	3,362	8,845	2,590	807	313

Source: Takizawa (1966:tables 6, 7, 12 and 20).
Notes: Data are for varying numbers of firms. Not all firms existed in the early years, and data availability differs for each item within each year. Sales appear to include all establishments, while wage data appear to include bonuses.

Table 2.3. Growth of the Soja Industrial Park, 1966-1982

Year	Firms	Employment	Sales (¥ mil)	Investment (¥ mil)	Ave Annual Wage (¥1000)
1966	23	2,670	8,330	1,300	247
1967	22	3,626	14,242	1,400	273
1968	22	3,690	15,239	1,600	334
1969	22	3,575	16,043	1,300	395
1970	22	3,570	18,793	700	479
1971	22	3,456	18,114	600	574
1972	19	3,557	21,389	400	684
1973	20	3,852	29,552	900	848
1974	19	3,791	32,283	800	1,108
1975	19	3,657	39,171	800	1,192
1976	19	3,493	•43,786	1,500	1,280
1977	18	3,596	53,199	2,500	1,352
1978	18	3,630	63,800	2,500	1,419
1979	18	3,777	79,300	2,700	1,492
1980	18	4,016	96,900	2,900	1,561
1981	18	4,003	96,500	—	—
1982	18	3,865	87,000	—	—

Source: Takizawa (1983:9, table 3) and a September 1983 Soja Park brochure.
Note: Sales appear to be only for factories located within the Soja Park, rather than for all sales of member firms. Sales for both the industrial park and MMC peaked in 1980.

left by their fourth year. In contrast, turnover was low at Mizushima.

The Soja firms in response adopted two strategies. One was to employ local women, who tended to stay rather than quit and end up commuting. Another was to employ older workers; the share of workers aged 20 to 35 declined steadily in the 1960s, in contrast to the trend at MMC Mizushima.[20] But turnover ceased to be a problem at the park plants only after 1974, when the first oil crisis made it much harder to find alternate employment. Except in the first two years following startup, however, employment in the park increased but gradually. During 1970–1980, sales by the park firms quintupled while employment in the park grew by only 12%. (In contrast, the number of vehicles produced by MMC Mizushima merely tripled, and employment there actually *fell* 13%.) Except at its inception, however, the growth of the park was not fueled by "cheap" labor. In response to tight labor markets the firms were

Table 2.4. Soja Industrial Park Members
(October 31, 1983)

Firm	Employment	Principal Products
Sankei Kogyo	376	Mufflers, Fuel Tanks, Air Cleaners
Soja Kogyo	130	Spindles, Flanges, Brake Drums
Kyoritsu Seiki	198	Bolts, Studs, Heat Treatment
Shinko Seisakusho	286 (414)	Driveshaft, Dashboard Assemblies
Ogino Tekko	39	Idler Arm, Steering Gear Box
Minori Kogyo	146	Interior Trim, Wood Products
Kyoei Kogyo	441 (481)	Frame & Door Assembly, Tools and Dies
OM Kogyo	344	Bumper, Door Sash, Cross Members
Mizushima Kanai Sharin	21	Disc Wheel Surface Treatment
Marubun	39	Trucking Services
Toyo Kogyo	55	Steering Gear & Mirror Assembly
Yonan Kogyo	230	Rear Suspension, Axle Housing
Hiruta Kogyo	316 (554)	Pedals, Hand Brakes, Steering/Suspension Arms
Sanyo Brake	341	Disc and Drum Brakes
Sanyo Hydric	46	Hydraulic Cylinder Piston
Knight Denso	129	Lamps, Seat Adjusters
Ibara Seiki	109 (360)	Brake Discs, Flywheels, Hubs
Soja Park Cooperative	400	Miscellaneous Joint Services

Source: 1984 Soja Park Firm brochure.
Note: All firms are incorporated. Employment is for operations located within the Park; figures in parentheses reflect employment including establishments located outside the Park, but do not include employment in affiliate firms. Direct employees of the Soja Park Cooperative include park management, a joint purchasing office, a transport center, a gas station and a cafeteria. The latter three were run on a profit-making basis.

ultimately forced to raise wages. The gap with MMC closed rapidly in the 1970s, and by 1984 wages in the park were "virtually the same" as at Mizushima.[21]

The Soja Park Firms: Technical and Management Change

From the beginning, Mitsubishi's aim for the park was the development of better suppliers; in Japanese this was referred to as an *ikusei seisaku*, literally to raise up suppliers (as one would a child). Improving supplier trust was but one element of this strategy. In 1965, Mitsubishi foresaw a continuing increase in output, even as it was reducing the number of models assembled at the

Mizushima plant. As the parent plant geared up for high-volume production on modern assembly lines, its Soja suppliers needed to make corresponding changes. One of the prime aims of bringing them together at a single site was thus to hasten the transition to mass production. This included helping them shift from specializing in a single manufacturing step to making subassemblies that required undertaking multiple processes.

A key part of Mitsubishi's policy was to locate exemplars within the park, both to show how really successful a firm could be, and to play a leadership role at Soja. Hiruta Kogyo was one such firm. It was the largest and most technically capable Mitsubishi supplier in the Mizushima area. As such—and unlike most local suppliers—it manufactured "critical" safety-related items such as pedal assemblies and brake parts. In addition, as early as 1964, it became a supplier to Toyo Kogyo (Mazda), thus developing customers outside the local market. MMC chose Hiruta to manage the day-to-day operations of Sanyo Brake, a joint venture between Hiruta, Mitsubishi and Akebono Brake. (A related firm, Sanyo Hydric, commenced operations in the park in 1973.)[22] In 1984, after twenty years, Hiruta remained the most prominent firm in the park.

While the industrial park was under construction, the parent firm set up a technical center, staffed with seventy full-time engineers. Each supplier assigned staff to what was called the industrial engineering center, while MMC Mizushima provided senior engineers and paid their salaries. At startup, MMC also assigned two of its management staff (including one senior purchaser) to work there full-time; two other MMC staff retired from their jobs at Mizushima to positions in park management.[23] While the Mizushima plant had provided technical guidance to its suppliers in the past, the Soja effort was far more systematic and substantial. At first the Soja suppliers worked to establish modern production lines; in some cases, Mizushima transferred its own subassembly lines to the premises of park firms as it concentrated increasingly on final assembly (Takeshita 1967:307).

The Soja suppliers were largely successful in their shift to mass production. By 1970, according to the local MMC Mizushima purchasing manager, "there was little remaining we could teach these firms." During the early 1970s, the technical center was reduced to a handful of permanent staff, and Mitsubishi engineers were no longer located there. This did not mean that technical assistance had ceased, only that problems common to all Soja Industrial Park firms were by then relatively unimportant. Instead Mitsubishi worked through the technical subcommittees of the 123–member Mizushima local of the MMC supplier cooperative association. For example, through these technical committees Mitsubishi encouraged suppliers to adopt common standards for die blanks and other materials, allowing them to obtain volume discounts on purchases and to shorten lead times. They also helped firms learn about and implement specific advances in stamping and machining, such as die design, rapid die changes and material-handling automation.

Mitsubishi also worked to improve supplier management, in parallel with its engineering assistance. In cooperation with its union, Mitsubishi Motors had long pushed employee enrichment and involvement programs. MMC therefore encouraged the systematization of labor relations within the Soja Park, beginning with the unionization of park workers (as noted above). Mitsubishi and its union then helped park firms implement QC circles in the late 1960s. (Quality control data and exhortations were on every bulletin board.) The Mizushima plant also implemented a just-in-time (JIT) system for production control. This aimed to achieve frequent deliveries of small lots, which meant that work flows needed to approximate those on a production line (the existing practice was to make parts in large lots and then carry a correspondingly large inventory). From its end, Mizushima worked to provide stable orders to its suppliers in advance. But while a few firms delivered multiple lots a day by the late 1970s, most suppliers made only daily or even weekly deliveries until 1980. Over time, then, Mitsubishi's technical emphasis had shifted from the shop floor (quality control and labor relations) to production engineering (work flow and JIT).

During the late 1960s the Soja firms strove to put production lines in place. By the early 1970s, the suppliers were beginning to redesign these lines, and by the late 1970s they were making most of their tools and dies and even building some of their own machine tools. (During 1979–1981, for example, several firms built or substantially modified welding robots.) To tie their knowledge of manufacturing into Mitsubishi's product development efforts, MMC's recent supplier development has centered on value analysis programs. Value analysis is a methodology for coordinating the design process across functional lines, including between engineers at suppliers and the design team at Mitsubishi.[24] Industrial engineering methods all along made up the most important area of management guidance; value engineering and value analysis were only the most recent applications of this methodology. Mitsubishi began to utilize value analysis internally in 1960, in purchasing and then in design. Several suppliers began to apply value analysis to their internal manufacturing operations in the late 1960s, but MMC did not begin systematic efforts to induce its suppliers to implement value analysis until 1979.[25] For the first time in several years a Mitsubishi engineer was assigned to the Soja Industrial Park full-time, and consultants were brought in at considerable expense to run training seminars. Now suppliers are increasingly undertaking design work for MMC. In fact, the Soja Park firms and other suppliers now play such a major role in the design process that Mitsubishi probably could not develop a car without them.

Over time, these various changes resulted in corresponding changes in contracting practices, as detailed in chapter 6. In the late 1950s MMC used competitive "market" prices obtained from bids by local suppliers when it contracted for machining and other commonly subcontracted processes. It discovered after 1958, however, that this was not practical as the complexity of subcontracted work increased. Pricing instead came to rely on cost breakdowns submitted by suppliers. Nevertheless, engineers from MMC Mizushima apparently did not make regular rounds of suppliers to audit costs. However often they might be consulted on specific problems, suppliers kept them away from the factory floor unless the problem at hand necessitated a visit.[26] As suppliers came to make first discrete parts and then entire subassemblies, it thus became increasingly difficult for purchasing managers to apply market rates to the cost breakdowns submitted by various suppliers. But instead of auditing suppliers and paying them on a cost-plus basis (a typical procedure in U.S. defense procurement), standard rates of productivity change were used to adjust prices. Thus Mitsubishi set and tried to enforce 3%-5% annual price reductions across the board, corrected for design modifications and movements in steel prices. This, of course, was possible primarily because of Mitsubishi's commitment to contracting on an ongoing basis with the Soja Park firms and its other suppliers.

Mitsubishi therefore paid careful attention to maintaining a close relationship with and monitoring the general management capabilities of its suppliers. The head of purchasing at the Mitsubishi Mizushima Plant on average spent one day a week in Soja, and he made it a rule to talk at least once a week by phone with management at major suppliers. He was an engineer by training, as were most purchasing staff, and had been in his position for four to five years. (Unlike many Japanese white-collar workers, purchasing staff at Mitsubishi were rotated infrequently.[27]) Mitsubishi purchasers had thus been in close contact with the top management of their suppliers for many years. Top management had also been stable; most of the suppliers at Soja were still owned and managed by the founder or his sons. Over time, then, the ties had become personal, not merely institutional, the stuff about which novels are written (Shiroyama 1982). These ties served an important function: they provided MMC a window into the developing strengths and weaknesses of its suppliers, and in turn provided suppliers access to current information on their primary customer. Each firm stood behind its representatives; personal trust was thus partially a product of corporate strategy.

Through these ties, one substantial weakness was apparent to MMC: the aging of its suppliers, or rather of their founders. At Soja, suppliers were still family-run, but the founding generation was beginning to retire, not always willingly, or with provision for capable successors. Mitsubishi tried to impress upon its suppliers the necessity for an orderly management transition, and helped locate new management when the owner had no successor *and* was willing to face the inevitable.[28] According to Mitsubishi purchasers, however, one-third of their nationwide network of two-hundred-plus suppliers in 1984 had neither found a viable successor nor (for larger firms) built up a professional management staff. Mitsubishi was greatly troubled by this prospect. Examples of now-defunct firms had not been enough to convince some that it was time to step aside. MMC also found it difficult to convince these typically strong-willed entrepreneurs that their sons did not have the "stuff."[29] Mitsubishi's guidance (*ikusei seisaku*) helped the Soja firms to grow strong, but in the end perhaps only half of the initial group will survive into maturity.

OM Kogyo

Mr. Namba, the founder of OM Kogyo (OM Industrial Company), had provided for succession. His only son was a skilled manager. The elder Namba remained as president in 1984, but he was also vice-president of the Soja Industrial Park Cooperative and a board member of various business and professional organizations, both prefectural and national. His son ran the firm on a day-to-day basis, while he served as elder statesman and advisor for the firm. He was kept busy in his varying official capacities, through which he also developed new business and information on forthcoming technologies.

Mr. Namba trained as a chemical engineer in a pre-WWII technical high school. After graduation he worked in Tokyo for an American supplier of plating chemicals and technology.[30] With the onset of the war its office closed, and he returned to his home in the Okayama area, starting a plating shop in 1943.[31] As the only one in the region with a technical knowledge of plating, he garnered subcontracts from nearby military factories. With a monopoly on a skill sought by the military, he was also able to obtain both labor and raw materials. Mr. Namba thus undoubtedly ended the war with a stock of materials (better than money, given the post-WWII hyperinflation) and a few experienced workers, even if his operations were initially curtailed. In 1950, with the start of the Korean War, he undertook work for the MMC Mizushima plant, which was then producing three-wheel vehicles. In 1960 Mitsubishi was but one of many customers, at 38% of OM Kogyo sales. The firm changed sites in 1947, 1953 and 1960, in part due to its water and waste disposal needs. The move to Soja Park promised better access to utilities, and a better locus in terms of roads. By 1964 he was committed to the park, and as noted above, MMC business jumped to 81% of sales. (This dependence decreased in the early 1970s to 60%, but with MMC's success in the 1970s it again climbed. In 1984 MMC accounted for 75% of OM Koygo's sales.[32]) For the past 25 years, then, he has been dependent on Mizushima business—and Mizushima on him.

Over time OM Kogyo added related manufacturing steps to plating. Seeing his management ability, MMC asked Mr. Namba to be responsible overall for the manufacture of specific parts. The firm began stamping operations in 1950, at the time it began supplying MMC. In 1956 the firm added welding and assembly operations, and thus became integrated from stamping to surface treatment (plating) and on to completing a subassembly (welding). OM Kogyo designed its own production lines, and their efficiency hinged on the firm's ability to design its own tooling. The firm began to experiment with cold rolling in 1966, and in 1969 began to manufacture bumpers with that process, using tooling developed in-house. In the late 1970s the firm added a 500–ton press line for large stampings, and more recently arc-welding robots. In 1984 it was therefore experimenting with injection molding as a substitute for large stampings. This constant change was necessary to keep up with evolving automotive technology. In fact, MMC switched to plastic (RIM urethane) bumpers in 1978. As a result, OM Kogyo lost that business and sales fell 14%. (Others were not so fortunate. Ueda [1987] described a bumper manufacturer in Tokyo that went bankrupt when its parent firm turned to plastic bumpers. That firm was also a plating specialist but it developed no independent technical capabilities.) OM Kogyo ongoing experimentation was an attempt to forestall such loss in the future, as they expected henceforth to be in a position to bid on such business. They kept up with advances in surface treatment, introducing alumite (1963), automating its plating operation (1968), adding a sophisticated waste treatment system (1974), and introducing electrostatic (1977), charged particle (1979) and other paint technologies. By 1984 plating constituted only 10% of its business; gradual vertical integration resulted in the eclipse of its original specialty. The automotive firms' avoidance of vertical integration has *not* been mirrored by their smaller suppliers.[33]

OM Kogyo increased its capitalization repeatedly, reflecting rapid growth in the 1950s and 1960s and slower growth thereafter, as outlined in table 2.5. This, however, understated recent growth, for OM Kogyo was in 1984 but one of a group of five affiliated firms, listed in table 2.6. The second member, OM Sangyo, was set up in 1970 to carry on the traditional plating side of the business.[34] It built a factory in Okayama in 1972, and absorbed an adjacent plant (built by OM Kogyo in 1960) in 1976, and its workers are therefore part of the OM Kogyo union. Diversification did not stop there. The cold-rolling technology developed for making bumpers and trim was applied to manufacturing aluminum building materials. A separate firm, OM Kiki, was set up in 1973 for this venture. The site

Table 2.5. Growth of OM Kogyo

Year . Month	Capitalization
1950.1	¥250,000
1955.4	¥1,000,000
1961.12	¥4,000,000
1963.12	¥8,000,000
1964.12	¥12,000,000
1966.12	¥20,000,000
1970.12	¥30,000,000
1978.12	¥45,000,000
1982.10	¥60,000,000

Source: 1984 OM Kogyo Brochure.

chosen for OM Kiki was in an area where labor was cheaper, and was far enough removed from Soja to avoid the OM Kogyo union. Another attraction was the cost of its factory: school consolidation left a vacant building, which the local government leased for a pittance ($300 a month) to attract jobs. The next venture was Takahashi OM, set up in 1974 to produce smaller stampings and assemblies, such as the pipe for filling up gas tanks. (OM Kogyo thereafter concentrated on large stampings.) The final venture, OM Kenso, was founded in 1976 to deal in real estate and construction.

In reality, then, the firm's operations were more extensive than they at first seemed. OM Kogyo, the parent firm, accounted for 73% of the sales of the group as a whole. While automotive products constituted 91% of its sales, for the group as a whole the proportion was 71%. Separately, each firm was capitalized at less than ¥100 million, and only one had more than 300 employees. All firms in

Table 2.6. OM Kogyo Group

Firm	Incorporated	Employees	Capitalization
OM Kogyo	1954	350	¥60,000,000
OM Sangyo	1970	40	¥5,000,000
OM Kiki	1973	100	¥32,400,000
Takahashi OM	1974	50	¥20,000,000
OM Kenso	1976	5	¥10,000,000
Total		545	¥127,400,000

Source: 1984 OM Kogyo Brochure.

the OM group were thus still classed legally as "Small and Medium Enterprises," maintaining their access to government small business financial institutions and other small business programs. In 1983 the combined group, however, had 550 employees, a total capitalization of ¥127 million and sales of ¥11.3 billion ($90 million). This could hardly be called a small- or medium-sized enterprise.

Splitting lines of business among individual firms had other advantages. Management was kept simpler; each firm was based on one manufacturing technology or product, and could be run independently. Labor and land costs have been held down; 25% of the group's employees are outside the OM Kogyo union. The top posts at OM Kogyo proper were occupied by Namba family members, but middle managers could aspire to a top post at a related firm. And should worse come to worse and one of the ventures fail, limited liability will protect the others from total loss.[35]

Toward the Future: Internationalization

While the Galant helped establish Mitsubishi as a domestic car manufacturer, growth remained modest: the firm lacked a strong dealership network, while its cars were stylistically unexciting.[36] Instead it was in large part MMC's ties to Chrysler that fueled growth: from 7% of production in 1970, exports rose to 42% in 1976, most to the U.S.[37] In contrast, domestic performance remained lackluster, and in the early- and mid-1980s MMC lost share in a generally stagnant domestic market. To make matters worse, the U.S. negotiated a "voluntary" export restraint with Japan in 1980. This coincided with similar restraints in Europe and economic problems in Southeast Asia, Mitsubishi's other major markets. Sales peaked at 1.1 million units in 1980, and actually fell in 1981 and 1982. (The firm made a modest recovery in 1983.) Needless to say, the Soja firms' sales likewise fell in the early 1980s.

There was little prospect of a substantial future increase in demand, while improved productivity made it more difficult for the Soja firms to utilize their increasingly skilled (and highly paid) workers. On the margin, the Soja firms worked to sell parts directly to the U.S. Big Three, but Japan was becoming an expensive locale for parts manufacturing. Another minor market was parts exports to MMC ventures in Southeast Asia which assembled CKD (completely knocked-down) vehicle kits. After 1980, however, these ventures gradually increased their local manufacture and purchase of parts. A final market was to Mitsubishi's affiliates in Taiwan and Korea, which were rapidly achieving an ability to manufacture a vehicle and all its parts. The Korean firm Hyundai was particularly successful; its subcompact was briefly the best-selling car in Canada. In the short run this resulted in additional parts sales, but the major revenue source to the Park firms was in designing and building new production facilities for these fledgling producers. By 1984, five of the firms in the Soja Industrial Park had sold technology to the Asian affiliates of MMC, in the form of miniature "turnkey" assembly line projects. This short-term increase in sales, however, served to strengthen firms that in the long run were potential competitors.

Still, the members of the Soja park remained primarily domestic in focus in 1984. To the extent that foreign production was being considered, thinking focused on Southeast Asia with its low wages. The Mitsubishi supplier cooperation association, the Kashiwa-kai, had sponsored study trips to the region, and further were being planned. This focus changed dramatically, however, in April 1985, when Chrysler and Mitsubishi announced plans for Diamond-Star Motors (DSM), a joint venture for assembling a Chrysler-styled, Mitsubishi-designed car in the U.S. (Mitsubishi was the last of the five major Japanese producers to announce such a venture. By 1985, Honda, Toyota and Nissan had plants in operation, and Mazda had made public its plans for a taking over a former Ford plant.) The motivations were complex. Chrysler needed additional models to feed to its dealers, and hoped to learn Japanese management methods. With apparently limited prospects for growth within Japan, Mitsubishi and the other assemblers were expanding into a market where they believed they would have room to grow. And with the U.S. dollar trading at ¥240, it appeared that an assembly plant could import most of its parts and still remain profitable, though for safety's sake a target of ¥200–¥220 was used. Since the plan was for DSM to produce cars unique to the venture—and in a niche where MMC had no car—it was clear that some vehicles were to be exported to Japan, and perhaps also to Europe (Mitsubishi has ties there with Mercedes-Benz). But with a planned capacity of 240,000 cars a year, one clear advantage stood forth: DSM would permit both Chrysler and Mitsubishi to effectively evade the voluntary export restraint.

By the fall of 1985, however, the yen had begun to appreciate, eventually doubling in value to ¥120. Wages and other costs in Japan effectively doubled, making production there more costly than in the U.S.—and making DSM unprofitable if planned levels of parts imports were maintained. In addition, trade friction with the U.S. was extending to encompass auto parts and not just autos; it became politically prudent to procure more parts locally. Of course, for many large parts shipping was impractical. But Mitsubishi's purchases were of subassemblies, not of simple parts, and both the design and manufacture of these subassemblies had long been handled by firms such as those in the Soja Park. While DSM could potentially locate suppliers of small stampings or other individual parts in the U.S., virtually no existing American firms (other than the Big Three) made subassemblies. Mitsubishi could not readily manufacture such subassemblies itself, nor was it in a position to transfer know-how it did not have to a U.S. firm wanting to enter the industry, presuming such a partner could be found. (It also wanted to limit its investment in the new plant.) Instead, MMC asked the Soja Park firms to undertake parts manufacturing for its new venture.

Mitsubishi's first overture to the Soja Park firms was in October 1985. The Board of Directors of the Park, comprised of the presidents of the member firms, requested the "Young Managers Association" to initiate a formal study, under the direction of a Mr. Isamu Kawasaki. Meanwhile, a group of the presidents paid a quick visit to the U.S. to tour the plants of American parts manufacturers. Before leaving they were pessimistic that operations in the U.S. were desirable; by the time they returned, they were convinced that a joint venture partner for stamping subassemblies would be hard to find, and in any case that their own technical abilities surpassed those of the firms they visited. In December 1985 detailed feasibility studies for a U.S. factory began, and a formal "go" decision was made in August 1986. Mr. Kawasaki was appointed president of the new firm, Eagle Wings Industries (EWI), a joint venture of the sixteen members of the park.

Within a couple months, a site was selected in a Rantoul, Illinois industrial park. Work on building the new plant commenced quickly, while the firm set about assembling a workforce.

Along with fifteen staff collected from managers and workers of the Soja Park firms, Mitsubishi Motors seconded three individuals to the new firm, including a former member of the purchasing staff with many years of experience overseas. (In addition, Mitsubishi guaranteed $24 million in loans.)[38] And while ironing out the details among sixteen firms was difficult, ownership and management were effectively separated: Mr. Kawasaki was more independent than if he had become head of the closely-held firm for which he worked in Japan. But most of EWI's managers were Americans; the Japanese staff concentrated on training and technical functions, rather than day-to-day management. With 95% of its employees Americans—most hired from the local community—the Diamond-Star venture has found in EWI one of the U.S. parts manufacturers it so needed.

To date the venture has gone very smoothly. The plant, which manufactures rear axle housings and other subassemblies, is now the largest factory in the community. Located in the midst of corn fields, EWI found that all of its new hires—including women—knew how to weld, worked well in teams and were otherwise at least the equal of workers at Soja. In addition, the plant has expanded rapidly, and will soon have 500 employees. This has given its workers an opportunity for advancement, as all of the foremen and team leaders have been promoted from within. (Other local factories, on the other hand, were resented in the community for tending to bring in outsiders for such posts.) EWI's main challenge was to expand its customer base, as it was initially 100% dependent on sales to DSM. Should its "parent" firm run into trouble, it too would face difficulties. For now, the prime problem is financing and managing expansion.

In 1987, for the first time ever, a Mitsubishi model was named car of the year in Japan. The timing was good: that year saw the beginning of a boom in the car market within Japan. Riding high, Mitsubishi Motors listed its shares on the Tokyo Stock Exchange for the first time in December 1988, selling ¥60 billion ($500 million) in new stock to the public to repay debt and expand its dealership network. This expansion, of course, was good news to the Soja Park firms. While the short-term prospects for the Soja Park firms appear good, one can but wonder about the longer haul. Of course, the owners of the park firms continue to age, and generational change may further erode their numbers. The auto assemblers are also increasingly willing to turn to the suppliers of rival vehicle manufacturers. In addition, technology is changing less rapidly in stamping, and the state of the art is being adopted by potential suppliers in countries with lower labor costs. Competition in the parts industry therefore remains strong, but it is likely to be at the cost of current suppliers. But for now, Mitsubishi remains dependent on its Soja suppliers for engineering, and as the workers in the park age, the Soja firms are also finding it attractive to concentrate on design. Meanwhile, more and more production capacity is being placed in the hands of foreign parts plants. (Several Mizushima-area suppliers are even setting up their own ventures overseas—although not all are going smoothly.) While for the moment the Soja Park firms claim not to be worried about a "hollowing out" of their market as production moves abroad, it is hard to believe that they will *all* become profitable multinational enterprises.

While the new overseas suppliers, especially those in Southeast Asia, still have weak management and especially technical abilities, that will not remain true forever. Nor is MMC likely to restrict its design and engineering efforts to a Japanese base. Mitsubishi struggled hard in the early 1960s to create goodwill among its suppliers, and while it succeeded, it did so in a growing market. In the future, it must replicate that feat internationally, a much more difficult task. Meanwhile, it must maintain the viability of the Soja Park firms and other key suppliers in a slowly growing market, and one where there will be more pressure to turn to foreign suppliers for their manufacturing cost advantages. But while the domestic Japanese supplier base may slowly deteriorate, there is as yet no evidence of a collapse of trust or an end to the structure of close, ongoing ties between auto and parts firms.[39]

The Evolution of the Automotive Parts Industry

The auto industry in Japan effectively began in the second half of the 1920s, when two firms set up commercially viable assembly operations. By the early 1930s, with the help of higher tariffs and a weaker yen, these two firms—Ford and GM—drove European and American imports from the domestic market. Following the onset of the Pacific War in 1937, however, the army closed down these U.S.-owned operations. In their stead three Japanese firms, Toyota, Nissan and Isuzu, succeeded as commercial producers of automobiles. And while there was much new entry into the industry after 1945, none of the U.S. Big Three chose to return to Japan. It was thus left to a dozen or more firms to fight for shares in the rapidly expanding domestic market, and for those that survived, ultimately to advance overseas.

Out of the immediate postwar environment came the decision by the auto firms to rely on outside suppliers rather than to integrate vertically into parts production. However, unlike the U.S., where parts firms antedated the auto industry and helped the initial entrants to develop, in Japan it was the assemblers that took the lead, encouraging their suppliers to improve their management and production capabilities (Helper 1990c). At the same time, implementing this subcontracting strategy required the development of new management methods to aid this learning process and to cope with close interfirm ties. (These innovations, sketched here, are detailed in chapter 6.)

This chapter traces these developments, dividing the history of the industry into three periods: the pre- and early post-WWII era,

1923–1953; the rapid growth era that lasted until the first oil shock, 1953–1973; and recent changes, 1973–1985. Each section surveys in order developments in final demand and the automotive assemblers, the evolution of the parts industry, and changes in contracting patterns and pricing. The final section summarizes the main points. Due to the chronological order of presentation, the key arguments from the book's perspective are made in the middle of the chapter: it was only in the rapid growth era that the adoption of a subcontracting strategy, the development of a network of increasingly efficient parts suppliers, and the transformation of interfirm ties took place.

The First Thirty Years: 1923–1953

The Automotive Market

1923–1945. Automobiles first came into wide use in Japan as a result of the Great Kanto Earthquake of 1923. This destroyed much of Tokyo, and with it the streetcar-based public transport system, so the Tokyo government imported 2,000 Ford buses to provide interim transport. They worked well, and soon even the National Railway was importing truck chassis for conversion to buses. But ocean transport of complete vehicles was costly; specialized car transport ships were not developed until the 1960s. Ford therefore built an assembly plant in Yokohama in 1925; GM followed suit in 1927 with a plant in Osaka, while Chrysler set up a joint venture in 1929. The market, however, was by today's standards minuscule: at their peak, the operations of the Big Three together produced only 30,000 vehicles a year.

Several Japanese companies tried making four-wheel cars in the late 1920s, but none were able to compete against Ford and GM. The Japanese military also produced a small number of trucks in their arsenals, and from 1918 subsidized domestic truck production; still, few were produced. Ford and GM supplied most of domestic demand through their assembly operations, though 30% of demand during 1926–1928 continued to be met by imports of assembled vehicles. But in December 1931 Japan left the gold standard, resulting in a sharp devaluation of the yen. Coupled with tariff increases, this doubled the price of imported vehicles. From the early 1930s, therefore, direct imports became negligible. However, since the locally assembled products of the Big Three depended on imported parts, their costs also increased. This led to the purchase of more parts within Japan, and it also provided an opening for niche vehicles, including the commercial production of small three-wheel trucks. (See table 3.1 on the output of the Big Three and of Japanese three-wheel and four-wheel producers.)

The winds of war created a second opening for would-be domestic producers. The Japanese Army staged the Manchurian Incident in September 1931, which provided an excuse for the annexation of the region. The growing strength of the army encouraged more firms to attempt to produce trucks for the military. Despite large subsidies they were commercial failures, though three of these firms merged in 1933 to form what eventually became Isuzu (Nis-

Table 3.1.   Pre-1945 CKD and Domestic Output

Year	GM CKD Assembly	Ford CKD Assembly	Total CKD Assembly	Domestic Three-wheel Vehicles	Domestic Four-wheel Vehicles
1925	—	3,437	3,437	—	—
1926	—	8,677	8,677	—	—
1927	5,635	7,033	12,688	—	—
1928	15,491	8,850	24,341	—	—
1929	15,745	10,674	29,338	—	—
1930	8,049	10,620	19,678	458	300
1931	7,478	11,505	20,109	434	552
1932	5,893	7,448	14,087	840	1,111
1933	5,942	8,156	15,082	1,612	1,822
1934	?	?	33,458	2,443	2,888
1935	?	?	30,787	5,355	9,837
1936	?	?	30,997	3,079	12,557
1937	?	?	28,951	8,029	15,233
1938	?	?	18,000	18,253	10,450
1939	—	—	—	33,203	7,953
1940	—	—	—	35,487	8,113
1941	—	—	—	43,161	4,503
1942	—	—	—	35,978	3,721
1943	—	—	—	24,439	2,259
1944	—	—	—	20,936	1,338
1945	—	—	—	6,861	686

Source: Nakamura, Seiji (1957:27, table 4) and Genther (1986:364).
Note: After 1928 CKD output includes Chrysler vehicles assembled by Kyoritsu. A question mark indicates no data available; a dash indicates minimal or no production. Data vary slightly depending on the source; compare Amagai (1982:71).

san also took over part of the operations of one of these firms; Cusumano 1985:16). As an invasion of China proper appeared increasingly likely, the military became more serious about promoting a domestic truck industry. Under pressure from the army, in 1936 the government passed an Auto Industry Law, designed in part to limit the role of the U.S. firms. With this inducement, Toyota and Nissan entered the four-wheel vehicle market, joining the now-viable Isuzu. Toyota and Nissan, who had begun their planning before the army's ascendancy, aimed at passenger car and small truck production. Isuzu, long dependent on the military, continued to target the manufacture of large trucks.

The fortunes of these three firms rose as those of the Big Three declined. (See table 3.2.) Japan invaded China in 1937, and the army stepped up pressure on foreign producers; the U.S. auto firms were denied import licenses, and were thereby forced to close their assembly operations in 1938. Despite the ground war in China, however, truck production was never a top military priority. The military did use its control over material allocation to force Nissan and Toyota to concentrate on making trucks. Nevertheless, output declined after 1941, as Toyota, Isuzu and Nissan were increasingly affected by inadequate steel supplies. (The three-wheel vehicle producers likewise saw their output plummet.)

From 1943 the ground war in China faded in importance and the auto firms were gradually forced to switch their output to aircraft engines and parts. The war affected the industry in other ways. Loans from government financial institutions dominated corporate balance sheets. The debt-equity ratio of the auto makers deteriorated from 40:60 in 1932 to 65:35 by 1943; by war's end the imbalance must have been far greater (Kobayashi 1969:sect. 4.9). The military intervened directly in management, with the army taking over Toyota's factories in the early 1940s. The indiscriminate draft, which swept up skilled workers and managers, made matters worse. By 1944, U.S. interdiction of shipping totally cut off Japan's access to raw materials. By 1945, the dispersal of factories to avoid air raids further disrupted production. Ironically, lack of truck transport added to the chaos: it sometimes required weeks to haul machinery to new sites by hand- and ox-cart. It took forty days to move one small parts manufacturer (Odaka et al. 1988:149). And even though U.S. bombing caused little direct damage to the automotive firms, machinery was often subjected to the elements dur-

Table 3.2. Pre-1945 Vehicle Output, Domestic Firms

Year	Trucks	Cars	Subtotal	Miniature Vehicles	4-Wheel Total
1936	5,004	847	5,851	6,335	12,186
1937	7,643	1,819	6,462	8,593	15,057
1938	13,981	1,774	15,755	8,633	24,388
1939	29,233	856	30,089	4,425	34,504
1940	42,073	1,633	43,706	2,335	46,041
1941	42,813	1,065	43,878	2,620	46,498
1942	37,653	1,362	39,115	—	39,115
1943	25,174	522	25,696	—	25,696
1944	21,434	19	21,453	309	21,762
1945	6,723	—	6,723	3	6,726

Source: Nakamura, Seiji (1957:61, table 11).
Note: These figures do not include US Big Three output. Data in different sources vary slightly. For example, Okumura et al. (1965, table 1.8) show 23,621 trucks in 1944.

ing dispersal. By the end of the war in August 1945, operations were in disarray and had in most cases ceased.

1945–1953. Management at war's end was oriented to coping with the demands of the military and the logistic chaos of wartime Japan rather than to the demands of competitive markets. The war, though, did leave one valuable legacy: Japanese firms had gained experience in manufacturing both vehicles and components. But at the start of the U.S. Occupation of Japan in 1945, the continued existence of the major automotive firms, Isuzu, Nissan and Toyota, was problematic. They faced serious labor and financial difficulties, facilities had been designated for reparations in kind and materials were unavailable. They also faced new rivals as former military contractors turned to automotive production, though the U.S. Big Three did not seek to reenter the market. Finally, industry output did not even reach the 1,500 per month quota of truck production authorized by the Occupation. Instead, firms kept busy making whatever products might sell, including agricultural implements and pots and pans for household use.

With the onset of the cold war during 1947–1948, the U.S. Occupation lifted reparations designations and permitted passenger car production to resume.[1] But the firms remained in a very weak position. One manifestation of this was an inability to borrow from commercial banks; most of Toyota's and Isuzu's loans were from the government Reconstruction Finance Bank (S. Nakamura 1957:103–4; Genther 1990:55–6). Their problems were accentuated by the deflationary Dodge Line policies of 1949, which sought to end the post-WWII hyperinflation. In the ensuing recession, current liabilities of the six main auto firms doubled while current assets increased only 60% — and many of those were of questionable value (S. Nakamura 1953:178). Toyota in particular was hit hard in the 1949 recession, as it was unable to collect on the installment financing it had provided purchasers. The government loaned money to bail out the firm, but the Toyoda family lost control of the company to its creditors, the firm's Tokyo-area factories were sold off, and new management was brought in. It and the other auto firms were forced to fire workers and to cut wages by ten percent.[2]

Contemporary Japanese observers believed that large firms in many industries would have failed if the Korean War had not broken out in June 1950. During the war, the U.S. sought deliberately to channel procurement to Japan, and Toyota and Nissan soon obtained substantial truck orders. The U.S. military purchased 7,624 trucks in 1950, 36% of Japanese vehicle output, and placed additional orders in 1951. The impact was significant: Toyota, which obtained the most orders, was able to pay off its considerable debts in 1951. U.S. vehicles, which had been abandoned throughout the Pacific theater, were also shipped to Japan for repair or to be cannibalized for parts; Hino, Komatsu, and forerunners of the current Fuji Heavy Industries (Subaru) and Mitsubishi Motors obtained lucrative contracts (S. Nakamura 1957:108, 114). In addition, U.S. military personnel were stationed in the auto factories, providing valuable technical and management assistance. Toyota, for instance, found American advice helpful in painting, plating and office management (Kodaira 1968:208).

Peace talks began in mid-1951, ending the Korean War boom. The industry faced renewed labor problems, and ultimately another round of strikes (including an especially bitter 100–day strike at Nissan). But by bringing in less hostile "second" unions, management undercut the militants and ended the threat of an industrial union. (See Halberstam 1986: chs. 8 and 9; Gould 1984 discusses the legal framework that permitted second unions.) Nevertheless, labor peace came at a price, including a greater emphasis on employment security. And demand for cars and trucks, while growing, remained small, and seemed likely to stay subject to periodic downturns.

Automotive Parts: 1923–1953

1923–1945. Before the 1925 entry of Ford into Japan, the market for automotive parts was very small. In the World War I era, car owners employed a full-time driver-cum-mechanic; while replacement parts might be machined locally, there was no ongoing production. After 1925, the number of vehicles increased sufficiently for local entrepreneurs to begin manufacturing common replacement items. The production of spark plugs, brake linings, belts, springs, pistons, piston rings and radiators all began at an early date; Nihon Kikaki even made carburetors.

Ford and GM, however, initially imported and assembled completely knocked down (CKD) vehicles, and so neither purchased nor manufactured parts in Japan. But after 1931, commercial three-wheel vehicle production increased parts demand, while the depreciation of the yen and tariff changes made local firms more competitive against imported parts. Several large firms entered the market, including Mitsubishi Electric and Hitachi. Similarly, Tobata Casting (the parent firm of Nissan Motors) obtained orders from Ford for malleable castings, and Teikoku Spring sold springs, bumpers and wheel rims.[3] In some cases, these firms used tie-ups or licenses with foreign firms as a route of entry. Sumitomo established a joint venture with Dunlop Tires in 1918 to make bicycle tires, and later made auto tires. The fledgling Toyo Kogyo (Mazda) licensed foreign casting technology in 1934. Hitachi licensed carburetor technology from a French firm in 1936. The military, to support diesel engine production, pushed for a domestic source of diesel fuel pumps and injectors. As a result, in 1939 Bosch (with Hitler's personal authorization) entered a joint venture, Diesel Kiki (Diesel Kiki 1981). Other firms with foreign ties included Nihon Air Brake and Japan Plate Glass.[4]

A handful of large and more technically capable firms thus were able to produce carburetors, filters and other components. But the majority of parts firms were like Kojima Press, whose seven employees began making washers for Toyota in 1937 using simple hand- and foot-powered tools (Odaka et al. 1988:143–153). (Kojima

Press is still a supplier to Toyota, for which it makes 500 different small stampings.) The simple production methods of the era are reflected in the composition of the early Toyota supplier association. At its formation in 1939, the association had but eighteen members; of these, five made screws, two made bolts and nuts, two made small stampings and three produced other small items; only six firms made more complicated parts (Matsui 1973). These firms carried out one or two simple machining steps or other operations on materials furnished by Toyota; some did not even produce finished parts. Relative to the auto firms, suppliers had older and poorer tooling (and sometimes only hand tools), and their workers were less skilled. Few firms had specialized machinery; even the automotive assemblers relied on skilled machinists operating general-purpose machine tools. Not surprisingly, auto parts purchasers complained that they had to inspect 100% of incoming parts, found most bad, and had to rework them themselves (Matsui 1973). (The assembled vehicle was little better: in the China war theater old GM and Ford trucks were preferred, as the springs, axles, driveshafts, distributors and pistons of domestic trucks frequently failed, with fatal consequences if the occupants were stranded outside a secure area; Shiroyama 1982.)

Existing firms in Japan, however, could not or would not produce many of the items the fledgling auto producers needed. This, together with price and quality considerations, led Nissan and Toyota to design their vehicles to make extensive use of GM and Ford parts, which they procured in the U.S. aftermarket. Forgings and castings seldom failed, however, and so were not available as repair parts, while gears and electrical components were extremely expensive. When neither domestic nor foreign sources could be found, the auto firms were forced to integrate vertically. Thus Toyota set up an electrical component operation (the now-independent Nippon Denso), a glass firm, a specialty steel maker (the current Aichi Seiko) and a shop to manufacture machine tools (now Toyota Machine Tool). (Note that in the U.S. Ford had a specialty steel mill, and Chrysler and Ford both had glass plants, but no U.S. auto firm made machine tools.) Nissan turned to fellow members of the Aikawa conglomerate such as Hitachi and Tobata Casting.

But as the war led to increased automotive assembly, so it also encouraged more domestic parts production. Formal policies existed specific to the auto industry. In 1938, an auto parts law was passed, modeled after the 1936 Auto Industry Law. The government drew up a list of 126 "outstanding" firms, including many companies prominent today. However, only one firm, Topy Industries, was formally licensed under the law (Press Kogyo 1975). Similarly, a control organization to oversee materials allocation for the parts industry was set up on paper in 1940. It only began functioning in 1943, however, and by that time the auto parts firms, as with the auto assemblers, were redirected to munitions and aircraft parts production.

Finally, wartime policy encouraged subcontracting. Large firms were given orders far beyond their own capacity, and were forced to turn to smaller firms for rough machining, even when such shops were inefficient. (The military did this deliberately, hoping to increase employment in the provinces and pull rural repair shops and textile firms into the war effort.) In addition, materials were rationed through industry control associations, of which only large, war-production-oriented firms were members; to obtain materials legally, small firms had to affiliate with association members. In turn, the more subcontractors a large firm had, the more materials it could claim, and the uncertainty of rationing made exaggerated claims essential. But the use of subcontractors also burdened large firms with the inspection and repair of parts and the management of material flows.

Subcontracting ties were thus often ephemeral, or existed only on paper; W. Mark Fruin (forthcoming) has dubbed the system a "wartime black market clearing house." Nevertheless, the unavailability of imports meant that by the end of the war all the components of a vehicle were produced domestically. Likewise, a large number of individuals gained experience in the machine industries. Finally, through munitions subcontracting large and small firms had worked together, albeit unwillingly and for their separate ends. But since automotive and aircraft production had ceased by the end of the war, most subcontracting ties were also terminated (S. Nakamura 1957:228).

1945–1953. At war's end there was a latent demand for automotive parts. Domestic truck output was below 500 units per month, and so was relatively unimportant, but the repair parts market did generate demand. During the war vehicles were converted to use a variety of ersatz fuels, causing engines to deteriorate rapidly, while roads were bad, adding to wear and tear. Spare parts were generally unavailable, and there was no rubber for tires; only half the trucks and cars in Japan were operable. However, trade controls under the Allied Occupation made it difficult to import parts from the U.S. aftermarket. Many firms therefore entered or reentered the auto parts market.

The Korean War, which began in June 1950, was a boon for the nascent parts industry as well. The automotive firms were reluctant to hire regular workers or to expand physical capacity. When they were added, it was as temporary workers (rinjiko) with the explicit understanding that they would be fired when the boom ended (S. Nakamura 1953:180). Firms therefore turned to subcontracting to expand their output. They could find outside suppliers readily, and neither they nor subcontractors needed to invest in additional capacity. This was possible because there was idle capacity among small machining shops, and because both parts and automotive firms relied on simple production methods. Overall, technology remained primitive; many operations were done manually, such as the bending and cutting of sheet metal for truck bodies using hammer, anvil and shears. Furthermore, accurate forgings and castings could not be made, so extensive machining to tolerance was needed. This was exactly the sort of work that subcontractors, with their general-purpose machinery, could be given when the auto firms' own capacity was strained. Subcontracting, however, was a short-term strategy to adapt to what firms thought might be a short-term boom. During recessions the automotive firms could and did pull production in-house to keep their own factories busy; this happened in 1949–1950 and again in 1954. (The long strike at Nissan in 1954 accentuated this; cuts among one group of fourteen suppliers were at least 20%, and for most were over 50%; S. Nakamura 1957:110, 235.)

While there was new entry, firms with prewar origins formed the core of the components industry, particularly those that had produced automotive and aircraft parts and components. For example, in a December 1939 list of firms recognized as "manufacturers of superior automotive parts and materials," at least 45 are prominent today as producers of major components such as pistons, coil and leaf springs, radiators, fuel pumps, batteries, bearings and brakes (Ozaki 1955:621–29). Similarly, in 1955, of the 231 members of the Japan Automotive Parts Industry Association, 60% (140 firms) started up before 1945 (Kodaira 1968:56, drawing on Jidosha Buhin

Kogyokai and Nihon Kikai Kogyo Rengokai 1957). Likewise, the advertising section of the first automotive parts yearbook provides a sample of 66 suppliers, including many of the leading parts firms. (The ads, in *Nihon no Jidosha Buhin Kogyo* 1965:411–496, normally included the date of founding and principal products.) Most were established before 1945, 54 of them as independent firms, while others were spun off from large firms. Half (33 firms) produced automotive parts before 1945, while many had supplied the aircraft industry and readily shifted to auto parts production. (For example, Kayaba Industries produced aircraft suspensions, while Aishin Kogyo's predecessor made aircraft engine parts.)

Through the mid-1950s, then, there were older and larger firms manufacturing components for which there was significant aftermarket demand, together with numerous firms carrying out simple processes or making simple parts. Among the small firms, some had previous ties with an automotive assembler, but even among the more specialized firms most were postwar entrants. (The 40% of the Japan Automotive Parts Industry Association members that started up after 1945 tended to be smaller firms.) These newer entrants often supplied only one auto firm, in contrast to the older firms, which typically supplied several or even all of the auto makers. As specialized producers, the larger firms tended to be dependent on the automotive market. Smaller firms, however, relied more heavily on standardized machining operations, so that the automotive firms were but one of a range of potential customers. Finally, while some firms depended on new vehicle production (e.g., truck body manufacturers), for most firms the automotive assemblers become a substantial market only after 1955.[5]

Contracting: 1925–1953

Subcontracting in the early 1930s and beyond consisted overwhelmingly of the purchase of simple manufacturing services, such as the drilling of a hole or deburring of a casting. A subcontractor received a semifinished part from the contractor (who sometimes was a broker and not the ultimate purchaser), carried out a simple operation, and returned the piece (often still only partly finished) to the contractor. This process-oriented subcontracting provided the starting point from which subsequent contracting practices evolved in the automotive industry.

Much of "modern" industry was concentrated in a few communities, such as the machining district in the area of the current Tokyo-Yokohama boundary (Ota Ward and Kawasaki City), or the Kawaguchi casting district, located just north of Tokyo. (Nissan and Isuzu were both in Tokyo, while Toyota evolved in a district of textile and textile equipment producers, of which it was historically the largest member.) These areas had myriad small shops with, for example, one drill press or a standard metalworking lathe. Competition among firms resulted in a "market" price for such services, in effect an hourly rental rate for the use of a standard machine and its operator. Since the contractor was often doing some of the same work itself, it could estimate how much time was required. Given the hourly market rate, neither bargaining nor cost accounting were required to set prices.

Continuity in contracting was not unusual, but it was not considered crucial. Given contemporary production volumes, an automotive purchaser was "small" in the market. It was not a primary source of demand for firms in machining districts where most suppliers were located, nor did it need to worry about the availability of subcontracting capacity. (After 1948, and especially in 1951, reparations plans were modified and the government sold off machinery from the old military arsenals. This permitted many auto and auto parts companies to purchase high-quality machine tools, but it accentuated excess capacity among machine shops.) The level of skills among shops in a machining district varied widely (and, grumbled most observers, from bad to worse), so experience with a given shop was useful in assessing likely quality and timeliness of delivery. But the major advantage of a given small supplier rested upon location and personal ties with brokers or purchasers—advantages, in other words, shared by many. In the literature of the period ongoing ties were viewed neither as normal in practice nor as an essential element of purchasing policy.

In practice, small firms in a machining district often obtained work through one or two brokers or "parent" firms. Portions of a large order were also traded back and forth among neighboring shops on an ad hoc basis. Brokers provided management decentralization; through proximity and constant contact they were better able to evaluate skill and reliability than the ultimate purchaser. Brokers also could post a surety, and took on the nuisance of managing material flows among a host of small firms. In most cases they were themselves subcontractors, but were older and larger in size, and hence well-connected among peers and protégés; it was natural for the head of a larger shop, acting as a broker, to give orders to a relative or former apprentice. Similarly, an auto firm might favor the shop of a former employee—and of course the other crucial element for a broker was to have ties with one or more firms that put out work. (See chapter 7.) The purchaser might not know (or care) whether a subcontractor-cum-broker did any of the work himself; what they wanted to purchase were his management and organizational skills.[6] And since there were many brokers and would-be suppliers, little was needed to cause work to be shifted to another supplier. In sum, arms-length, "market" ties prevailed with the typical parts subcontractor.

Contracting patterns fit those of a competitive market, but for manufacturing processes rather than for parts production per se. Large firms did not pay much attention to their suppliers or to contracting methods. Since subcontracting was effectively a market purchase, the auto firms were unwilling to invest in suppliers as the benefits would accrue to others. In Japanese firms of this period, cost accounting was at best rudimentary, and statistical quality control, industrial engineering methods and other management tools for manufacturing were unknown; production technology was equally backward. The stationing of U.S. personnel to assist Japanese producers during the Korean War, and a series of management consultants from the U.S. (such as Juran and Deming for statistical quality control) provided a window on U.S. best practice, not just in technology but also in management systems. But these did not in general filter down to suppliers. (The exception in this era was Toyota, which preceded the other automotive firms by several years in attending to its suppliers.)

Rapid Growth: 1953–1973

The Automotive Market

A recession hit Japan during 1954–1955, but thereafter the economy began to grow rapidly, and the auto companies soon were faced with the need to systematize their factory operations. As incomes rose, so did the demand for vehicles; the growth of the auto market outpaced GNP. Furthermore, this growth accrued increasingly to domestic firms. Until 1955, foreign vehicles constituted half of apparent consumption: not only were there direct imports (despite a 40% tariff), but there were significant indirect imports via the purchase of used cars from U.S. military personnel and the assembly of CKD vehicles under one of four licensing agreements (calculated from Okumura et al. 1965:144). In 1955, however, the government raised trade barriers, channeling growth to domestic producers. Thus, while the automotive assemblers began the era with their attention focused on labor relations, they soon shifted their focus to rationalizing their production system and bringing out new vehicles in a rapidly expanding market. This ultimately engendered many other changes.

For Toyota the timing of the boom was good, since in 1955 it introduced the Crown, the first domestically designed passenger car of the post–WWII era. Toyota was the first firm to begin a thorough rationalization program, as part of its efforts to stave off bankruptcy in 1950. It sought to adopt American management techniques, and by 1956 was experimenting with an early version of "just-in-time" production controls.[7] A symbolic turning point was reached in 1959, when Toyota's output (combining both trucks and cars) reached 10,000 units a month. (In contrast, Toyota's 1990 output was over 10,000 units a day.) At Nissan labor problems took the fore until 1954, but it, too, began expanding after 1955. During the period leading up to 1960, therefore, the leading auto firms began implementing mass-production methods, and this soon extended to the construction of new plants. Toyota again preceded its rivals, completing the first specialized assembly plant in Japan in 1960.

Given their recent battles with labor unions and frequent recessions, the auto firms were cautious in adding employees and capacity. Instead, they continued to utilize outside parts suppliers whose workers were in addition often not unionized. The industry remained small in relation to manufacturing as a whole, while as noted above, supplier capacity was a ready substitute for that at the auto firms proper. In fact, despite four- to six-fold higher output, direct employment initially fell and in 1957 was barely above 1952 levels. (See table 3.3.) Employment at parts suppliers in turn rose, increasing from 40% of industry employment in 1950 to 60% by 1960. Thus employment at parts firms went from only 20% above that at assemblers in 1950, to 100% over assembler levels from 1956 on. (See figures 3.1 and 3.2, though these data must be treated with caution.)[8] Thus, during the middle and late 1950s, there was a quantitative shift toward greater subcontracting.

However, contrary to expectations at the time, passenger car demand not only continued to increase rapidly, but did so without going through periodic downturns. This led to several changes. First, as output expanded, the auto firms were forced to hire additional workers, first as "temporary" employees, but increasingly as regular (unionized) employees. (See Chapter 4.) Second, by 1960 it was difficult to find skilled workers, or to train new workers fast enough to keep up with demand. This encouraged the adoption of production lines and other mass-production technologies, which made possible the use of relatively unskilled workers. On the other hand, once dedicated equipment was adopted, it was no longer possible to pull work in-house should demand suddenly slow. And suppliers in turn were forced to adopt "modern" production methods and change their own employment mix (Tomiyama 1973:128–29;

Table 3.3. Nissan and Toyota Output and Employment

Category	1952	1953	1954	1955	1956	1957	Increase 1952-57
TOYOTA							
Regular	5,115	5,311	5,271	5,182	4,989	5,830	14%
Output							
Sm Trucks	4,950	4,416	8,434	9,184	25,289	43,423	877%
Reg Trucks	6,838	7,906	9,688	6,030	8,940	15,847	231%
Cars	2,049	4,253	4,624	7,827	13,454	19,885	970%
Total	13,837	16,575	22,746	23,041	47,683	79,155	565%
NISSAN							
Regular	7,725	7,671	7,605	6,858	6,448	8,384	9%
Output							
Sm Trucks	3,687	3,693	4,714	7,556	11,000	26,937	731%
Reg Trucks	7,224	7,307	9,976	6,998	9,006	12,709	176%
Cars	2,213	3,933	4,191	8,008	15,361	18,801	850%
Total	13,124	14,933	18,881	22,562	35,367	58,447	445%

Source: Car production and labor force data are from S. Nakamura (1957, tables 28, 57), respectively and truck output data are from Amagai (1982:200).
Note: The car totals for Nissan include CKD assembly. For 1957, car production is calculated from total production and market share data, and are not consistent with the data for prior years.

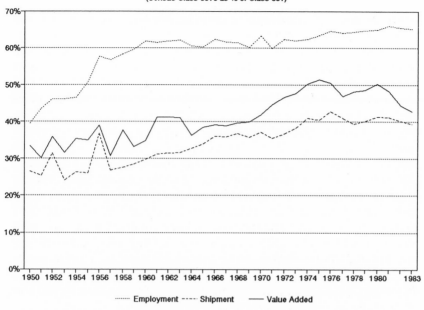

Figure 3.1. Parts Share of Industry
(Census Class 3613 as % of Class 361)

······ Employment ----- Shipment —— Value Added

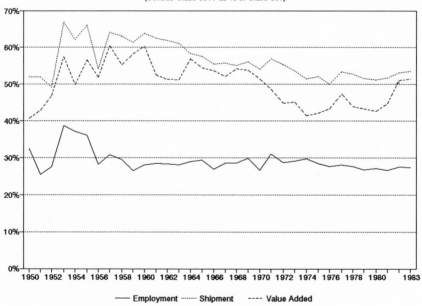

Figure 3.2. Assembly Share of Industry
(Census Class 3611 as % of Class 361)

—— Employment ······ Shipment ---- Value Added

Matsui 1973). In consequence, the qualitative nature of the sub-contracting relationship was also altered. (See figure 3.3.)

Expanding volume at existing producers and evolving production technologies were not the only changes; there was also greater competition. Within the automotive industry proper, expanding demand—and the lack of alternatives for wartime producers of aircraft—encouraged substantial new entry. One avenue was through CKD assembly under foreign licenses, which the Ministry of International Trade and Industry (MITI) encouraged. Isuzu, Nissan, Mitsubishi and Hino all participated in such ventures, starting in 1953.[9] Another route was through motorcycle manufacture. After WWII, a host of firms in the vicinity of Hamamatsu City in Shizuoka Prefecture started making motorcycles and scooters. Four firms soon dominated the market (Honda, Suzuki, Yamaha and Kawasaki), and two—Suzuki and Honda—ultimately entered the passenger car market. Similarly, twelve firms tried their hand at making three-wheel trucks. By the end of the 1958 recession, only Toyo Kogyo (now Mazda) and Daihatsu remained significant producers; both later entered the four-wheel vehicle market. (See figures 3.4 and 3.5.)

By 1960, therefore, there were fourteen manufacturers of four-

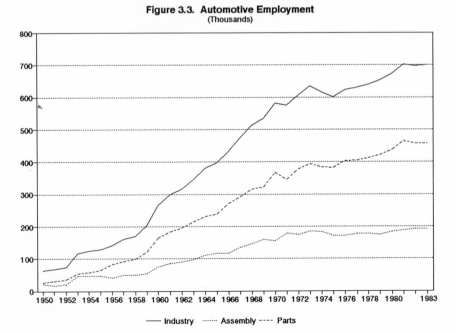

Figure 3.3. Automotive Employment
(Thousands)

— Industry ⋯⋯ Assembly ---- Parts

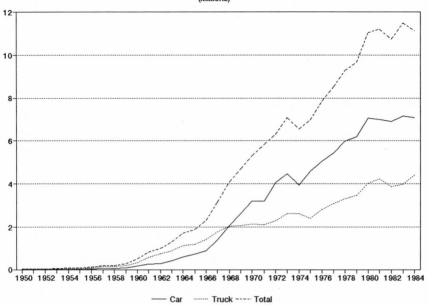

Figure 3.4. Vehicle Output, 1950-1984
(Millions)

Car ——— Truck ········ Total ----

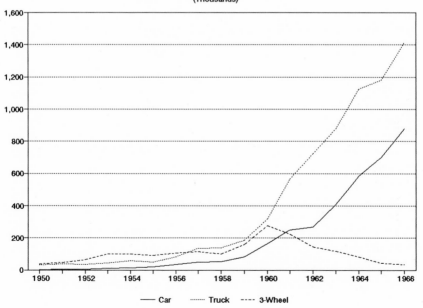

Figure 3.5. Vehicle Output, 1950-1966
(Thousands)

Car ——— Truck ········ 3-Wheel ----

wheel vehicles, though most initially concentrated on making min-icars and subcompact trucks. (Table 3.4 summarizes changes in the number of producers by vehicle class.) The largest market at that time was for trucks, not cars, and the next largest segment was for subcompact and light vehicles, not full-sized cars. Thus Hino, Nissan Diesel and Isuzu concentrated on large trucks, and Daihatsu and Suzuki on midget vehicles. (At the time both Isuzu and Daihatsu tried unsuccessfully to enter the regular passenger vehicle market. In the 1980s both did enter, with Isuzu producing cars for distribution by GM and Daihatsu for Toyota.) But truck and bus demand was strongly affected by the business cycle, and thus was stagnant during the slowdowns of 1951–1952, 1955 and 1958, while the three-wheel market went through a shakedown (as noted above). In addition, CKD assembly by Japanese firms peaked during 1960–1961. Thereafter no foreign vehicles, CKD or otherwise, were available on the domestic market. (See table 3.5 on post-1945 output.)

It was only the standard passenger car market that grew continuously throughout this and subsequent eras. Car demand doubled in 1960, and increased by at least 20% most years during 1950–1970; even in the recession years of 1958 and 1962 demand was up over 7%. But with new entry the two dominant firms, Toyota and Nissan, faced increased domestic competition and saw their market shares decline. Three firms—Honda, Mazda and Mitsubishi—did particularly well (Itami et al 1988:13; Cusumano 1985:98–99). In

Table 3.4. Number of Producers by Market Segment

Type of Vehicle	1952	1955	1960	1964.6	1967.6
Regular trucks	6	7	7	7	8
Buses	6	6	7	7	8
Small trucks	5	5	11	8	8
Light trucks	—	—	8	8	7
Small cars	5	7	8	10	10
Light cars	—	—	2	4	6
Small three-wheel	9	11	6	2	2
Light three-wheel	—	2	8	2	2
Scooters	3	7	5	2	1
Motorcycles	43	48	16	6	6
Mopeds	—	—	15	5	5

Source: Kodaira (1968:404, table 96) drawing from MITI vehicle production data.
Note: Engine displacement of "small" vehicles was under 2,000cc, of "light" under 1,000cc.

Table 3.5. Post-1945 Japanese Motor Vehicle Production
(1,000 vehicles)

Year	Trucks	Cars	Buses	Total	Three-wheel Vehicles
1945	1	0	0	1	0
1946	15	0	0	15	3
1947	11	0	0	11	7
1948	19	0	1	20	17
1949	26	1	2	29	27
1950	27	2	3	32	35
1951	31	4	4	38	44
1952	30	5	4	39	62
1953	36	9	5	50	97
1954	50	14	6	70	98
1955	44	20	5	69	89
1956	73	32	6	111	105
1957	127	47	8	182	115
1958	130	51	8	188	99
1959	177	79	7	263	158
1960	308	165	8	482	278
1961	553	250	11	814	225
1962	711	269	11	991	144
1963	863	408	13	1,284	117
1964	1,109	580	14	1,702	80
1965	1,160	696	19	1,876	43
1966	1,388	878	21	2,285	33
1967	1,743	1,376	27	3,146	26
1968	1,991	2,056	39	4,086	22
1969	2,022	2,611	42	4,675	17
1970	2,064	3,179	47	5,289	14
1971	2,058	3,718	35	5,811	12
1972	2,238	4,022	34	6,294	3
1973	2,571	4,471	41	7,083	3
1974	2,574	3,932	46	6,552	1
1975	2,338	4,568	36	6,942	0
1976	2,772	5,028	42	7,841	0
1977	3,035	5,431	48	8,515	0
1978	3,237	5,976	56	9,269	0
1979	3,397	6,176	63	9,636	0
1980	3,913	7,038	92	11,043	0
1981	4,103	6,974	103	11,180	0
1982	3,783	6,882	67	10,732	0
1983	3,904	7,152	56	11,112	0
1984	4,320	7,073	72	11,465	0

Source: Three-wheel vehicle data are from Odaka et al. (1988). Other data are from the Japan Automobile Manufacturers Association, cited in Genther (1986:370).
Note: Data from different sources are not consistent.

addition, in 1959 the Japanese government committed itself to a free trade policy that would eventually open the domestic automotive market to foreign trade and investment. But Japanese vehicles were neither price competitive with European subcompacts nor comparable in quality, and Japanese auto manufacturers were painfully aware of the gap (Halberstam 1986:ch. 24). While they fought to delay liberalization, they took seriously the threat that they might face foreign competition in the mid-1960s. However, the primary impetus to improve product and price came from numerous domestic rivals, not the distant foreign specter.

Over the period as a whole, then, the auto firms had to strive to increase capacity while lowering price and improving quality to match their numerous rivals. Throughout the 1960s new plants were built, while firms that had entered niche markets moved into the production of standard passenger cars. Production technology, of course, became much more sophisticated, while management methods such as statistical process (quality) control, value analysis and just-in-time scheduling were adopted. (See chapter 6.) Price also declined during continuously through the late 1960s, despite constant improvements in styling and performance (Itami et al. 1988:8; Tomiyama 1973:116–17). But 70%–75% of the manufacturing cost of a vehicle comprised purchased materials, components and parts. Virtually no small stampings were made internally, and even most small subassemblies were made by suppliers and shipped directly to the final assembly line. The auto firms concentrated primarily on design, marketing, final assembly, large body stampings and engine and drivetrain manufacture. It was therefore impossible for the auto firms to remain competitive unless they also improved the capabilities of their suppliers. And, as discussed below, suppliers did in fact contribute more than the auto makers themselves to cost reduction.

By the late 1960s, firms and government anticipated a slowdown in growth, or the "maturation" of the domestic passenger car market. While exports to the U.S. had reached over 400,000 units a year in 1970, foreign demand was also expected to increase but slowly. MITI officials thus talked about how the total market would grow "only" 6%–7% a year in the 1970s, and not the more than 10% a year of the previous fifteen years. In fact, already during the 1960s several smaller firms had run into difficulties: Prince merged with Nissan in 1966, Aichi Kikai became primarily an engine builder for Nissan, and Ota (Tokyu Kurogane) exited altogether. Neither industry nor government officials anticipated the explosion of foreign demand for small cars that arose after 1975.

Automotive Parts: 1953–1973

After 1955, the auto makers became the main source of demand for auto parts manufacturers. New vehicle sales grew rapidly; the ratio of new vehicle sales to the stock of existing vehicles increased from 12% in 1955 to 30%–35% throughout the 1960s.[10] The relative importance of the replacement parts market therefore declined. At the same time, the growth in new vehicle sales was coupled with increased utilization of suppliers by the auto makers, as noted above. Equally important was the qualitative shift in the nature of subcontracting that accompanied the adoption of mass production technology as the use of production lines affected the "make" versus "buy" choices of the auto firms and led to different types of work being subcontracted. This led as well to changes in contracting patterns and the overall subcontracting relationship.

Statistical data illustrate this qualitative and quantitative shift. (Again, see figures 3.1 and 3.2.) Before 1945 from 30%–50% of machining steps were subcontracted (gaichu), but purchased parts constituted as little as 14% of the cost of a vehicle (S. Nakamura 1953:243). (This figure does not include related items such as tires, glass and batteries.) In 1955, at the start of the shift of the subcontracting paradigm, parts purchases accounted for 20% of costs, while tires were a further 16% of costs, and small stampings, machining and other process subcontracting composed another 17% of costs. But even in 1955, the Japanese auto industry purchased more than the U.S. industry. Corresponding to the higher level of parts purchases, in 1955 labor costs at four Japanese auto firms averaged 14%, but were 27% at GM and 32% at Renault (Kodaira 1968:318–19).[11] By 1965 process subcontracting was minimal for most automotive firms (Nihon no Jidosha Buhin Kogyo 1967:60). Data available for one firm in 1970 show parts purchases as 63% of manufacturing costs, and steel purchases a further 14% (Tomiyama 1973:126–27). The level varied across different facets of a vehicle. Purchases were lowest for the transmission (30%) and the frame and car exterior (38%, the "metal" line); they were highest for trim (88%, including seats, dashboard, and glass) and the chassis (73%, including the starter, battery and tires). While the total quantity of subcontracted work may not have shifted much thereafter, the content continued to evolve.

This evolution encouraged new entry into the parts industry, as the automotive firms (and their primary subcontractors) sought additional suppliers. Aggregate data, such as that presented in table 3.6, provide an image of continuous growth and entry. *Census of Manufactures* data, for example, shows a steady increase in the total number of automotive industry establishments. (Since few firms have multiple establishments, this is virtually identical to the number of parts firms.) The data are not totally consistent across time, but do suggest that rapid growth in the early 1960s generated substantial new entry, with entry slowing thereafter.

This shift resulted from rationalization and the adoption of mass-production technology by the automotive assemblers. As a result of their efforts, their production flows were reorganized. Initially similar machines had been grouped together into job shops, with each machine used to manufacture a variety of parts. To rationalize production, machines were physically regrouped into production lines, and hence were dedicated to a specific type of part. With production lines, the use of process subcontracting became difficult, as volumes increased and the production line made new demands on quality and timeliness. When production was organized around job shops, a skilled worker could carry out another task until a part was available, including repairing a defective part. This flexibility could not be attained when machines were made integral to a production line and were manned by semiskilled workers. The cost of an interruption to the flow of production increased: if not initially caught, defective parts could stop a line or be worked on instead of a good part, and the idle capacity could not be redeployed.

Even with job shops, process subcontracting increased inventories and made it hard to manage the flow of production. Most parts required several machines, so that work-in-process tended to pile up. Parts also were shipped out for plating and other intermediate steps, adding to the piles on the floor. (This chaos was one stimulus for the development of just-in-time methods. In 1956, Japanese visitors to Ford were amazed to find "not a single warehouse in the plant" (S. Nakamura 1957:179). Ironically, in 1980 it was American visitors to Japan who were amazed by clean floors.)

As volumes increased and production lines were implemented,

Table 3.6. Selected Auto Industry Establishment Data
(Census Industry Code 361)

Year	Establishments with 4 or more Workers	Employment	Shipments	Value Added	Establishments with under 4 Workers
1950	1,087	62,949	32,085	11,203	—
1951	1,251	67,208	64,201	20,822	—
1952	1,398	75,186	78,360	32,463	—
1953	2,029	117,503	153,372	47,338	—
1954	2,172	124,309	181,488	58,683	1,013
1955	2,406	127,082	190,606	63,690	1,003
1956	2,417	140,674	261,514	86,743	913
1957	2,972	160,477	390,585	121,429	1,020
1958	2,999	168,343	387,787	107,266	1,104
1959[a]	2,465	203,171	513,228	155,693	1,939
1960	2,983	264,397	854,629	279,661	2,446
1961	3,208	299,394	1,099,080	286,876	2,441
1962	3,321	315,567	1,248,774	352,286	2,667
1963	3,447	344,861	1,445,060	458,865	4,305
1964	3,348	379,874	1,815,229	554,755	4,366
1965	3,539	395,933	1,979,305	588,877	4,270
1966	3,790	433,081	2,336,559	676,204	4,846
1967	3,967	475,113	2,984,166	902,991	5,454
1968	3,993	512,214	3,774,788	1,163,183	5,347
1969	3,976	533,603	4,544,708	1,335,793	5,773
1970[a]	10,418	579,974	5,467,372	1,644,888	—
1971	10,717	574,818	6,028,103	1,607,339	6,565
1972	11,835	607,173	6,767,090	1,843,894	—
1973	12,162	634,447	8,172,769	2,241,436	—
1974	11,841	614,774	9,466,906	2,367,074	—
1975	12,473	601,156	10,524,07	2,701,838	—
1976	12,622	622,251	12,424,26	3,502,332	—
1977	12,765	629,400	14,451,20	3,989,414	—
1978	13,701	637,841	16,384,02	4,275,421	—
1979	13,557	651,342	18,402,76	4,896,338	—
1980[a]	9,775	673,466	21,282,09	5,252,364	—
1981	10,007	700,078	23,798,55	5,829,025	—
1982	10,109	696,384	24,143,27	5,943,333	—
1983	10,580	698,690	25,450,87	6,610,225	5,275

Source: Drawn from the Census of Manufactures.
Note: An "a" indicates years when data classifications changed.

some work previously subcontracted was pulled back in-house, but more often the production of parts was subcontracted in full. In the aggregate, these shifts were quite large. By 1965 the number of manufacturing steps carried out by the automotive assemblers declined to 41% of their 1957 level, while the share of specialized and automatic machine tools increased from 22% to 41% and the total number of machine tools roughly tripled (Kodaira 1968:358). At Toyota, the initial rearrangement was largely completed by the early 1960s, though items such as valves and brakes were shifted out only in the mid-1960s. (In 1964, Toyota moved its lines for torque converters to Aichi Kogyo and for engine valves to Aisan Kogyo; in 1968, brake production went to Hosei Brake; Kikai Shinko Kyokai 1981.) But at Mitsubishi Motors and other firms this transition did not start until after 1960.

Another element of this shift was access to financing. While Toyota and Nissan were granted World Bank and U.S. Export-Import Bank credits, they used these funds to build assembly and engine plants, not to expand parts production. Even before 1960, additional parts capacity was needed, and suppliers were able to tap sources of funds unavailable to the auto makers. In 1965, there were at least forty parts firms with 1,000 or more employees, and 75 with over 500 workers, most of which were component manufacturers with roots going back to the 1930s (Nihon no Jidosha Buhin Kogyo 1967:45). These firms met MITI's ideal for a parts supplier: they had clearly identifiable products and technologies and high market shares. Hence from 1956, these larger firms were granted preferential access to government financing under the Machinery Industries Promotion Law; they also qualified for accelerated depreciation and were permitted to license foreign technology. (During 1956–1964, for example, the Japan Development Bank granted loans to 63 auto parts manufacturers, almost all of which were relatively large "component" manufacturers; Sei et al 1976:59. Such component firms may also have benefited from the tie-ups of Japanese and foreign car firms in the 1950s, which required the licensor to help the Japanese firms achieve 100% local content.) And by 1960 component suppliers could borrow more readily from commercial banks, or even raise equity on the stock market. (Eighteen parts firms were newly listed during 1961–1962.) Even smaller firms had their sources of capital, such as mutual savings banks (sogo ginko) and credit unions (shinyo kinko), governmental and private small business banks prohibited by law from lending to large firms. In the face of rapidly expanding output, differential access to credit in a segmented financial system undoubtedly increased the ability of the industry as a whole to raise funds.

The large component manufacturers not only had access to finance, but controlled key patents and key technologies. They were thus distinguished from smaller, less specialized suppliers in that the auto firms *had* to go to them. Many were on a par with the auto makers in the introduction of the latest management techniques. A firm like Akebono Brake used its license of American technology to develop ties to all the Japanese assemblers, including both Toyota and Nissan. (It was even able to force them to make equity investments.) With 2,700 employees, Akebono maintained 226 "secondary" suppliers and several affiliates and joint ventures in 1984; its secondary suppliers included twenty for machining, nineteen for stampings and twelve for screws.[12] In particular, they faced the same labor problems as the auto firms, and for the same reasons developed their own network of "secondary" subcontractors. Work carried out by such firms fell into three categories. First, primary suppliers subcontracted steps that did not fit readily into a "line" or used special processes such as heat treatment and plating. Second, both labor-intensive and skill-intensive (craft) tasks were put out to other firms. Finally, small volume products were subcontracted, which was important for firms that made items both for assembly and for replacement and other low-volume market niches such as large trucks, which were typically customized to the end-user's requirements. Overall, then, specialized component makers resembled the auto assemblers more than they did the bulk of auto parts firms.

In any event, from the perspective of the smaller "primary" parts suppliers and the larger "secondary" suppliers, the changes that occurred during the rapid growth era of the 1960s were reflected in a shift by their customers to the purchase of finished parts and subassemblies instead of a single process. As a result, the stronger suppliers were encouraged to carry out additional steps. (As noted in chapter 2, OM Kogyo added small stampings and subsequently welding and related assembly operations.) Parts firms' own operations became more complex, as they in effect integrated vertically. As production volumes rose during the 1960s, these operations in turn were organized into production lines.

Many of these firms initially did work for a variety of nonautomotive customers. But the explosive growth of auto demand meant that in most cases their business came to be dominated by a single automotive customer. (The parts firms with prewar origins tended to have multiple customers, but one firm was often still dominant.) With subassemblies subcontracting, these firms became important to the auto assemblers, but they received little government assistance. Even when they were able to borrow from government small business financial institutions, the amounts were limited to a small portion of total needs. These firms were also too small to be listed on the stock exchange, and were unable to recruit at the leading universities. Yet the increase in demand ultimately forced these suppliers to adopt new production technologies. Skilled labor was scarce; increased demand could not be met using general-purpose machine tools. Over time they built either production lines or evolved into specialized job shops, and all developed considerable expertise in their respective manufacturing processes. But, given their importance, they were given substantial aid by their customers toward that end, as will be seen below.

Contracting: 1953–1973

The shift to a subcontracting strategy by the automotive assemblers in the 1950s and early 1960s forced them to manage suppliers effectively. This was particularly critical once production volumes transcended the limits of a batch-oriented production system. Furthermore, as capacity utilization in manufacturing as a whole increased, the auto firms found their subcontracting environment changing. In response, they made incremental adaptations during this period, which over time evolved into the contemporary subcontracting system. The emphasis in this section is on the historical process; the practices themselves are detailed in chapter 6.

As noted above, prior to 1955 there was idle manufacturing capacity in Japan and output could be increased with little net investment. After 1955, body manufacturing and stamping plants were fully utilized, and new investment was required. By 1958 this was true for most types of automotive capacity, as the increased automotive demand coincided with expansion elsewhere in the economy. In particular, capacity was strained for items such as castings, forgings and sheet metal work. The automotive firms therefore chased after potential suppliers, trying to lock in access to their capacity. One alternative to investing, or having one's suppliers invest, was to "steal" the supplier of a rival auto firm. To prevent this, from 1956 the auto assemblers (and large firms in other rapidly expanding industries) formed vertical networks of affiliated suppliers, or *keiretsu*. (See chapter 5 and Okumura et al. 1965:289.) The auto firms demanded that suppliers dedicate most —preferably 100%—of capacity to them. This made it difficult for suppliers to defect to a rival, as it limited their ability to gradually develop other business relationships. And to further cement ties, Nissan, Toyota and to a lesser extent Isuzu bought stock issued by their key suppliers, though (unlike the Big Three) they were never merged into parent-firm operations. Later entrants faced less of a problem. They were initially small in the market and could purchase parts more readily from existing suppliers, including those of Toyota and Nissan. While they, too, developed *keiretsu*, the links were less likely to be exclusive, and they seldom developed shareholding ties.

But even without pressure from a parent firm, one company often came naturally to dominate a suppliers' business. Parts suppliers saw demand increase even more rapidly than did the automotive firms as the shift to purchasing units meant that the number of parts going into each vehicle increased. But while in the late 1950s and early 1960s the established firms tried to lock in their suppliers' capacity, by the mid-1960s the auto firms saw advantages in having suppliers diversify their business.[13] The existing auto firms saw their market share decline with the entry of Honda, Mitsubishi, Mazda and other firms and by the latter 1960s the overall market was expected to grow more slowly. The new entrants were eager to attract suppliers, and in fact their entry was eased by the existence of the supplier networks of Nissan, Toyota and Isuzu. Toyota and Nissan welcomed this—indeed, urged suppliers to broaden their base—because with multiple customers, a poor model year would be less likely to damage their suppliers' health. They also hoped that other customers would pay higher prices: Toyota did not mind if it was Mitsubishi who provided their suppliers with profits. Suppliers also saw their bargaining position improve: they could use other customers to obfuscate the source of their profits, by blaming a rival's ineptitude in pricing.

As noted in the previous section, parts firms became more

specialized and tended to complement rather than substitute for parent firm capacity. This was particularly clear when production lines were shifted to a supplier. The cost of switching suppliers increased, as more specialized assets were utilized by suppliers, and without internal capacity the auto firms no longer had the ready option of pulling work back in-house. The incentive to maintain an ongoing relationship with a given supplier therefore increased. The devolution of subassembly production to suppliers also changed the nature of purchasing management. Before, the logistics of moving parts to and from different factories threatened to overwhelm purchasing and production. Now, with subassembly subcontracting, the number of items purchasers in the auto firms had to track was vastly reduced and they could concentrate on helping existing suppliers improve.

Increased specialization placed new demands on suppliers to improve their technical abilities. But only the large auto firms had both the engineering and management resources to sort through the new American learning, and it was they that aided and abetted the adoption of the more useful techniques by their suppliers. Parts firms grew rapidly in size, and were able to (or found themselves forced to) develop middle management. Initially many suppliers were run by an owner/operator with at most a family member as an assistant. Books, if kept, were rudimentary, cost accounting unknown; financial know-how was minimal, labor management personalized. In some cases the owner was an engineer, but in many cases he was a machinist or even a brash entrepreneur, so that the ability to adopt new manufacturing methods was hampered by lack of technical background. This was viable as long as parts firms supplied simple manufacturing services in a competitive market. But as volume increased, more specialized machinery and manufacturing processes and a larger scale of operation became essential. Modern (which meant "American") management and technology were believed to be a necessary accompaniment. The auto firms, with their greater experience, stepped in to help their suppliers learn modern management, develop systematic labor relations and implement new production methods. As parent firms (oya kigyo), they worked both directly with individual firms and through their supplier associations to develop (ikusei suru) their supplier base. In turn, they often picked up new ideas from their more innovative suppliers which could be implemented elsewhere in their subcontracting network.

Finally, pricing policies changed because of greater interdependency, the purchase of more complicated products, and the change in the scale of operations. No longer could a market price be directly observed, as subcontracting no longer centered on single processes or simple parts. Furthermore, purchasers wanted to attract and retain suppliers and have them invest in new manufacturing and management technology. To do this, purchasers had to offer subcontractors a reasonable profit and assurance of continuity. Yet stiff competition in the final market required that the cost of even minor parts had to be held in line; given the sheer number of parts, it was quite possible to be nickeled and dimed to death.

In meeting these problems, the automotive firms developed a pricing mechanism derived from the previous system of market-oriented process subcontracting. For each part or subassembly a detailed bid was required, in which the manufacturing process was broken down into steps and a price attached to each step. In this it mimicked the earlier system, in that the cost of these steps could in principle be compared to the "market" rate for that process, and not merely to the final unit price quoted by rival suppliers. To this cost base was added a margin to cover overhead and profit. The linkage to market rates forced suppliers to keep costs in line. But firms that could run their operations more efficiently than rivals found this pricing mechanism very attractive. Given the stable contracting environment, firms had the confidence to invest in new plant and equipment. By making subassemblies, they also had more parameters under their control, further improving their ability to lower costs. Finally, given the use of a slowly changing cost base, innovation was often highly profitable; a firm that could lower costs faster than rivals reaped substantial benefits.[14] Improving supplier management and technology was also necessary. Beginning in the early 1960s there was vigorous price competition in the passenger car and other vehicle markets. And despite the qualitative improvement of the assemblers' own operations, parts suppliers proved to be the primary source of manufacturing cost reductions. (See table 3.7.)

The automotive firms obtained the assistance of suppliers in improving overall performance in large part because they established a trusting and cooperative relationship with their suppliers. Formal supplier associations were one tool they used to foster this. While supplier associations existed during WWII, many were moribund from their inception. The renewed interest in supplier

Table 3.7. Changes in Manufacturing Costs

Category	1958-60	1961-63	1964-5	1958-65	Total
Total Reduction in Manufacturing Costs	24%	22%	11%	53%	(100%)
Cheaper Materials (Steel)	4%	3%	1%	8%	(14%)
Cheaper Purchased Parts	13%	13%	5%	29%	(54%)
Internal Cost Savings	7%	7%	4%	17%	(32%)

Source: Adapted from Kodaira (1968:348, table 79). The underlying data are from MITI surveys of five assemblers of four-wheel vehicles.

networks in the 1950s led to the formation or formal reorganization of supplier associations, as detailed in chapter 6. These associations served to channel information on market developments, brought suppliers together to hear about advances in management and technology, and were a locus for the development and maintenance of purchaser reputation. Their name was apt: *kyoryoku kai*, "cooperative associations." (They were also organized legally as cooperatives, which qualified them for note discounting by the government bank for cooperatives, the Shoko Kumiai Chuo Kinko.)

In sum, during the 1960s the automotive firms consciously "developed" their suppliers, raising them up (*ikusei shimasu*) to be mature firms. Suppliers and their automotive customers became closely linked, as suppliers undertook the manufacture of subassemblies and discrete parts. They were partially integrated into their parent firms' operations, and not surprisingly there was considerable stability in the supplier-purchaser relationship. In turn the auto assemblers provided management consulting, engineering assistance, and created an environment of trust. Suppliers were then willing to invest and change in response to their customers' needs for lower costs and improved quality and performance.

The Contemporary Era: 1973–1985

The Automotive Market

The recession following the 1973–1974 oil crisis was a shock to Japanese industry, particularly as it came after two years of very high inflation. In the face of expectations of future price increases, firms increased wages by 40% in their annual contract settlements in April 1974. But inflation quickly fell to negligible levels by mid-1974, and firms found themselves not only with excess capacity but also paying sharply higher real wages. Automotive firms did not resort to layoffs, in line with the policies they adopted twenty years earlier, though many requested their unions to solicit "voluntary" early retirements. And while the workforce was being reduced through attrition, tremendous efforts were put into developing new means of cost-cutting. Investment remained low at most firms for several years; automation was not viewed as the answer, and was introduced only selectively before the 1980s (Kyoikusha 1980:104).[15] Instead, Toyota and other automotive firms turned to the systematic application of "just-in-time" production control and shop-floor improvement programs (*kaizen*), and to the implementation of value engineering programs for product design and parts purchasing.

The explosion of U.S. small-car imports after 1974 (and especially after the second oil crisis in 1978) took the Japanese auto firms by surprise, and not just Detroit. Exports to the U.S. doubled from 422,000 units of cars and trucks in 1970 to 814,000 units in 1971, but increased slowly thereafter to reach an apparent peak at under one million units in 1974. (In 1975, both exports and domestic demand fell.) But exports to the U.S. then surged to over two million units in 1979. U.S. tastes changed, Japanese firms had kept quality high to meet their domestic competition, and wage increases in Japan were capped after 1974. Meanwhile, labor costs in UAW plants mounted under the impact of COLA (cost-of-living adjustment) clauses and increasingly more expensive benefits packages, while quality was hurt by shotgun cost-cutting. Toyota and Nissan exports were 28% and 32% of production in 1973; by 1980 their exports reached 50% of output. At Honda, which had a weaker domestic position, they reached 70%.

While Japan capped its inflation by 1975, prices continued to rise in the U.S. throughout the 1970s and inflation increased to double-digit levels after the second oil crisis in 1978. Finally, to quell the inflation, the U.S. Federal Reserve System imposed stringent monetary policies in 1980. Interest rates skyrocketed, and car (and housing) sales plummeted. The North American operations of the Big Three hemorrhaged; Chrysler teetered on the edge of bankruptcy. Even though most of Detroit's short-term problems stemmed from the overall decline in sales, the visibility of Japanese imports brought a political reaction. Under the threat of congressional action, the Japanese government agreed to a VER ("voluntary" export restraint) in 1980. This restricted Japanese exports to 1.68 million units, or about 20% of the U.S. market. Car prices—both Japanese and American—rose immediately. This allowed the Big Three to return to profitability, but also generated huge windfall profits for the Japanese. While they therefore benefited in the short run, the VER (along with similar restrictions in Europe) implied that exports had probably reached a permanent peak. Attention thus turned to developing upscale cars with higher profit margins, rather than increasing sales volume through low-cost vehicles. After 1981, then, any substantial increase in auto production in Japan would be contingent on stronger domestic demand.

The construction of assembly plants in the U.S. and Europe by the major Japanese auto firms accentuated fears that production within Japan would shrink. As the North American and European "transplant" operations reached their planned capacity, their output would tend to displace direct exports. Exports by Japanese-affiliated plants in Korea and Thailand would only compound the effect. In addition, the strengthening of the yen after 1985 combined with steady wage increases within Japan eroded the Japanese labor cost advantage over the Big Three. Exports to the U.S. in 1989 fell to 2.0 million units, 10% under the then-higher VER cap of 2.3 million units. European car exports to Japan increased at 70% per annum during 1987–1989 while Japanese firms began exporting cars from their foreign plants back to Japan. For the moment domestic demand in Japan is very strong (up over 10% annually during 1988–1990), more than compensating for the decline in exports. But clearly the days of rapid expansion within Japan are over, and the possibility of an occasional recession—and the weeding out of weaker firms—appears very real for the first time in twenty years.

Automotive Parts: 1973–1985

The first oil crisis resulted in tremendous pressure on suppliers as well. For the auto firms, decreased parts costs were an important element in holding overall costs in line. To help achieve this, the assemblers increasingly integrated their subcontractors into their overall production and design process. Toyota, for example, began their almost fanatical extension of just-in-time processes to suppliers only in 1974. Value analysis also began to be systematically applied on joint design projects, as parts firms became responsible for the design of entire systems or subassemblies, and not merely for their manufacture. Taking advantage of this, suppliers, of course, had to work hard to reduce their own manufacturing costs.

The slowdown entailed redundant capacity at parts suppliers. This was accentuated by increases in productivity, which rose more rapidly at suppliers than at the auto firms themselves. Excess plant capacity and surplus workers led many primary suppliers to increase their vertical integration. Unlike the auto makers, they were able to do this because their facilities often partially duplicated those of small secondary subcontractors. In addition, individual subcontracted operations were often small, so that they could be taken over without building a new factory or making similar non-marginal changes. Furthermore, few secondary suppliers could offer their customers unique technical skills. Pulling operations in-house thus permitted primary suppliers to make fuller use of their human resources, and gave them greater internal control over technology and costs. While this had been occurring since the mid-1960s, the pace accelerated in the 1970s.

After the first oil crisis, market forecasts did not encourage new entry into the automotive parts market, while established suppliers continued for one or another reason to exit. With the painful reminder that the industry could not forever be immune to business cycles, firms encouraged their suppliers to diversify customers. This had been done to some extent from the mid-1960s, but it now had a new urgency. In turn, when the automotive firms wanted to locate another supplier, the readiest source was among the suppliers of other, rival automotive firms. The *keiretsu* of the auto firms were no longer used to exclude rival producers, continuing the trend of the late 1960s.

Technical change intensified, with the substitution of new materials and the development of value analysis and other tools for managing the process of innovation. The advent of plastic parts made an impact on suppliers in the late 1960s, as had developments in stamping and rolling technology (Osaka Furitsu Shoko Keizai Kenkyusho 1968). In some cases the automotive firms pulled "new" work in-house; the automotive firms, after all, had excess capacity and workers as well. But this was generally limited to processes for which no current supplier had facilities. The auto firms found it difficult to emulate the primary suppliers' strategy of increased integration because that would have them competing with the suppliers on whom they were so dependent. In addition, their capacity seldom replicated that at suppliers and they often had few technical skills in areas that had been the exclusive province of suppliers. They would have to develop expertise and build and bring on-line new facilities, which was almost always more costly than continuing to rely on existing suppliers. (Surveys of suppliers in the late 1960s showed they had little fear that their customers would use them as "safety valves.") Still, firms with inadequate technical staff found it difficult to meet purchaser demands for cost reductions and improved designs; many were effectively dropped, as rival suppliers won more and more of their business (interview, Mitsubishi Motors; Ueda 1987).

The unanticipated boom in exports to the U.S. did not relieve the pressure on suppliers. If higher volumes resulted in higher profits, then clearly unit costs could be lowered and still leave suppliers a competitive return. Suppliers in response introduced labor-saving equipment, spurred on as their labor costs approached those of the auto firms themselves; labor at large suppliers was no longer "cheap." Suppliers also become more involved in the design process. This was valued by the auto firms, who were concentrating on front-wheel drive and other novel features. In turn, suppliers gained a degree of control over costs unavailable when they worked strictly to blueprints supplied by their customers (Asanuma 1985a, 1985b).

Finally, in the 1980s the Japanese vehicle manufacturers began to diversify their production base internationally. During the 1970s Japanese auto firms set up assembly operations for knocked-down vehicles in Asia. After 1980, they built plants in North America and Europe. Parts firms were forced to respond. In the early 1980s, sales of tooling to overseas parts firms and exports to the Big Three provided a short-term increase in sales. After 1985, the strong yen and pressure for domestic content led the Japanese auto firms to seek parts suppliers located overseas, and simple parts were increasingly imported into Japan. Suppliers that remained purely domestic faced the threat of being slowly squeezed out of the market. For the employees of these firms, building a factory overseas would not prove much of a palliative; few workers could expect to find jobs as expatriates in the U.S. or elsewhere. For that matter, profits might not arrive quickly, if at all. But suppliers wishing to remain in the automotive business—or that, because their specialties were in making large items, found few prospects for diversification into electrical machinery or other expanding areas—had little choice but to become multinationals. To date, they have set up 250 factories in the U.S. and Canada (Mair et al. 1988). Others, of course, may eventually exit. This portended heightened difficulties for the auto firms in maintaining a stable domestic supplier base.

Contemporary Contracting: 1973–1985

Contracting practices continued their gradual evolution during this period. The need for adaptation stemmed from the increased role for suppliers in design and development, the systematic integration of suppliers into overall production through "just-in-time" and other management techniques, and increased pressures for cost reduction. An active stance of cooperation in these areas became a prerequisite for continuing as a supplier. Firms were formally rated on their provision of technical inputs, in addition to having to satisfy stringent just-in-time delivery and "zero" defect requirements. The ability of an existing supplier to meet these criteria was valued more highly than a small cost advantage over a would-be supplier. Parts firms were expected to supply more than just parts.

Prices were set accordingly. For one thing, suppliers were directly compensated for technical innovations, even when the impact on costs was felt only by the assembler. In the face of severe competition, suppliers were also expected to reduce prices according to a prior schedule, set for the supplier network as a whole ("our suppliers should lower prices by 3% every six months"). And while explicit penalties for late delivery and poor quality were instituted in the 1960s, their gravity increased: under "just-in-time" schedules, late delivery or unusable parts stopped the assembly line, and suppliers were expected to foot the bill. Finally, to permit accurate cost calculations at smaller suppliers, purchasers guaranteed their volume projections. Under "take or pay" clauses the auto firms made supplemental payments when demand fell—and received price reductions when volume exceeded projections (chapter 6; Asanuma 1985a, 1985b).

In all this, suppliers and the auto firms became more interdependent. The integration of suppliers into the overall design and manufacturing process made it more costly for an automotive firm to use a new supplier. For one thing, it became difficult for a firm without a proven track record to win a substantial order; too much was at risk. In addition, the engineers at an outside firm would not immediately be able to coordinate with in-house engineers; bringing a supplier on-line, getting its personnel to know their counterparts at the "parent" auto firm, was time consuming—and time was of the essence in new model development, for a delay at one point could create a bottleneck that would slow down related work throughout a new car project. (The slow pace at which existing U.S. suppliers have been brought on board by the Japanese "transplant" operations is thus hardly surprising, but not therefore easily palatable to traditional suppliers to Detroit.)[16]

Despite vigorous competition, data show increasing continuity among existing suppliers and a decrease in new entry. In the 1950s Toyota and Nissan adopted a stated policy that they would not change suppliers without due cause, and even then would try to avoid dropping a supplier without first offering it the opportunity to improve. (In fact, many of the current component manufacturers began supplying Toyota and Nissan fifty years ago, in the 1930s.)[17] Since Toyota, Nissan and to a lesser extent Isuzu hold equity in suppliers, such continuity should not be surprising. It is the continuity among relatively small suppliers of stampings and other "simple" items that distinguishes Japanese from American purchasing practice.

One source of evidence comes from the membership lists of the automotive supplier associations. Table 3.8 presents data on the total number of members for the ten firms that maintain formal supplier organizations, drawn from the lists published in *Nihon no Jidosha Buhin Kogyo* in 1965, 1967 and annually since 1971. The data on total membership illustrate relatively modest shifts over time. Of course, this does not preclude high turnover, with new suppliers taking the place of those that exit. Firm-by-firm comparison of membership lists for different years helps indicate that this was not the case, at least once an auto maker was well established.

For example, the Kanto Kyoho Kai (Toyota's cooperation association for the Tokyo area) had 46 members in 1963; it grew to 59 members in 1971, the next year for which a complete membership list was available. Of the original members, 4 were dropped and 11

Table 3.8. Changes in Supplier Association Membership

Firm	1947	1964	1967	1971	1975	1980	1985
Toyota							
Tokai	108	114	?	136	129	137	136
Kanto	31	46	46	59	?	63	62
Kansai	16	?	?	23	25	25	25
Nissan							
Takara Kai		106	106	115	113	110	105
Shoho Kai		—	31	43	46	49	56
Prince Motors		320	305		(merged with Nissan)		
Mitsubishi		—	292	337	340	340	333
Mizushima		?	44	114	120	124 ('83)	
Toyo Kogyo (Mazda)		103	?	88	96	91	178
Isuzu		230	221	206	276	275	279
Fuji Juko (Subaru)							
Mitaka		53	48	48	53	55	73
Gunma		98	94	99	132	160	157
Daihatsu		?	?	152	129	142	152
Hino		79	78	164	236	243	240
Suzuki		11	56	83	105	101	98
Nissan Diesel		33	?	64	64	60	56

Source: Membership data are drawn from Nihon no Jidosha Buhin Kogyo, various years.
Note: A dash indicates no association existed, a "?" that data were unavailable. The Suzuki association
includes no large firms; that of Toyo Kogyo initially included only local suppliers in Hiroshima and Kure.
For Fuji Juko, there is overlap; 8 firms were members of both associations in 1971, so total membership
was 139 firms. Prince merged into Nissan in 1966; only 16 of its 300-plus suppliers became new suppliers
to Nissan. Honda has no supplier association.

were new suppliers. Over an eight-year period, attrition was thus
10%, new entry 30%. Similarly, the Tokai Kyoho Kai (Nagoya-
Toyoda City area) had 105 members in 1963. By 1971 there were
120 members; only 5 of the old members had been dropped, while
20 were added. Exit was 5% over eight years, and new entry 20%,
showing even greater stability than for Tokyo suppliers, despite the
members on average being smaller firms.[18]

A more comprehensive analysis was made of data on Mitsubishi suppliers. (The results are summarized in tables 3.9 and 3.10.)
As noted in chapter 2, the pre-WWII firm was split into three
companies during the Occupation; they merged in 1965 to form
Mitsubishi Heavy Industries (MHI), and then in 1971 MHI's automotive operations were spun off to form a new company, Mitsubishi Motors. In 1965 there was thus no unified supplier organization;
there were, however, plant-level associations; lists of their members

Table 3.9. Changes in Mitsubishi Kashiwa-kai Membership

Year	1966	1971	1975	1980	1985
1966	292	217	199	183	173
1971	—	337	301	270	256
1975	—	—	339	304	286
1980	—	—	—	340	316
1985	—	—	—	—	333

Source: Membership lists for Mitsubishi were drawn from Auto Trade Journal, Nihon no Jidosha Buhin Kogyo, various years.
Note: It is exceedingly difficult to correct for name changes, especially for early years when addresses frequently changed. For later years the president's name makes it easier to catch name changes. The data therefore tend to understate continuity.

were available for 1966. By the time MMC was formed there was an overall association of automotive suppliers; lists of members were available for 1971 and subsequent years through 1985.

These data indicate much greater flux than at Toyota. In 1966, Mitsubishi's four auto plants had 292 suppliers. By 1971, there were 337 firms, most of which were members of the companywide Kashiwa Kai; in 1985, total membership was 333 firms. But while membership grew by 15% between 1966 and 1971, in fact 75 suppliers dropped out of the Kashiwa Kai, and there were 120 new entrants. Thus 25% of the members were dropped over a five-year period, while (relative to the original size) 40% were new members. During the longer period of 1971–1985, only 81 firms were dropped and 77 firms added as new members; entry and exit were thus substantial,

Table 3.10. Entry and Exit, Mitsubishi Suppliers

	1966	1971	1975	1980	1985
Total # of Firms	292	337	339	340	333
# Dropped	-75 (-26%)	-36 (-11%)	-35 (-10%)	-24 (-7%)	—
# Added	+120 (-36%)	+38 (+11%)	+36 (+10%)	+17 (+5%)	—
New Total	337	339	340	333	—
# Present only that year	70 (24%)	11 (3%)	0 (0%)	4 (1%)	15

Source: Nihon no Jidosha Buhin Kogyo, various years.
Note: The number of firms is biased for initial and final years, so percentages are not given. As with table 2.10, some name changes could not be traced, so totals are overstated. Five firms dropped in 1966-1971 also reappeared later.

but now each was under 25%. And after twenty years, 173 firms (60%) of the original membership remained—or, from the opposite perspective, 40% had exited. They constituted, however, only about half of the total supplier base in 1985.

The greater change relative to Toyota reflects in part the greater product variety of vehicles manufactured by Mitsubishi, together with the relative newness of Mitsubishi in the industry. (Ironically, many of the "new" suppliers had worked for Mitsubishi's aircraft plants during WWII, but after 1945 became suppliers to Toyota. Only after what in some cases was a twenty-year hiatus did they again begin working for Mitsubishi.) Among new entrants, firms supplying new technology stand out. Very few large firms exited, while many small machining firms supplying Mitsubishi's Kyoto engine plant dropped out. Thus, even at Mitsubishi there was a substantial core of stable suppliers and during the most recent period, 1980–1985, turnover fell to its lowest level. Nevertheless, such smaller firms continued to differ from the larger component manufacturers. While firms with 200 or more workers were typically unionized, they made heavy use of (relatively) low-cost unskilled labor and batch-production operations. They also had many rivals. For example, subcontractors of Oi Seisakusho, a supplier of door locks for Nissan, were at one time direct Nissan suppliers. In 1963 three firms were regrouped under Oi; four more were added in 1967. They continued to ship items directly to Nissan, though their formal contract was with Oi. (Even though all made small stampings, they specialized in slightly different items.) Their primary-firm customer (here Oi) also carried out similar processes internally, though their concentration on particular parts meant that over the short run they complemented their parent firm's production, rather than merely substituting for internal production. Thus, as with the primary suppliers and the auto firms, they and their customers tended to become interdependent.

Large parts firms have increasingly paralleled the automotive assemblers in the development of formal supplier associations and other contracting practices. The primary suppliers have extended "just-in-time" systems to their own secondary suppliers, and are similarly making high demands for quality. Over 300 primary parts firms now have their own supplier associations (Dodwell 1986). Akebono Brake, for example, set up an association in 1968 (Akebono Brake 1979:212–15, 344–47, 369). (See also the Kato Shatai case study in chapter 5.) The larger parts firms thus have come to resemble their auto customers in many ways. Meanwhile, as automotive suppliers, second-tier subcontractors lead a tenuous existence, similar to that led by their "primary" supplier customers four decades earlier, in the early 1950s. Other sectors, however, are booming. So while the primary suppliers have become narrowly focused on autos, *their* suppliers are in some cases diversifying away, into electrical equipment and other, more lucrative fields.

Conclusions

At an older, established automotive firm (Toyota) the continuity of the supplier relationship was extremely strong. At a younger, more diversified manufacturer without a web of subsidiaries (Mitsubishi Motors) there was a strong core of suppliers, but less continuity, especially in the earlier period when new technologies (car radios, power steering) were being introduced. Firms *were* dropped, but not readily. Despite this—or rather, in part because of this— the Japanese automotive industry was able to grow from a group of small, backwards producers to the world leaders of today. Suppliers were provided sufficient assurances of continuity that they were willing to invest in new plants and worker training. In turn, the automotive firms were willing to invest in them by providing management and technical aid. In the end, the efforts of suppliers were more important than those of the auto firms themselves in helping the industry become cost-competitive. Subsequent chapters trace in more detail the Japanese labor relations structure that provided the impetus for the automotive and other industries to turn to subcontracting. They also provide greater detail on the logic and techniques of Japanese contracting practices, since innovations in management were central to making an ongoing, interdependent relationship not only workable, but a source of competitive advantage.

Labor Markets and Subcontracting

The structure of Japanese labor markets explains much of the reliance on subcontracting. The simplest interpretation is that the auto companies use outside suppliers to finesse the strength of labor unions. That, after all, was one explicit motive given by the Japanese automotive firms for their initial decision to adopt a subcontracting strategy. Put crudely, outsourcing (as it is called in Detroit) lets firms use nonunion (in the U.S., read "cheap") labor (Helper 1990b).

This, however, is too simplistic an interpretation. While unions have helped mold the pattern of labor relations, they are but one factor. At a deeper level, there are other elements of Japanese society, such as a strong egalitarian ethic, which constrain employment practices. As a result, firms tend to employ a relatively homogeneous set of workers, and in turn specialize in a narrower set of tasks than might otherwise be the case. Instead, large firms employing skilled, blue-collar workers that wish to tap unskilled (and hence low-wage) labor choose to subcontract work to firms specializing in such workers. Subcontractors in Japan may offer cheap labor, but that is because the characteristics of their workers and the tasks they carry out do not warrant high pay. The impetus is thus not ultimately from labor union demands, but rather from the Japanese vision of appropriate labor relations, of how job and social status and pay should be related.

To manufacture its products, the auto industry utilizes a tremendous range of technologies and skills. Some tasks potentially can utilize low-skill labor, should it be available, while other tasks will require highly trained workers. Since compensation is in large part a function of observable individual characteristics—age, education, experience, skill, location, gender—we should thus expect the auto industry, or for that matter any industry, to employ a wide variety of individuals. But this is not what is found in Japan. Instead, firms both large and small respond to wider social norms, including an egalitarian ethic. They therefore limit themselves to employing a relatively homogeneous subset of individuals from this heterogeneous universe of potential workers. In particular, even smaller firms tend to employ a homogeneous work, despite the lack of the unions or of the bureaucratic dictates of large organizations. Similarly, while relatively harmonious labor relations have prevailed in Japan since the early 1960s, large firms continue their reluctance to fire workers as an adjustment mechanism, and the egalitarian ethic remains strong. Labor market considerations thus help account for the continued Japanese reliance on subcontracting —although, as other chapters stress, it is not the only consideration.

In any event, subcontracting was initially an adaptation to the societal norms of appropriate pay and status that developed during the post-WWII era. One key element was an "egalitarian ethic," which held that peers should be treated alike. "Peer" is a social concept, and in Japan a peer is someone who works in the same establishment or firm, and secondarily is someone with similar personal characteristics, such as age. (Job title and content are less important in determining who is a "peer" than they are in the U.S.) This egalitarian ethic makes it difficult for management to make (socially) unwarranted distinctions in status and compensation among members of the same peer group.

This does not imply that compensation is flat.[1] Social status in Japan changes as a result of education, experience (age), geographic locale and gender, and pay distinctions can be made on that basis. (In contrast, in the U.S. "job" tends to be the dominant criteria, as otherwise disparate individuals can be commonly found next to each other, doing the same job for the same pay year after year. That would be unthinkable in Japan. On the other hand, the status of women in Japan makes it still acceptable to make distinctions that are unthinkable here.) Nor do Japanese deny that performance should matter, though they do stress that performance is best evaluated over long periods of time (e.g., 10–20 years). Nevertheless, the work group or even entire factory is ideally comprised of "similar" individuals who can view each other as peers, and among peers compensation should be closely linked to objective criteria such as age and education. Only with promotion into middle management, at about age forty, is the status of peer finally sundered. The impact of the egalitarian ethic is seen most clearly in large firms, but as the statistical data and case studies below demonstrate, even smaller firms (and their employees) view it as a principle that should be honored, even if the reality is that it is honored in the breach.

More narrowly, the objectives of the Japanese labor movement in the late 1940s and 1950s accentuated the advantages of subcontracting. Unions strove for job security, so when business boomed from 1955, employers initially utilized outside suppliers, whose workers were not guaranteed jobs. But over time unions were also influential in establishing the egalitarian social ethic of labor relations. From the 1920s, unions in Japan insisted that objective criteria be used in fixing compensation and deciding on promotion. Labor relations were tumultuous during the decade following World War II (1945–1955), and by the end of that period the egalitarian ethic, along with the ideal of "permanent" employment, had spread throughout society. These intertwined forces gave the impetus for the adoption of a strategy of subcontracting parts production in the automotive and other industries. The timing of these two developments coincided with the evolution of the present subcontracting system, traced in chapters 2 and 3.

Three things are required for this interpretation to be true. First, it must be shown that there are widely varying wages in the workforce as a whole. Second, and most critical, it must be demonstrated that there is a relatively homogeneous workforce at the establishment level. Finally, industries must use technologies that make it desirable to employ a mixture of educated, skilled and unskilled labor. This third characteristic is assumed to hold for the automotive industry. The present chapter will thus address the first two points. In the following section the heterogeneity of the workforce in the Japanese economy as a whole is detailed. The homogeneity of the workforce within firms and the use of subcontractors to work around this is then documented, using case studies and statistical data. Finally, the development of labor relations and the egalitarian ethic is traced, showing that it is indeed a "modern" phenomenon (with the exceptions declining in importance since the 1950s), and that the timing of its development coincides with the rise of subcontracting.

Heterogeneity in Japanese Labor Markets

It should not be surprising to find a great range of wage rates in the Japanese labor market, since most market economies have such variation. Nevertheless, it is useful to review the extent of the variation, and the criteria used to differentiate among workers in the labor force. First, the wages of the lowest-paid group of workers, part-time workers, are contrasted with the compensation of automotive firm executives. Part-timer wages are then compared to that of workers at Nissan Diesel. Finally, wage differentials accruing to education, gender, age and blue/white collar distinctions are set forth.

In Japan the lowest-paid group of workers are part-time student and female workers. The going rate in 1984 stood at ¥500 per hour ($3.33 per hour) at restaurants in Tokyo, and while wages there may have since risen, in 1989 the average nationwide "minimum wage" for part-timers still stood at that level.[2] At the opposite extreme are the top managers of large corporations. In the automotive industry the annual cash compensation for the directors of the four largest firms averaged ¥18 million ($120,000) in 1978. (This, of course, is not very high by U.S. standards.[3]) Assuming a 3,000–hour workyear (reflecting long evenings and weekends) gives top executives an income of ¥6,000 per hour ($40/hr), or twelve times that of a part-time restaurant worker.

But alongside truly part-time workers, in Japan there is also a distinct labor market for *paato*, regularly-employed women working a 35–hour week. Together with the truly part-time, they make up 19% of the labor force.[4] (See the case study below of Kakaa Denka, which relies on such workers.) Table 4.1 presents data on wages paid to *paato* by age and firm size. In large firms the average *paato* wage rate is ¥590 per hour. Fringe benefits at small firms are minimal; most legally mandated benefits apply only to full-time workers. And while large firms may pay a small bonus and offer vacation time, on average labor costs are only 10% above the wage rate. One striking feature of *paato* is the small variation for tenure or firm size; older workers in large firms are paid only 15% more than young workers in small firms, suggesting a well-functioning interfirm market. Nevertheless, there is some variation, and it is important to note that average *paato* wages are less than those paid by large- and medium-sized firms. Most *paato* must therefore work in firms with fewer than 100 employees, at wages not much above that paid to students and other truly part-time workers.[5] In contrast, regular (full-time) female employees in large firms earn on average ¥900 per hour, and ¥1,200 with bonuses, twice the average for *paato* in large firms; furthermore, their benefits are greater.

More important, the cost of *paato* is only a fraction of that of regular male workers. An analysis of total compensation at Nissan Diesel, the smallest of the eleven Japanese automotive firms, illustrates this. In June 1983 Nissan Diesel employed 6,970 workers, who on average were 31 years old and received ¥204,670 in base pay.[6] (Nissan Diesel had been faring poorly: another 841 "employees" were on loan [*shukko*] to other firms.) Table 4.2 presents data from the Annual Report on labor costs. Adjusted for bonuses and benefits, average labor cost was ¥358,000 per month, 1.75 times base pay.[7] Annual executive compensation averaged only 4 times this amount, while (using ¥2,200 per hour) Nissan Diesel workers earned only 3.5 times more than *paato*.

The 1984 *Chingin Kozo Kihon Tokei Chosa* ("Wage Census") provides data on compensation and hours worked for a large sample

Table 4.1. Female (*Paato*) Wage Rates, 1983
(¥ per hour)

Age	Average (All Firms)	Large	Medium	Small
30–34	550	576	562	531
35–39	543	575	541	530
40–44	552	587	551	536
45–49	565	597	570	542
50–54	572	612	582	545
55–59	571	615	596	545
All	560	590	565	542

Source: From the Chingin Kozo Kihon Tokei Chosa (Japan. Rodosho [1984]).
Note: The "all" age class includes workers younger than 30 and older than 60. Paato in large firms often receive bonuses, so that the above data understate their compensation.

Table 4.2. Per Employee Labor Costs, Nissan Diesel
(Fiscal Year 1982, ¥150 = $1)

Item	Annual Cost	Monthly Cost	Hourly Cost	US$ Cost
Labor cost of production:	¥3,474,319	¥289,527	¥1,810	$12.06
Labor cost of sales:	¥581,349	¥48,446	¥303	$2.02
Retirement funding:	¥109,755	¥9,146	¥57	$0.37
Management pay:	¥28,551	¥2,379	¥15	$0.10
Management bonuses:	¥7,174	¥598	¥4	$0.02
Mandated benefits:	¥49,928	¥4,161	¥26	$0.17
Other benefits:	¥21,377	¥1,781	¥11	$0.07
Loan subsidy:	¥16,360	¥1,363	¥9	$0.06
Deposit subsidy:	¥10,712	¥893	¥6	$0.04
Total:	¥4,299,525	¥358,294	¥2,239	$14.93

Source: Data are from Yuka Shoken Hokoku Sho (semiannual financial statements).
Note: A 160-hour month was used; the large-firm automotive average in 1982 was 180 hours, but here the standard 8-hour day was used. Labor costs include bonus payments. Subsidies are estimated at 1% of the balance of loans to and deposits by employees. Employment does not reflect shukko, whose salaries were paid primarily by the receiving firm.

of the Japanese labor force. Table 4.3 uses data on the monthly wages of high-school graduates in the *Wage Census,* adjusted to reflect bonuses and converted to an hourly rate.[8] Assuming the differential between cash compensation and labor costs at Nissan Diesel is typical, actual costs are 20% greater than those reported in Table 4.3 and 75% greater than pre-bonus "base pay." Using this correction for the 30–year old large-firm male category gives an hourly cost of ¥2,136 per hour, approximately the same average labor cost as at Nissan Diesel. In the U.S., automotive wages far exceed average manufacturing wages, as detailed in chapter 8. In contrast, there is little or no industry premium in Japan.

In sum, there is significant heterogeneity in the Japanese labor market, as measured by differentials in compensation. At the low end of the scale, *paato* compensation is on average less than one-half that of regular female employees, and less than one-quarter that of (male) workers in large firms such as Nissan Diesel. These differentials, as the number of *paato* and the case studies here and in chapter 5 demonstrate, are indeed sufficient to give rise to organizational forms that permit them to be tapped.

Table 4.3. Male High School Graduate Wages in Manufacturing
(¥ per hour)

Age	Large ¥	Firms as % of large	Medium ¥	Firms as % of large	Small ¥	Firms % of lg
18-19	933	100%	850	91%	745	80%
20-24	1048	100%	984	90%	895	82%
25-29	1457	100%	1256	86%	1163	80%
30-34	1780	100%	1605	90%	1466	82%
35-39	2273	100%	2000	88%	1721	76%
40-44	2678	100%	2289	85%	1983	74%
45-49	3106	100%	2642	85%	2096	67%
50-54	3195	100%	2766	87%	2048	64%

Source: Data are from the Chingin Kozo Kihon Chosa (Japan. Rodosho 1984).
Note: Monthly data were converted to an hourly rate using average monthly hours worked by males in manufacturing and average bonus rates by firm size from the May 1984 Rodo Tokei Chosa Geppo. Large firms have 500+ employees, medium firms 100-499 and small firms 30-99. By size class, the average monthly hours and bonus paid (in months' wages) were 178 hours and 4.5 months (large firms), 182 hours and 4 months (medium firms) and 188 hours and 3 months (small firms).

Homogeneity within Firms

The case study below of Kakaa Denka demonstrates the use of *paato,* and shows that even in such enterprises the egalitarian ethic exerts pressure on employment practices. Maruzen Kogyo illustrates again the systematic difference in the labor force employed at small firms, as well as suggesting the difficulties that a large firm would face in utilizing such workers. It is followed by an analysis of data from standard statistical sources. This and subsequent case studies are drawn from a sample of over thirty firms interviewed in Japan in 1982 and 1984. While each firm has its unique features, both here and later at least one other firm from the sample could have been substituted to illustrate the same features. The Japanese small business literature provides many similar vignettes, which serve as an additional check that these firms are in fact illustrative in their labor practices.

Kakaa Denka

Kakaa Denka assembled computer printers in an old school building in a rural area in the mountains of Japan.[9] It was one of eleven such subsidiaries of Kachikachi Corporation, the watch and

printer manufacturer described in chapter 7. Outside of ten management and supervisory personnel sent from the parent firm, all Kakaa Denka's 200 workers were *paato*. All were married women
from the same village; most were farmers' wives whose children
were in school or had already left home.[10] They worked five seven-
hour days, with the factory's schedule timed to mesh with that of
the local schools. All were paid ¥600 per hour, with only a slight
increment with tenure. The village social structure made it difficult
to do otherwise. At one time the firm attempted to use local women
as supervisors, but found they could not function well: the resulting
ranking conflicted with the social hierarchy of the village where the
women lived.

Kakaa Denka was not legally obligated to provide bonuses or
other benefits to its workers. To reduce turnover, however, it offered vacation and sick time and paid semiannual bonuses that
totaled about 4 months' base pay. (This was still less than the 5.5–
6 months' bonus paid by Kachikachi, its parent firm.) The pay was
also 10%–15% higher than that of smaller but otherwise similar
operations located nearby, which typically provided no benefits and
paid only a one-month annual bonus. With its rural location and
flexible work schedule, Kakaa Denka initially had found all the
workers it needed, but was acutely aware of its (monopsonistic)
impact on the local labor market. Subsequently many similar firms
located nearby, competing for the same type of workers, while
increasing automobile ownership had rendered the village less remote. Good *paato* were now clearly in demand, and wage rates were
rising. The firm was for the first time actively considering locating
future plants in truly remote parts of Japan; it already had made
initial forays into manufacturing in Southeast Asia, and has since
set up plants in the U.S.

Kachikachi had ten similar subsidiaries nearby, but its practice was hardly unique; female labor-intensive subcontractors are
common in Japan. Yazaki Sogyo, which assembles wire harnesses
for automobiles, had twelve branch factories and twenty other subcontractors. Yazaki's subcontractors were set up in densely popu-
lated areas, and staffed with housewives who worked three-to-four
hour shifts. As at Maruzen (see below), Yazaki maintained excess
capacity at its subcontractors, since peak demand could be 50%
over their regular operating rate. As at Kakaa Denka, all managers
of these subcontractors were full-time male employees of the parent

firm. At one time Yazaki directly employed substantial numbers of women, hiring recent high school graduates rather than house-wives. Such hiring ceased with the oil crisis in 1973, and attrition soon brought numbers to a low level. In the 1970s *paato* became the preferred form of lower-cost labor, though in the late 1980s Yazaki also expanded into less developed countries; it is now one of the largest exporters in the Philippines.[11]

Maruzen Truck Body

Maruzen Truck Body is one of three suppliers of small stamp-ings to Kato Shatai, which manufactures truck bodies for Mitsubi-shi Motors and Isuzu. It is a second-tier subcontractor, in that it does not directly supply any of the automotive firms. Maruzen is one of the 46 firms in the Kato Shatai supplier association; Kato Shatai is Maruzen's only customer.

The owner and president of Maruzen, Mr. Nakazawa, began his career as a mechanic for a transport firm at the end of WWII. He started doing repair work for Kato Shatai in 1953, and in 1960 moved to a site just outside of Yokohama, adjacent to a new Kato plant. Initially he had no machinery. Only in 1964 did he buy his first stamping press, financed by a loan from a small business bank.

The Maruzen factory was a clean, open building with four stamping presses, three spot welders for attaching nuts to stamp-ings, and other small machines. Most of the site, however, was taken up by row upon row of neatly stacked dies. Kato Shatai owned virtually all of the dies, and supplied the primary material, sheet metal.[12] The factory was in fact a repository for old Kato Shatai dies, with Maruzen setting them up to do production work for infrequently ordered options and to make spare parts. In 1984 the shop was not particularly busy, as it was a slow year for truck sales. Mr. Nakazawa in any event maintained excess capacity for rush orders.

While the building was clean, his twelve workers were scruffy. His male employees were unreliable in demeanor, and his female employees all appeared to be over fifty years old. Absenteeism was, he said, "high." Mr. Nakazawa normally asked employees to work one or two hours overtime; in a pinch, he had several people he could call upon who did not want regular work. Two sons helped

Mr. Nakazawa run the plant, and his wife assisted with paperwork. The sons intended to succeed him; only one had gone to college. His sons and two younger workers drove the forklifts and did other physically demanding or less routine tasks. In fact, the other workers could not set up equipment or otherwise work on their own. Among the younger employees, no one remained for long—and, because of age, the same was true of the older workers. The exception was one worker who had been with him eighteen years, in part because he was only a junior high school graduate and so had limited mobility.

Mr. Nakazawa was quite frank in stating that his livelihood depended on cheap labor. His four female employees were paid only ¥670 an hour, even though they worked fulltime; his elderly men were not paid much more. They were not rapid workers, but he could not afford to pay younger workers enough to keep them around. With irregular orders, the firm needed neither staffing consistency nor workers with the stamina, high motivation or skill to run a production line. For difficult tasks Mr. Nakazawa's two sons were adequate help.

A large firm could not readily staff part of its factory with elderly, unreliable labor, as did Mr. Nakazawa. The manager of such a shop would need total discretion over hiring and firing, wages and scheduling—little short of the authority to run it as if it were his own business, without regard for corporate policy. It would also be impossible to run such an operation as anything but a small shop; labor relations were intrinsically personal. Like many small companies in Japan, Mr. Nakazawa's firm could not readily expand beyond the size at which it could be managed comfortably (and when need be, operated) by one family.

Statistical Data

The case studies above suggest the capability of small firms to employ homogeneous sets of workers that might be difficult for larger firms to employ directly. While smaller firms on average pay lower wages, it is because they employ workers who vary systematically from those in larger firms. Here the emphasis is on using statistical data to show that different size firms do specialize in workers with different characteristics, such as gender, education and age. (The next sections ask whether, in fact, larger firms are so constrained.) Specifically, the wages of similar workers are compared across different size firms. This variation is less across firms than is the variation in average wages, which can only be true if small and large firms systematically employ workers with different characteristics. In other words, small firms pay less because their workers have less education, or are older, or are women. This makes them attractive as subcontractors for many types of labor-intensive work—assuming, as will be argued below, that large firms cannot simply employ such individuals directly at low wages.

Labor Ministry data show that average wages indeed differ with firm size. In 1981, the average wage in manufacturing firms with 20–99 employees was 63% that of firms with 300 or more employees, and 58% that of firms with over 1,000 employees. Similarly, the average wage in incorporated firms capitalized at ¥10–¥50 million was 58% that of firms capitalized at ¥1 billion or more (*Chusho Kigyo Hakusho* 1983:appendix tables 11, 17, 19). Likewise, fewer fringe benefits are provided by smaller firms, though comparable data were not available. This is true not only for industry as a whole, but also for the automotive industry, as can be seen in Tables 4.6 and 4.7. Smaller parts firms pay on average 60% or less what workers receive in larger parts firms—and the pay even at large parts firms is 10% below that at the auto companies themselves. Small firms also tend to be labor-intensive, and large firms capital intensive. Thus, despite employing lower-wage workers, labor costs make up 78% of value added in smaller firms, as opposed to 60% of value added in larger firms. (Value added is the difference between sales and purchased inputs, and hence includes profits, capital costs and labor costs.)

While average wages vary nearly twofold with firm size, rates for similar workers change surprisingly little. Table 4.4 shows average male wages by age and firm size, as a proportion of large-firm wages. For example, at worst production workers at small firms make 74% of those in large. Most blue-collar workers make at least 85% of what their counterparts in larger firms make. (Table 4.1 showed that peak *paato* wages were only 16% more than the minimum at small firms.)

The above data, however, are not adjusted for experience and education, and therefore exaggerate the variation in wages across firm size for similar workers. Analysis of the wages of "standardized" workers, male high school graduates who have been in the

Table 4.4. Male Wages by Age and Firm Size
(as percentage of level of comparable workers in large firms)

¥1,000 per month

Age	Average		Production Workers			White Collar Workers		
	Medium	Small	Medium	Small	Large	Medium	Small	Large
18-19	94%	92%	93%	91%	¥122	98%	97%	¥116
20-24	95	96	93	95	140	99	100	142
25-29	93	95	91	93	176	96	100	178
30-34	92	92	91	91	209	93	97	231
35-39	91	86	91	88	234	92	91	282
40-44	89	80	90	85	251	90	83	336
45-49	86	73	90	81	258	87	77	376
50-54	84	69	86	77	263	87	73	392
55-59	82	68	82	74	251	85	74	360
All	88	82	88	87	¥216	89	86	¥281

Source: Rodo Tokei Chosa Geppo (May 1984), 36(5), table 6 for the indices and table 4 for large firm wages.
Note: Large firms have 1,000 or more employees, medium-sized firms have 100-199 employees, and small firms have 10-99 employees.

same firm since leaving school (so that tenure with the employer is identical) partially corrects for this (*Rodo Tokei Chosa Geppo*, May 1984, p. 20, table 7; 1983 data). In 1981, the wages of "standardized" workers in firms with 10–99 employees were 90% or more of those paid by firms with over 1,000 workers until age 44, and wages for young workers were actually higher than those paid by large firms. (However in 1961, at the start of the rapid growth era when subcontracting was spreading, wages were uniformly lower in small firms, at 80% or less those paid by large firms after age 35; *Chusho Kigyo*

Table 4.5. Auto Industry Labor Force Composition by Firm Size

Firm Size	Age Under 20 Yrs		Age 20-29 Yrs		Age 30-49 Yrs		Age Over 50 Yrs	
	Male	Female	Male	Female	Male	Female	Male	Female
1-3	0.4%	0.4%	9.2%	3.9%	31.8%	27.8%	19.3%	7.1%
10-19	1.2	0.2	12.7	4.5	28.8	27.5	15.3	10.0
30-49	2.9	0.7	14.8	5.4	34.2	21.2	12.8	8.1
100-199	5.7	1.0	20.6	6.4	33.2	16.1	12.2	4.8
300-499	5.3	1.4	24.6	6.0	40.4	9.9	10.0	2.4
1000+	6.0	1.9	30.2	5.1	46.9	3.2	5.9	0.8

Source: Drawn from the Kogyo Jittai Kihon Chosa Hokokusho: Sokatsu Hen (Dai 5-kai) (Fifth Basic Survey of Manufacturing: Summary Volume), 1979 for the survey of year-end 1976, table 2.
Note: The survey gives data on eleven classes. For brevity, only six size classes are reproduced here.

Table 4.6. Census of Manufactures Auto Industry Data, 1983

Size of Firm (Employees)	Number of Establish-ments	Number of Employees	Wages ¥ billions	Shipments ¥ billions	Value Added ¥ billions	Wage as % of 1000+ firm wages
Automotive Industry (Census Class 361)						
All Estab.	10,580	698,690	¥2,602	¥25,451	¥6,611	83%
4-9	5,275	31,972	61	200	118	42%
10-19	1,986	27,697	65	276	123	52%
20-29	1,111	27,301	66	327	132	54%
30-49	645	25,261	67	394	134	59%
50-99	689	47,644	132	848	259	61%
100-199	384	52,364	162	1078	290	68%
200-299	151	36,812	122	866	217	64%
300-499	125	47,975	175	1,222	321	81%
500-999	119	83,525	314	2,403	711	83%
1000+	95	318,139	1,436	17,838	4,306	100%
Assembly (Census Class 3611)						
All Estab.	47	191,480	¥893	¥13,643	¥3,400	100%
30-199[a]	4	360	1	8	4	60%
300-499	3	1,135	5	41	6	93%
500-999	5	3,651	14	247	65	80%
1000+	35	186,334	873	13,347	3,325	100%
Truck and Auto Body (Census Class 3612)						
All Estab.	200	51,005	¥208	¥1,790	¥378	91%
20-29	59	1,461	4	20	8	69%
30-49	42	1,593	5	18	7	69%
50-99	34	2,385	8	31	11	71%
100-199[a]	24	3,458	12	87	28	78%
200-299	10	2,390	9	44	14	84%
300-499	7	2,669	11	73	22	89%
500-999	11	7,933	30	260	89	95%
1000+ empl	12	29,266	130	1,260	201	100%
Automotive Parts (Census Class 3613)						
Total/Avg.	10,333	456,205	¥1,501	¥6,702	¥2,832	78%
4-9[a]	5,274	31,972	61	200	118	45%
10-19	1,986	27,697	65	276	123	56%
20-29	1,052	25,840	62	306	124	57%
30-49[a]	602	23,668	62	376	127	62%
50-99[a]	653	45,259	124	817	248	65%
100-199	359	48,906	150	991	262	73%
200-299	141	34,422	114	821	202	78%
300-499	115	44,171	160	1,107	293	86%
500-999	103	71,941	270	1,896	557	89%
1000+	48	102,539	432	3,232	780	100%

Source: Kogyo Tokei Hyo (Census of Manufactures), 1983 using establishment data.
Note: An "a" indicates interpolated values.

Hakusho 1983:141). At age 55 to 59, when the gap was the greatest, standardized small-firm wages were 82% of the large firm level. The wage rates in medium-sized firms varied even less.

These data show that the composition of the workforce in smaller firms must be more important than differences in wages for workers with similar characteristics in explaining variations in wages by firm size. Direct measures of employee characteristics bear this out. The data in table 4.5 above show systematic variation in the age and gender composition of employment by firm size in the automotive industry. Smaller firms employ more women, especially older women, and employ more men in the oldest wage class.[13] This same pattern is found in manufacturing as a whole.

To rephrase this, firms tend to draw on workers with a narrow set of characteristics, relative to the variety in the labor force as a whole. This relatively homogeneous group of employees is then paid wages as dictated by the market. Most variation can be explained by statistically observable information, such as gender, education and tenure, and characteristics that are not readily observable or were not corrected for in the data—geographic location, skills, ambition, personality (ability to work with others, honesty and so on)—would surely account for most of the remaining variation. While, for example, smaller firms are found to pay systematically lower wages on average, this is not due to exploitation of their workers, as the long-standing Marxist interpretation within Japan insists, but because they are (as dictated by the market) inherently low-wage labor. Correspondingly, even large unionized firms do not pay excessively high wages.

Origins of the Egalitarian Ethic

Why do Japanese firms have a relatively homogeneous workforce, rather than a variety of workers within the firm, paid as the market dictates? The argument here is that this stems from the Japanese social structure, which developed in part under the influence of the labor movement. This section therefore traces the development of the egalitarian ethic, and notes the exceptions permitted at the enterprise level—exceptions that have declined considerably in importance since the early 1950s. From this perspective, the egalitarian ethic serves as a constraint on management. Quite sim-

Table 4.7. Auto Industry Wages by Firm Size
(¥ 1,000)

	1959	1961	1966	1971	1983
Automotive Industry (Census Class 361)					
Average	251	309	507	1,005	3,713
4-9	135	187	269	541	1,901
10-19	154	209	385	775	2,364
20-29	163	224	415	835	2,431
30-49	168	236	409	810	2,653
50-99	184	235	428	804	2,770
100-199	186	252	446	885	3,086
200-299	210	278	450	945	3,327
300-499	250	258	457	969	3,655
500-999	236	308	480	985	3,765
1000+	376	415	593	1,164	4,514
Automotive Assembly (Census Class 3611)					
Average	180	180	620	1,184	4,661
10-19	164	238	438	x	—
20-29	191	273	—	x	—
50-99	134	x	—	x	—
100-199	272	265	—	x	—
200-299	235	351	—	x	—
300-499	313	252	—	x	4,339
500-999	218	346	574	870	3,743
1000+	407	422	622	1,192	4,684
Automotive Parts (Census Class 3613)					
Average	197	266	439	897	3,291
4-9	134	187	267	541	—
10-19	154	207	382	771	2,364
20-29	160	220	411	834	2,395
30-49	165	232	403	795	—
50-99	180	229	418	797	—
100-199	177	248	434	870	3.069
200-299	209	268	436	919	3,300
300-499	232	260	441	961	3,618
500-999	249	303	463	983	3,765
1000+	314	409	543	1,086	4,221

Source: Kogyo Tokei Hyo (Census of Manufactures), selected years.
Note: Data are calculated by dividing total employment by total wages as reported in the census tables. A dash indicates that data were missing or that no firms existed in that size class, while an "x" denotes data were withheld to preserve confidentiality.

ply, over time workers in Japan came to demand the treatment accorded those around them. The objectives unions sought in the 1950s aided and abetted underlying sociological factors, and made the realization of this ethic part of the social vision of the Japanese nation.

Sociological Factors

There is clearly a stronger group orientation and greater attention to vertical relationships in Japan than in the U.S. Works by sociologists and anthropologists such as Nakane (1970), Vogel (1971), Cole (1971, 1979) and Rohlen (1974) depict both the concern with keeping harmony within a group and the importance of distinctions other than those of income to perceptions of status. One prerequisite for maintaining this group cohesiveness is that members should be similar in age and personal characteristics. For workers in large firms, their peers are almost exclusively fellow employees, or as it would be phrased in Japanese, are "members" of the same firm.

When a firm desires to provide an incentive to employees, it is possible (and generally necessary) to do this through more than merely the provision of a monetary reward. For example, the rearrangement of the mechanisms by which promotions and pay increases are governed may increase motivation without any change in average compensation. In addition, in Japan the emphasis on egalitarian ties means that relatively small differentials in compensation set someone apart.[14] In other words, very small changes in pay can have a very large impact. Furthermore, firms are embedded in local society, which is particularly important in rural areas, as the Kakaa Denka case study illustrates.[15] Where peer and superior are determined by factors external to the firm rather than the individual's skill and effort, differences in pay can be divisive, and so the only feasible policy is to minimize distinctions among individuals in the work place. (In many American universities, pay scales are confidential for just such reasons.)

Unions and the Development of the Egalitarian Ethic

The current stereotype of Japanese labor relations, as perceived in both Japan and the U.S., stresses the lack of merit pay and hence indirectly the strength of the egalitarian impulse. The accuracy of this stereotype, however, must be assessed. For that purpose, the development of Japanese labor relations is traced, drawing particularly upon Gordon (1985).[16] In addition, the ability to create exceptions must be analyzed, such as the utilization of temporary male workers (rinji-ko) and paato in the large firms in which egalitarianism is most often said to exist. The data available for large firms suggests that such exceptions are severely limited. Case studies show that the ideal created by large-firm labor relations also applies to small firms (comparable statistical data are not available), even if their practice typically falls far short of the ideal.

The Rise of Permanent Employment

Workers in Japan were initially craft-oriented. In the early years of the metalworking industries in the 1920s, a skilled worker moved among large plants, often in different parts of the country, as well as periodically running his own shop. If successful, he might become a straw boss or foreman (oyakata) inside a larger firm, directly employing the workers under him in a manner reminiscent of inside contractors and foremen of the early years of the U.S. automotive industry (Buttrick 1952; Chandler 1964). These foremen functioned by hiring, firing, setting pay and (sometimes) training their own crew of workers.

In the 1930s large firms in Japan began to intervene directly in labor relations as the volume of production increased, and as technology diverged further from the traditional craft base in which skilled workers (and hence foremen) had been trained. More and more specialized production equipment was used by large firms, and they therefore required a more stable and specialized workforce than the traditional foremen were capable of providing (Gordon 1985:52ff). But wages continued to reflect previous craft practices, which included a component reflecting skill-cum-age, as mobility was only partially dampened. Identification with the firm by blue-collar workers remained minimal. In contrast, managers and technical personnel had substantial tenure and identified with and gained status from the firm. This provided a model and goal toward which blue-collar workers later strove.[17]

While the stereotype is that Japanese firms have traditionally provided permanent employment, and that wages and promotion were dominated by seniority, it was only at the end of the 1950s that these practices became sufficiently widespread to be noted by contemporary observers. Impetus toward new patterns was provided by the U.S. Occupation, when labor unions were encouraged (especially in 1945–1947). A period of considerable ferment ensued, during which a militant labor movement pressed for the extension of the prewar white-collar practices to blue-collar workers. They also held forth egalitarian ideals, one reason that the separate white- and blue-collar unions that had existed in many firms merged. A *modus vivendi* was achieved following the highly ideological labor strife of the late 1940s and early 1950s. It was thus then, during the period when the auto companies began to systematize their use of subcontractors, that the "typical" features of Japanese industrial relations—strictly enterprise unions, seniority wages, employment security and the hiring primarily of new school-leavers—became common in large firms.[18] These practices are traditional only in the sense that they drew on existing cultural images, since they unambiguously do not represent traditional employment norms in industry.

Simultaneously, the compensation system at unionized firms changed. Workers demanded a "living wage" as the prime component of base pay, while rejecting the use of piece-rate compensation. With the postwar hyperinflation, adjustment for price increases remained important to unions, and so the "living wage" was simply a continuation of the wartime "cost-of-living" pay indices.[19] Piece-rate compensation was disliked both because of egalitarian concerns, and because managers tended to abuse such systems by revising rates arbitrarily. The widely publicized April 1947 "Densan" (electric utilities) contract became the prototype. In that contract, the prime pay component was based on a cost-of-living table reflecting age, marital status and number of children. This was a foundation of the seniority wage ideal, and it remained influential into the 1970s.[20]

The emphasis on employment security reflected the slack labor markets of the late 1940s and 1950s. Firms pared employment during the Dodge Line recession (1949–1950) and after the Korean War (1952–1955); bitter strikes resulted. Most strikes were soon broken and militant labor leaders were ousted, but firms remained leery of increasing the size of their unionized labor force. The auto industry was no exception. Unions at Nissan, Toyota and Isuzu coordinated their efforts, in one of the few attempts in Japan to form an American-style industrial union. The near-bankruptcy of Toyota in 1949–1950 helped quell the union there, but only in 1954, after a 100–day strike at Nissan, did the industry finally rid itself of militant unions.[21] As noted in chapter 3, this turmoil was one factor leading to the adoption of a subcontracting strategy in the industry.

The impact of these changes was felt throughout the Japanese labor market. Contributing to this was the presence of unions not only in very large firms, but also in most medium-sized firms of 200 or more workers. For example, workers at Kato Shatai, then still a small firm, formed a union and went out on strike in 1953. (See chapter 5.) Furthermore, Japanese labor legislation required that firms maintain a consultative mechanism between management and workers. Bookstores in Japan offer manuals that help managers meet the paper requirements of consultation, for which the Ministry of Labor checks. Still, at firms of 200 or more workers, the tendency is that consultation does not occur merely on paper. As a result, even where no union exists, the consultative bodies provide a mechanism through which workers can formally voice their concerns to management.[22]

The evolution of new labor relations patterns can be traced not only through the development of formal institutions, but also through the Wage Census. This survey presents data from a large sample of workers by job classification, industry, age and other criteria.[23] Contrary to the homogeneous seniority-wage model, the 1954 Census classified wages by detailed craft criteria. In the transport industry alone, data were broken down by over 42 different trades, including such detailed job classifications as lathe operators, press operators and assemblers. (The data were otherwise categorized primarily by experience.) The labor market was clearly viewed as horizontal and interfirm, and the data show that workers could choose a smaller shop without a substantial wage penalty. But after 1954, the organization of wage surveys changed rapidly. In 1964 there were fewer classifications, and of the thirty reported for the transport industry, only twenty were for skilled trades. By the 1974 survey, only three classifications remained. Similar surveys, using the same three classifications, are now made by many other groups to serve as a starting point for small firms in devising their own pay scales.[24] Unlike in 1954, the emphasis everywhere is on large-firm age, education and tenure characteristics.

Firm-level data on pay and promotion standards reflect a similar evolution. Honda formalized its "basic system" in 1953, five years after its foundation. It incorporated 52 job categories, though it apparently also had a seniority component. By 1974, "job pay" accounted for less than 5% of base pay, while base pay itself varied a maximum of ±3% until a worker was in his late twenties (Okamura 1974:283–85). The only differential was for "rank," which itself appeared primarily to reflect seniority. Likewise, Kato Shatai, described in chapter 5, moved away from a craft-oriented apprentice system after 1953. During the subsequent decade it hired personnel managers away from larger firms to gradually install a "modern" employment system (chapter 6; Kato Shatai Kogyo 1971:171–78).

In the early 1950s, then, Japanese employers were oriented toward interfirm labor markets, and wages were linked to the external market. Only after the mid-1950s did well-defined internal labor markets develop and become recognized in society at large as normative. During the 1960s, the system continued to evolve, and while on the face this involved a lessening of the strictures of the Densan model, in fact the salary system of firms on the whole became more egalitarian.

Homogenization of Pay

Few if any Japanese firms ever used seniority as their sole compensation criterion. Even in the Densan settlement, the seniority element was only 60% of total pay, and this was modified almost immediately. Rapidly growing firms needed to hire mid-career workers, and the structure of the external market was at odds with the idiosyncratic internal salary structure—especially as older worker's pay scales had been "grandfathered." This resulted in an unwieldy and strife-riven wage structure. At Honda 2,000 workers were hired in 1954 and "They differed greatly both in terms of ability and salaries, which caused some confusion in the internal organization of the factory." Hiring new entrants to the labor market avoided this difficulty (Sakiya 1982:110).

Another adjustment was to restrict the importance of seniority. During the first few years' tenure, "promotions" based on ability remain virtually automatic, but for older workers greater differentiation was possible. By the early 1960s pay was increasingly linked to rank, which explicitly reflected ability. Thus Suzuki began basing pay on rank in 1959 to facilitate shifting workers among jobs. This was particularly important as the firm was moving rapidly from the production of textile machinery to making motorcycles and cars (Suzuki Jidosha 1970:442). In large firms, therefore, the rank component (*shokumu-kyu, to-kyu*) increased from an average of 21% of pay in the mid-1950s to 33% of pay by 1962 (Takagi and Fukami 1974:80–83; Gordon 1985:353). Corresponding changes were made in the job structure; steel firms, for example, revised their job classification systems from 1962 (Marsh and Mannari 1976). By the mid-1960s, at only 9% of firms did workers consider their base pay to reflect primarily age, though in 49% of the firms it was judged the most important single component. On the other hand, in 9% of firms compensation was based solely on job and ability, and in 33% of firms these were the primary criteria (Suzuki 1969:80, table 35).[25]

The evolution of the Honda wage structure illustrates these changes. Employment at Honda grew ninefold during 1960–1965, while production shifted from a reliance on skilled labor (which was increasingly scarce) to production using semiautomated machine tools and other less skill-intensive equipment. In the early 1960s, seniority was dominant and rank relatively unimportant as determinants of pay. In 1968, however, Honda shifted to an emphasis on worker performance and ability (Okamura 1974:177–203).[26] The new pattern was formalized in 1972. Under the new system promotions were to be linked more closely to ability, and bonuses and the annual increment to base pay on performance evaluations. Management had made efforts to implement such a system for over a decade, but had been unwilling to confront the Honda union over the issue (Sakiya 1982:177).

At the same time, the age/wage gradient became flatter, and now resembles that in the U.S. (Sterling 1984). For example, in 1962 there was a 4.2–fold differential between the pay at age twenty and at retirement at Honda. In 1973 it had narrowed to a 2.5–fold differential. Pay also peaked at an earlier age; on average pay reached a maximum at retirement in 1962, while in 1973 pay increases on average ceased at age forty, except for those who began to be promoted into management positions. The salary system came to include explicit bounds on the deviation from the "model" wage. For the first two ranks at Honda, promotion was virtually automatic, hinging solely on tenure; differentials accruing to ability and performance appeared only gradually. Thus, as noted above, pay varied by only 3% from the "model" level at age 27. (Sources show equivalent changes at the Daihatsu, Nissan, Isuzu, Toyota, Suzuki and Mazda.)[27] While some firms maintained three parallel salary systems (at Suzuki Motors, for production workers, technical personnel, and office personnel), during the initial years of work pay for men of the same age remained similar across all three scales. Thus for ages 25 to 29, labor force surveys found the pay of high school graduates in white collar jobs to be the same as that of college graduates, and only 4% more than that of junior-high school graduate production workers (*Rodo Tokei Chosa Geppo* 36:5 [May 1984], p. 20, table 7). (Note, however, that at age 25 a junior high graduate had ten years' experience, a high school grad seven years, but a college grad only three.) Over time, then, there was a sharp diminution of pay differentiation among workers at large firms.

The net impact of the evolution of labor relations in the Japanese economy was thus to severely constrain the ability of firms to pay their regular workers dissimilar wages. Only individuals who made their way into management or accumulated substantial technical skills deviated from the model, and that only occurred well into their career with the firm. And in particular, the framework did not provide for low wages to be paid for those performing unskilled tasks—or for young workers with unusual skills to be paid more. The remaining issue is to examine whether firms had leeway to employ nonunion workers who fell outside of these egalitarian constraints.

Loopholes: The Strictness of the Model

The labor relations system sketched above applied formally only to the unionized regular employees of large firms. Regular male workers, however, account for only one-fifth of the labor force in Japan. Large firms thus could potentially diminish the impact of the egalitarian ethic by employing individuals other than regular workers. Firms did hire young women who soon quit (or in the 1960s, were fired upon marriage) and so never became expensive. Young male workers were likewise inexpensive, but this merely postponed the day of reckoning, since they stayed on to become well-paid middle-aged workers—and will in the next two decades begin receiving retirement benefits. Firms also employed *paato* and temporary or seasonal (male) workers.

Women, however, have not been a substantial part of the workforce of large firms in the automotive industry. This was true in other heavy industries, but not the electronics industry, which historically employed large numbers of women. Part of the reason was that household consumer goods required more unskilled light assembly work, while skilled metalworkers and machinists were dominant in the early automotive industry. The automotive industry also involved physically demanding work, shift work and substantial overtime, while until 1985 Japanese labor legislation precluded employing women for such work. Thus in 1962 less than 8% of Toyota's employees were female, and very few were in production work. Similarly, in 1965 less than 6% of Toyo Kogyo (Mazda) employees were women, and only a few were production workers. Even in 1989, only sixty of Mitsubishi Motor's 15,000 production workers—as opposed to 15% of its white-collar employees—were women.[28] Neither regular women employees nor *paato* have been or are a substantial component of the factory labor force at the auto firms themselves, though this is not the case at smaller parts suppliers—or in the U.S. at the Big Three.

Nonregular male employees were more important. They included "temporary" workers employed under short-term or annual contracts (*rinji-ko*) and "seasonal" workers employed during the agricultural off-season (*kisetsu-ko*), who on paper had neither the security nor the pay of regular workers.[29] Nonregular workers in various categories were pervasive in large manufacturing firms in the 1930s, but with unionization and the economic collapse after 1945, such workers were either dismissed or became regular employees. In the automotive industry temporary workers reappeared in 1950 at Isuzu, and by 1952 they constituted 12% of the labor force of the three largest auto firms. At Nissan, union pressure resulted in fewer temporary workers being employed in the mid-1950s, but in the auto boom of the early 1960s the proportion increased dramatically, to peak at 44% in 1963. The expansion of the automotive industry, and of large firms in general, outstripped their ability to increase their workforce solely through the hiring of new school leavers. Given the labor turmoil and sharp economic downturns of the late 1940s and early 1950s, firms were reluctant to add to their roster of permanent employees, and turned to temporary workers as a supplement to their increased use of subcontracting.[30]

By the mid-1960s, however, firms were pressured by their unions to limit non-regular employment, and were in any event willing to encourage temporary workers to stay. After 1963, the number of temporary workers therefore dropped precipitously. At Nissan and Toyota, temporary worker numbers declined in part because at least half went on to become regular workers; the same was undoubtedly true elsewhere. By 1967 they were only 9% of the workforce, and their numbers were only slightly higher in the boom years of 1972–1973. In the 1980s, they were 7% or less of the workforce.[31] Thus from the early 1960s through 1974, temporary worker status appears to have been a transitional one into which middle-aged workers were placed before becoming regular employees, and did not therefore serve as a permanent means of circumventing union wage scales; except for a short transitional period, they were not a source of cheap labor.[32]

Thus while there have been some exceptions within large firms to the egalitarian ideal, they were of limited duration. Women were never important in the automotive industry, and the use of large numbers of temporary workers had ceased by about 1965. While there continue to be temporary workers, unions prescribe their roles and numbers. In 1984, the Honda union had an informal agreement limiting temporary workers to 10% of the workforce, all of them in production jobs; about 20% of the workers in Honda factories were therefore "temporary." But Honda appears exceptional in the large number of such workers, which may reflect its late start in the industry. Elsewhere the caps are stricter, at 5% at both Nissan and Kachikachi (chapter 7), and they were only used in material handling and other low-skill tasks. They were thus the in-house equivalent of subcontractors, rather than an exception to the rule.[33]

Conclusions

Societal pressures are an important factor in firms choosing to maintain an egalitarian workforce. From a management perspective, an organization probably functions more smoothly, or at least can be run more readily, when its members are individuals with similar characteristics. Communication is easier, interpersonal conflicts are moderated and the response to incentives and discipline is more uniform. In contrast, an establishment with a variety of workers performing different jobs will have to cope with social friction. Those with more valuable skills will expect to receive recognition, yet their erstwhile peers will resent such upstarts. Likewise, jobs carrying prestige or other rewards may be viewed as reflecting no more than luck. Rather than making what others view as arbitrary distinctions, it may in fact be more efficient to pay the same wage to similar workers. In theory, different types of skills and jobs involve different technologies, different types of interpersonal interaction, and presumably different incentives. But interpersonal distinctions are likely to be invidious to cooperation and morale, and will often outweigh such benefits as might come from stronger pecuniary incentives.

Clearly the latter is the case in Japan. On the surface, it was union pressure that prevented large Japanese firms from paying widely divergent wages to regular employees, and limited their resort to nonregular workers who fell outside of the pale of union compensation and promotion criteria. Since they could not make significant pay distinctions, firms tended to specialize in hiring a uniform group of workers. In the case of large firms, they are typically high-quality workers (e.g., men with better-than-average education and social skills). For large firms, the only way to tap inexpensive labor was to subcontract unskilled, labor-intensive work.

But even small Japanese firms appear to strive for homogeneity in their workforce. Relative to the heterogeneity of the workforce in the economy as a whole, an individual small firm is also conspicuous in its specialization in workers with a similar set of gender, age, or other characteristics. In turn, through subcontracting the individual firm—small as well as large—is linked to other firms specialized in other lines of work, and (equivalently) other types of workers. As stressed in chapter 3, over time the line of work undertaken by suppliers came to complement rather than substitute for those at the auto firms; this was true of workers as well. Ironically, this then precluded using suppliers as a "safety valve," since suppliers could no longer be cut to save regular employee jobs. Subcontracting did not enhance flexibility directly, at least in terms of dealing with sales fluctuations. (This undermines the claim of Piore and Sabel [1984] that small firms and subcontracting contribute to flexibility.) More generally, as noted in chapter 3, the ability to arbitrage around sociological and union constraints was not the only motive for (or benefit from) subcontracting. Labor was not the whole story.

Finally, in the U.S. the popular image is that we work primarily for money, and in parallel economists and even businessmen focus heavily on pecuniary incentives. The Japanese experience suggests that this may be misguided as other, peer-based incentive schemes are potentially more powerful. The realization that peer pressure can be mobilized to motivate workers is certainly one factor in the recent discovery of "teams" by U.S. industry.[34] Given status criteria, economic models of compensation (e.g., wage *versus* experience) serve to explain pay. But sociological considerations determine status and the associated concept of "appropriate" pay, as economists are increasingly willing to admit (Akerlof and Yellen 1990). It is important to remember that low-wage labor does not automatically mean "cheap" labor: workers in small firms were paid less in part because they were less productive. But they were also paid less in part because their status did not demand higher pay. Status is culturally determined, through a historical process only indirectly affected by economic forces. (Chapter 8 will speculate on the implications of this point.) Its determinants will in general not be invariant across time or culture, and yet may be the most critical element in determining the overall structure of earnings.

Case Studies: Kato Shatai Group and Sembokuya

Three of the four case studies in this chapter focus on "secondary" subcontractors, firms without direct ties to an auto company. They therefore serve to counterbalance the emphasis on direct ("primary") automotive suppliers in chapters 2 and 3. Nevertheless, they also provide further illustrations of the general historical trends outlined in chapter 3 and of the labor market issues raised in chapter 4. They also provide additional background for the analysis in the next chapter of contracting patterns. Several points stand out.

First, the Kato Shatai case study vividly illustrates the interdependence of customer and supplier. When Kato ran into financial difficulty, Mitsubishi Motors was obliged to bail it out—and Kato in turn needed to look after its own suppliers. But the history of these firms also serves as a reminder of the great extent of direct rivalry among secondary as opposed to primary suppliers—several were allowed to fail, and new entry was readily encouraged. Second, these case studies show other facets of labor relations and incentives. On the one hand, Jidosha Kogyo was self-conscious of its use of large differentials based on performance—the exception, as it were, that proves the importance of egalitarian concerns. On the other hand, the examples here also depict the use of inside contractors, which is unusual in firms making passenger car parts but common in truck-body manufacture and (as noted in chapter 7) steel, shipbuilding and other industries. While on paper indistinguishable from subcontracting, in fact inside contracting resulted in outsiders toiling next to "regular" workers.

Finally, the case studies demonstrate how contracting patterns affect incentives. For example, inside contractors were not used primarily as "cheap" labor, but because they could be offered incentives and provided options different from those available using regular workers. In another direction, in the Sembokuya case study ongoing contracting provided both an incentive and an opportunity for technical change. Sembokuya was willing to invest in new equipment, but as an independent company it was also able to interact with firms in other industries, and through them learn technologies that had automotive applications. Similarly, the continuity of ties meant that even Kato was willing to help its suppliers improve their production processes.

The Kato Shatai Group

Kato Shatai manufactured truck cabs and bodies.[1] The cabs were bought directly by Mitsubishi Motors, its largest customer. But in Japan as in the U.S., commercial customers often buy only the chassis, and order the truck body separately. Mitsubishi, of course, preferred to sell standard types such as flat-bed and delivery trucks directly, and in that case it was Kato that actually made the truck. Kato also made some items directly for Isuzu. In addition, Kato offered body types it designed and marketed itself for fitting onto any company's chassis. Most of its products, therefore, were made in low volume, and many were adapted to the customer's particular needs. In its own factory Kato concentrated on making the truck beds and large body panels and frame pieces; it also carried out final assembly. Subcontractors made grillwork and smaller metal fittings, rubber parts, hydraulic and refrigeration fittings. This section includes a case study of Kato Shatai and two of its three principle suppliers of stampings, Suzuki Bankin and Jidosha Kogyo. (The third, Maruzen Kogyo, was briefly described in chapter 4.)

What makes Kato particularly interesting is that in 1976 it filed for protection from its creditors—went bankrupt—and in 1984 it was still in receivership. As with many primary parts firms, Kato not only made heavy use of subcontractors, but also had its own supplier association. But while Kato was bailed out by Mitsubishi, six of the forty original association members were not so fortunate, and went out of business. Jidosha Kogyo, as noted below, also ran into trouble, but in its case Kato helped find a new manager who ultimately took over the firm and kept it in operation. In 1984, Kato and its suppliers were only marginally profitable; unlike the passenger car industry, truck sales were highly cyclical, and had in fact been falling for 3 years.

Kato Shatai Kogyo

Kato Shatai began as a maker of wagons in 1901 in Numazu, a small port on the far side of Mt. Fuji from Tokyo. The founder, one Mr. Kato, had spent a year as an apprentice at a traditional Japanese cartwright before striking out on his own. It was not until 1924 that he made his first truck body, and during the next ten years he received only an occasional order. Then, in 1934, Teikoku Jidosha, a forerunner of Isuzu, received an army truck body contract too large for its own capacity. They subcontracted part of it to Kato Shatai, which thereafter made twenty to thirty truck bodies a month using materials supplied by Teikoku. During the war, however, rationing affected their operations; to try to obtain materials, Kato and its rivals organized a Truck Body Control Association in 1943. They were largely unsuccessful, and production at Kato ceased in 1944, as materials were unavailable and most employees had been drafted. While most of Numazu was destroyed by U.S. firebombs in 1945, however, the Kato plant survived unscathed with one of the city's few stocks of wood, a valuable resource.[2]

By 1948 Kato was again producing truck cabs and bodies for chassis assembled by Nissan, as well as for Toyota and the other truck manufacturers. It soon began expanding, setting up a small branch factory in Tokyo and a new firm to continue the production of wooden truck beds. With its roots as a traditional cartwright, Kato initially used all-wood construction for its cabs; the firm was not familiar with steel, and (equally important) wood body prices were not subject to price controls. Customers, however, wanted composite wood/steel construction, and as a result Kato lost its Toyota business in 1951—but it took until 1956 for Kato to introduce and successfully market an all-steel cab; only then did it finally drop its all-wood products.

Kato products sold particularly well in Hokkaido, due to ties to Nissan dealerships there, and in 1956 a branch plant was built in Sapporo; plants in other regions followed. Kato proved unable to manage operations in disparate locations, however, and the Sapporo venture proved unprofitable. It was spun off as a separate firm in 1960. This both provided its managers with greater autonomy, and meant they faced the prospect of bankruptcy should they fail to turn the operation around, which in fact they quickly proceeded to do. At least two other plants were similarly spun off as independent firms, run by separate branches of the Kato family. (The Kato family also bought a Nissan dealership in 1959 in Shizuoka Prefecture, near Numazu.)

The truck body market continued to evolve. After two years of stagnant demand, the market for trucks took off in 1960. Kato received an order for 100 cabs per month from Mitsubishi; about the same time Nissan also received a large order for chassis with cabs and initially contracted production to Kato. The change in customer tastes and in the volume of demand was obvious to all, and so Nissan designed its own cab and from 1961 pulled produc-tion in-house, where it could guarantee capacity.[3] Toyota and Hino likewise began marketing chassis with cabs, placing their orders with "captive" firms, while Isuzu set up a joint venture with Press Kogyo.[4] Thus in the space of two to three years the market shifted totally. In 1960 Kato's primary business was making cabs and its largest customer was Nissan, though it sold to all the truck manu-facturers. By 1964 all the truck manufacturers bought their cabs from tied or captive (keiretsu) suppliers; Mitsubishi turned to Kato, and in turn became Kato's dominant customer. (See table 5.1 on Kato's growth. Note that while revenues increased five-fold during 1960–1970, employment remained flat at roughly 600 workers dur-ing 1961–1969, and rose to only 687 workers in 1970. This is in large part because Kato, as noted below, increased its subcontract-ing during this period.)

Labor relations evolved rapidly. In 1952 Kato Shatai was a medium-sized firm with perhaps 100 workers, based in a provincial town (but with a growing Tokyo operation). Most employees were craftsmen trained in woodworking under a traditional apprentice-ship system, and had little formal education. The main Numazu plant concentrated on making special-order truck bodies, while the Tokyo plant turned out truck cabs. But given that choice, produc-tion at Tokyo far surpassed that at Numazu, and locally hired work-ers, often with a noncraft background, soon outnumbered workers transferred from Numazu. It was workers at Numazu, however, who organized a union and called a strike in 1953. (Work rules had

Table 5.1 Kato Shatai Revenues and Employment

Year	Revenues	Profits	Employment
1951	187	26	—
1952	196	8	c. 200
1953	314	28	—
1954	292	14	—
1955	203	3	—
1956	533	15	—
1957	—	18	—
1958	—	6	—
1959	716	13	—
1960	917	21	—
1961	1,281	37	550
1962	1,251	24	605
1963	1,566	27	591
1964	1,864	33	604
1965	1,533	28	522
1966	2,037	36	569
1967	2,774	61	588
1968	3,792	89	615
1969	4,455	128	635
1970	—	—	687
1980	16,390	729	—
1981	15,015	420	—
1982	13,695	284	540

Source: Kato Shatai Kogyo (1971).
Note: Data are partial and due to changes in accounting period are not consistent over time.

been promulgated in Tokyo in 1948, but there was no union until 1956.) Not coincidentally, in 1953 a labor relations consultant was hired to head up the first personnel department, and a management lecturer at Waseda University was brought in to head the new corporate planning department and to design a proper management structure. An organization chart, formal written rules, and payment and retirement standards were all drawn up for the first time. (Among other provisions, a bonus was to be paid only to workers with an attendance rate of *over* 50%, suggesting extraordinary levels of absenteeism.)

The pay system was soon revised, in light of the settlement

with the new Nissan labor union in 1954. Emendations followed in 1955 and 1956, and in 1959 the earlier system was modified to recognize the education and previous work experience of incoming workers. (While Kato hired its first new school-leaver in 1948—a junior high school graduate—the first new college graduates were hired only in 1960. Most workers were *chuto saiyo*, midcareer hires.) Labor relations were gradually systematized; the last "strike" occurred in 1963, when bandannas were worn to protest the lack of a dining hall and other amenities at a new factory. By the early 1960s, therefore, the firm had come to reflect the new "Japanese" employment system, in part as technology had made the old apprentice skills obsolete.

Kato Shatai adopted modern management practices during this period as well. While it employed a hundred workers in 1950, the firm had only a very rudimentary accounting system. Management had a poor grasp even of profitability: all it could state with certainty was that both expenses and revenues were higher in Tokyo. Then, in 1951, the truce in the Korean War and consequent decline in truck sales hit Kato Shatai hard, and management discovered it had no cash. The treasurer had to beg hat in hand at Nissan for payment so that Kato could meet its payroll. With recovery, therefore, a CPA was hired to develop an accounting system. At the same time, the Tokyo plant hired a Musashino Technical School professor to provide technical assistance, including quality control.

Thus in the early 1950s Kato Shatai modernized its management, accounting, labor relations and production systems by bringing outside experts in as managers and consultants. Not all of their advice proved useful. Management set up seven departments at the end of 1959 and imposed common accounting systems on Numazu and Tokyo. The two operations were made formal rivals in 1963, with their own cost accounting and control over hiring and other variables; and with bonuses given for performance in line with goals set by the Kato family. The business lines of the two sites were quite different, however, and the accounting system became a constant source of friction. It was eventually scrapped in 1970.

Kato Shatai did not obtain its first bank loan until 1955, though it had used banks to discount notes from Nissan and other customers. With the sudden increase in sales in 1959, it thus found itself against its credit limits. But sales to Mitsubishi continued increasing, while during the 1960s Kato developed and eventually patented truck bodies of its own design. (For example, it designed and made the bodies for Coca-Cola delivery trucks, and a "wing-top" body that swung up at the center so that forklifts could unload from both sides simultaneously.) The firm accordingly boosted its capitalization five times in the 1960s, and sought outside shareholders to finance part of this increase. With a controlling share, the Kato family wanted stable shareholders who would not be likely to sell to potentially hostile outsiders. It thus established an employee shareholding plan and requested that its suppliers purchase blocks of stock.

By 1970, however, the family began an expansion binge. Given its woodworking history, a major product continued to be wood-floor flatbed trucks. The Kato family therefore bought up forest reserves in Malaysia in the early 1970s, and then purchased a ship to transport timber to Japan. To finance this, though, Kato Shatai and the other firms owned by the Kato family went increasingly into debt. Preparations were therefore made to list the firms' shares on the stock exchange. The Kato descendants who ran the company, however, were not only adventurous, but were according to both suppliers and customers poor managers. When the oil crisis struck, truck sales plummeted and Kato Shatai began losing money. Soon the entire group of Kato operations unraveled, and the various family firms were forced to declare bankruptcy in 1976. The Kato family lost everything, as they had not isolated the constituents of their empire from each other financially. Suppliers took a bath as well. Not only did they own shares in Kato, but (as is typical in Japan) they were paid largely by promissory notes of three months' or more term, and were able to collect only 20% of their due.

Kato's factories, however, continued in operation: Mitsubishi, dependent upon the firm's production, bought up the assets. And while a handful of top managers were replaced by men seconded from Mitsubishi, few workers at the Tokyo plant were fired. (Mitsubishi, however, disposed of the all non-Tokyo operations.) By 1984, Mitsubishi accounted for 70% of sales, Isuzu for 20%, and Nissan and other firms for the remaining 10%. Kato Shatai was in stable condition, despite several poor years; while truck sales were down almost 25% from 1980, an order of 800 truck beds for Mitsubishi chassis for export to China restored profitability. (The truck market improved in the late 1980s, and Kato was finally able to move out of bankruptcy.)

The Kato factory was similar in appearance to that of other large primary suppliers. It was clean, with a large press line set up for rapid die changes and robots for welding, and made multiple daily deliveries to customers. In 1984, employment stood at 540, about 300 of whom were blue-collar workers. There were, however, about 600 workers on the factory floor: half of factory operations were carried out by inside contractors rather than Kato employees. At the time of its initial efforts to build steel cabs in the 1950s, Kato Shatai had no experience with welding or other fabrication techniques, and so turned to contractors to organize crews who could work with sheet metal. Kato at that time was busy with orders for its wooden cabs, and so these men worked at a separate site. Though it gradually moved work into its own plant, the influx of orders in 1960 again surpassed internal capacity, and so much of the metalwork continued to be done by subcontractors at other sites.

When in 1963 Kato built a new plant and again moved metal-working operations to its own site, the work continued to be done by the subcontractors rather than by Kato employees. In the late 1960s, when production lines were instituted, it formalized its network of regular suppliers, and established a formal supplier association. (See figure 5.1.) Kato employees operated the presses and other machinery and ran the regular assembly line. But in 1984 inside contractors ("straw bosses") still ran portions of assembly lines for special orders, managed one of the paint shops and did all of the hand welding. The hourly wage paid by these inside contractors to their workers was more than that received by similar Kato employees, but Kato did not have to provide any nonwage benefits. Kato managers estimated that the real income of the employees of its inside contractors was thus slightly lower. The main difference was not pay but the type of tasks for which they were employed, and the incentives they faced. Those aspects are discussed in the following case study of Suzuki Bankin.

Suzuki Bankin

Stepping into the Suzuki Bankin factory felt like stepping back in time. Unlike the modern, clean plants maintained by primary automotive suppliers like Kato Shatai, the Suzuki building was clearly twenty years old, with an oil-covered asphalt floor, dim

Figure 5.1. Kato Shatai Group Customers / Suppliers

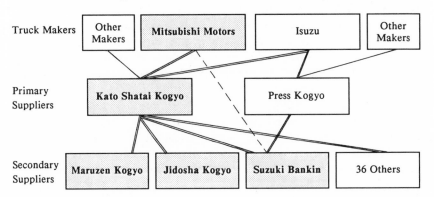

lighting and older vintage stamping presses. Even more surprising, the largest part of the plant was devoted to workers doing freehand welding, and forming sheet metal with hammer, anvil and shears. In the plant's twenty years of operation, production technology had changed little for Suzuki's products, which ranged from the front grillwork of a cab to body panels and bumpers. He seldom made items in volumes of more than a few hundred a month. His business depended in part upon being able to schedule a craft-like production process. He also had to be able to devise temporary dies and jigs and other short-cuts that maintained quality while lowering the cost of small-volume production.

Suzuki's success also hinged on retaining and motivating independent-minded skilled tradesmen, including inside contractors. In fact, that was how he got his start. Mr. Yoshio Suzuki was by training a sheetmetal worker, and by all appearances a car enthusiast. As with traditional craftsmen in the pre-WWII era, he built up his skills by moving from firm to firm. He first worked for Yanase Motors, an independent car importer and dealer that forayed into manufacturing in the late 1930s and 1940s. He then continued working for Press Kogyo, an Isuzu affiliate, when they took over Yanase's auto body business. During World War II he switched to Nissan, and in 1950 moved to Kato Shatai. At that time Kato Shatai itself had no experienced metalworkers, as noted above, and so his first task there was building the Kato all-metal cab. In particular, Mr. Suzuki helped find and manage subcontractors for Kato as well as doing subcontract work himself.

Suzuki began his own venture by leasing part of a run-down factory, which he and his seven workers shared with other small subcontractors. In 1963 he set up a plant on his own, and as his firm grew he brought in others to assist him with management. One of Suzuki's brothers-in-law joined him in 1965, and another brother-in-law (that man's younger brother, Mr. Ohkawa) quit a job as a newspaper journalist at the Tokyo Shimbun to join him the following year. At that time (1966), Suzuki Bankin employed thirty workers directly together with thirty inside contractors. Suzuki peaked in size in 1969–1970 with one hundred workers (sixty of them inside contractors). While employment shrank slightly, business kept improving until 1975, just before Kato Shatai's bankruptcy.

In 1984 the firm had 80 workers, of whom 45 were direct employees (20 office workers, 25 in the plant), and 25 were inside contractors working alongside Suzuki's men. Along with his inside contractors, Suzuki utilized six outside subcontractors, ranging in size from two to twenty workers. He turned to these firms only in part because of labor costs. The outside subcontractors did stampings and other sheetmetal work for a variety of customers, concentrating in particular on small items, while he did larger stampings himself. More important, when he was busy he depended on subcontractors to supplement his own capacity, even though he paid a premium over his normal production costs. Nonetheless, to maintain ties Suzuki tried to order some work from them even in slow periods—such as in 1984—albeit at lower prices. Of course his outside contractors were free to (and did) find other business, such as supplying electronics firms.

In contrast, his inside contractors worked at his plant on his machinery, though as skilled tradesmen they generally owned their own hand tools, in part as they drifted back and forth to auto repair "bump" shops. Suzuki paid his inside contractors on a piecework basis at a rate giving good workers a slightly higher hourly income than his direct (salaried) employees. Inside contractors, however, were not provided with benefits or paid bonuses, and so in fact cost Suzuki less money. In return, they were free to set their own hours (generally shorter), and could be lackadaisical in attendance, though total indolence was not tolerated. Some simply valued their freedom, and used Suzuki to make only enough to get by.

But all were craftsmen, carrying out semiskilled or skilled

tasks where quality and speed were dependent upon effort. Direct incentives were therefore more important than for tasks where the work pace and quality were governed by machines. And unlike white-collar work, output and quality could also be quantified ("x good parts per day"). Some worked as individuals; others had banded together and incorporated themselves for tax reasons. But unlike regular employees, they could be (and on occasion were) fired; in particular, when Suzuki's business slowed, their work was shifted to regular employees to keep them busy. Many viewed themselves as part way up the ladder that led from apprentice to skilled worker to inside contractor to independent subcontractor. A few were presumed to be doing work on the side, prior to becoming independent. Being an outside contractor resulted in higher earnings—if successful. The flexible arrangement of inside contracting provided them with a way to make a gradual transition to independence, and increased their likelihood of making it. In this they were part of the skilled trade tradition out of which Mr. Suzuki himself had come forty years earlier.

Suzuki Bankin, of course, was not a fledgling firm with ties to only one customer. Along with Kato Shatai, Mr. Suzuki had maintained ties with Press Kogyo over the forty years since he had worked there, and 20% of his output went to them and hence (indirectly) to Isuzu. Suzuki was also a racing fan, and helped Mitsubishi out with their rally cars. But the Kato bankruptcy badly hurt Suzuki's capacity for expansion. To finance his business, he had borrowed money from local commercial banks since the building of his factory. (Government small-business finance programs had been of little value to him.[5]) His financing needs were relatively modest. He purchased his steel on a cash basis from Kato Shatai, which had a large-volume, fixed-price contract; this together with labor composed his needs for working capital.[6] His investment needs were also modest, as his production process was neither capital intensive nor changing rapidly in technology, and his firm was not growing.

That was not his choice. While he was not locked into business solely with Kato Shatai, to diversify away from the large truck segment of the auto industry would take more capital. He was interested in producing stampings for one of the light pickups then being designed for export to the U.S., but he could not readily expand at his current site, and with Kato's bankruptcy could not afford to move to a new one. In fact, had it not been for low funding requirements, Suzuki Bankin might not have survived the Kato bankruptcy. Kato owed Suzuki about ¥100 million in promissory notes and accounts payable when they failed in 1976. Suzuki recovered only 20%, and so was forced to absorb a loss of ¥80 million ($533,000), though his firm had a capitalization of only ¥25 million. His reserves, however, were adequate. As with many small firms, he had bought additional land just outside Yokohama in the late 1960s, in the expectation of future expansion and as an investment. For accounting purposes, this land was carried at acquisition value, but since he had bought it prices increased over tenfold. By selling land Suzuki was able to cover his losses, while Mitsubishi Bank, cooperating with Mitsubishi Motors, stepped in to cover temporary working capital requirements. But he could not borrow a sum large enough to permit him to expand, and did not have enough resources left to do it on his own.

Another problem was that no successor was apparent. Mr. Suzuki had two sons, but one was running his own firm and the other, the graduate of a Boston-area college, was happily employed at a trading firm. (His brothers-in-law might have been interested, but the company was his, not theirs.) Ironically, the most profitable area for the firm in 1984 was financial arbitrage, not manufacturing: after 1980, note discount rates had fallen sharply, and in 1984 they were below short-term money market interest rates (just as on occasion scrap rates rose above the fixed price of the steel they obtained through Kato). Until the truck market improved, manufacturing would not be profitable and there could be little hope of borrowing enough money to expand. In the meantime, they had to concentrate on keeping enough inside contractors and subcontractors in place.

Jidosha Kogyo

Jidosha Kogyo was founded by a relative of the Katos of Kato Shatai in the early 1960s. However, the firm was for all intents and purposes only five years old. When Kato Shatai went bankrupt, it was one of the suppliers that met insurmountable problems. A new manager, Mr. Kiyohashi Fukumura, was brought in to try to turn around the operation; in the end, he bought out the previous owners, and all but three of the firm's original 40 employees either left or were fired. Fukumura succeeded where the old owners had not; in 1984 Jidosha Kogyo had 76 employees and was still expanding.

Mr. Fukumura started as a banker and later moved on to be the manager at a trading firm tied to Kato Shatai, but he had wanted to run his own firm for some time. When he moved to Jidosha Kogyo in 1978, the firm had only 17 employees at its factory; the remaining 23 were divided among three inside contractor crews at the Kato Shatai plant. The firm, however, continued to have problems and in 1980 Kato Shatai (and, as Kato's main creditor, Mitsubishi) closed it down. The Kato relative and the three foremen of inside contractor crews had been shareholders. They were bought out by Fukumura for a minimal sum, and he was willing to invest the remainder of his life savings in the firm. With new capital and an assurance from Kato Shatai that it intended to buy from Fukumura, banks refinanced the firm's outstanding debt. Fukumura now had his own firm, but would have to rebuild it from the ground up.

Fukumura was willing to do the building. His demeanor was not that of a staid banker or trading firm manager, but of a rough-and-ready factory hand: his fingers were calloused, and he was dressed in wrinkled and slightly dirty work clothes, ready to pitch in on the factory floor whenever necessary. Jidosha Kogyo reflected his vigor and nonconformity. In contrast to most Japanese firms—including Suzuki Bankin—he set pay separately for each worker and did not use formal wage criteria; pay varied by as much as ¥1.5 million a year ($12,500) among individuals of similar age and education. Jidosha was unconventional in other ways.

Other Kato suppliers such as Maruzen Kogyo (described in chapter 4) and Suzuki Bankin undertook only one or two manufacturing processes. In contrast, Jidosha Kogyo did many types of work, and with the help of Kato Shatai was experimenting with new types of machinery. Three technical workers, including two computer programmers, were on loan to him (shukko) from Kato Shatai, which continued to pay 20%–30% of their salaries.[7] Their main project was the integration of a new type of machine (an NC turret punch) into the firm's production, in the hopes of speeding up the cutting of irregular-shaped blanks from heavy-gauge sheet metal when the volume was too low to build a proper die.[8] When Kato Shatai found Fukumura reliable, it also ceased in-house painting and chrome plating operations and shifted them to Jidosha Kogyo; the firm also planned on purchasing two spot-welding robots.

The unconventional moves paid. Within four years, the firm was larger than in its previous incarnation, with 39 workers in its factory and 37 others manning a line as inside subcontractors at the nearby Kato Shatai plant. It appeared likely that Jidosha Kogyo, with the guidance of Kato, its parent firm, would soon be in a position to carry out subassembly work using technology that none of its rival subcontractors possessed. Kato stood to benefit, as it purchased 95% of the firm's output. Mr. Fukumura and the Kato manager working with him hinted they had been quite successful in reducing costs without foregoing profitability. And at least they (if not the other workers) enjoyed what they were doing: it was purposeful and challenging, and their responsibility. The senior Kato man laughed at the suggestion he would have more fun if he stayed where he was rather than return to Kato Shatai for a promotion with his peers into middle management.

Sembokuya Seisakusho

As he told it, Mr. Sembokuya yearned for a motor scooter while in high school, so when he graduated in 1953 he apprenticed to a local stamping shop for three months and then set out on his own.[9] Thirty years later, he had moved from his initial backyard shed to several buildings filled with state-of-the-art machine tools; in 1984 he employed 150 workers and had revenues of ¥3 billion ($20 million). Yet Mr. Sembokuya remained a family-oriented small businessman. His residence, a large house on a treed-in plot of land, was a few minutes' drive away, close enough for him to have dinner with his family every night—and then return to work.

Sembokuya's father made a living using hand tools to file rough castings to tolerance for a Hitachi supplier. The son disliked hand operations, so he chose to do stamping. At the beginning, his sole machinery was a foot-treadle press purchased on credit, while his father's connections got him his first order, from Jidosha Denki, a Hitachi-related firm supplying electrical parts to Nissan. (See figure 5.2.) As someone running one of many such shops in the area, he was simply paid the going piece rate, while Jidosha Denki supplied both the die and materials.

Sembokuya established a reputation as a reliable worker, and within five years obtained more substantial orders. His capital re-

Figure 5.2. Sembokuya Seisakusho Customers

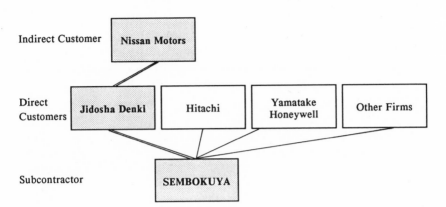

quirements thereby increased. With the boom in autos (and hence the capital needs of his parent firm), he was required to procure materials and dies himself, but only by going to the firm supplying Jidosha Denki with materials was he able to obtain credit.[10] His business continued to grow; he made heavy use of prefectural and Yokohama City leasing and loan guarantee programs, and at the time he incorporated his business in 1962, he already had borrowed several times his capitalization. With a good reputation (and relatives and business friends as guarantors) he obtained sufficient additional loans in 1984 to finance his move to a larger site near Yokohama.

The growth of the automotive market in the early 1960s meant "good money" even for primitive stamping operations such as his. This encouraged entry; Sembokuya was but one of fourteen suppliers of small stampings to Jidosha Denki. But stamping technology gradually became more sophisticated. In 1964 Sembokuya visited the in-house stamping operation of Hitachi, and was impressed by the automatic (continuous cycle) presses and progressive dies he saw there; at the time it was the electrical appliance industry, not the automotive, which had better mastered mass production technology. He tried to imitate what he saw there but was unsuccessful in developing a die on his own, and so scouted out a skilled machinist from Hitachi, Mr. Aoyama. He soon left Hitachi to become Mr. Sembokuya's right-hand man with responsibility for technical matters.[11] Aoyama thus worked on designing and making progressive dies suitable for an automatic press, and rebuilt old presses to make them automatic.

While Sembokuya was several years behind the state-of-the-art in stamping technology in Japan, in the middle and late 1960s he introduced progressive dies and automatic presses far ahead of his rivals. For him the late 1960s were therefore "*very* good money," helped after 1965 as the exit of small stamping shops from automotive work increased and entry slowed. He nevertheless continued his experimentation. During 1969–1970 Sembokuya purchased several different types of automatic presses to test their effectiveness, and in 1971 he began moving aggressively into using the newest vintage of such equipment. Though he had only 25 employees, he committed to purchase forty automatic presses at the rate of five a year, with financing through the Yokohama City Small Business Center under a national small business modernization program. This made him the low-cost supplier to his parent firm when the oil crisis hit. While other firms were struggling, his firm expanded rapidly; new entry in stamping virtually ceased after 1973, and the number of Jidosha Denki suppliers gradually shrank, leaving Sembokuya in a strong position.

By 1975 the firm had doubled employment to fifty workers and had sales of ¥600 million ($4 million). Part of this expansion was due to vertical integration and diversification into new types of production. Sembokuya began light assembly work for Jidosha Denki in 1972, using *paato,* and in 1973 he set up his own tool-and-die shop to manufacture progressive dies. By the mid-1970s, other small stamping firms were beginning to introduce more automated equipment, and his technological lead was shrinking. Thus while he was briefly the sole supplier of small stampings to Jidosha Denki in the late 1970s, the parent firm soon located two additional suppliers.[12] (Despite this, in 1983 Jidosha Denki still accounted for 70% of sales.)

Mr. Sembokuya therefore sought more lucrative business. He and Mr. Aoyama constantly visited other plants and themselves hosted visitors, and thereby observed a growing demand for high-quality tools and dies and prototype parts for electrical and precision machinery. In 1976 Sembokuya therefore imported one of the first two EDMs (electric discharge machines) into Japan,[13] and worked to tie them into a CAD (computer-aided design) system. By 1984,

Sembokuya had installed nineteen EDMs and had twelve more on order, all from Mitsubishi Denki. In the mid-1970s the firm also bought its first machining center; in 1984, six systems were in operation and six more on order, all from Mitsui Seiki. He used this equipment to produce prototype parts and dies for manufacturers of cameras and electronics. By using previously prepared, standardized die blanks, the firm could receive a fax order in the morning, do the programming the same day, have the machining centers and EDMs working unmanned all night, and assemble, ship and deliver a completed die the next day. Furthermore, since under the old technology skilled labor was the largest cost, he could do all this not only faster but for far less than traditional tool-and-die shops.[14] Business was sufficiently good that he was building a second factory.

Nevertheless, he continued experimenting with other products and processes. He had set up an injection molding operation for the manufacture of thermal fuses under license from Lucas Industries (UK). However, the production setup, which used small robots to automatically burn in and then sort out bad fuses, was of his own design. Sembokuya was looking for other products that would help extend his firm's abilities in injection molding, while taking advantage of his staff's ability to devise innovative manufacturing and testing setups. He had also purchased an experimental laser-based machine tool, and was otherwise keeping up with what he saw to be his future core business.

Sembokuya's success did not lie in his own technical ability or financial or other expertise. His skill was in working with others and with selecting successful strategies. Mr. Sembokuya had long delegated the technical side of the firm to Mr. Aoyama, and in early 1984 he added a former bank branch manager to run the financial side of the firm. (His ability to raise funds was constraining his ability to expand.)[15] Freed of much of the day-to-day detail, Mr. Sembokuya devoted extensive effort to interacting with individuals outside the firm (and encouraged his staff to do likewise). He visited the factories of other firms regularly, and was active in prefectural manufacturing and civic associations. (Over the years he had benefited significantly from prefectural technical and business consultant programs, along with the financing of his initial purchase of modern machinery.[16]) His own plant was always open to outsiders, even potential rivals. In 1984 about 3,000 individuals toured his facilities, and Mr. Sembokuya or Mr. Aoyama met most of them;

he had also appeared three times in nationally broadcast small business programs. His technical staff made presentations at professional association meetings and published articles about their innovations, including detailed lists of pitfalls and ways to avoid them. His openness resulted in significant publicity at low cost; he used this to keep the suppliers of his machine tools attentive to his needs (their names were always mentioned), as well as to garner new orders. More important from his perspective was that as a result he and his staff kept abreast of trends in industry, and so could remain a step ahead.

While his was a family business (his oldest son was studying engineering and planned to work in the firm), he brought in outsiders to create a team of professional managers. His was a typical small firm in that he made use of the *paato* available in his suburban location, but he did not use them merely for menial tasks; one young woman, still in school, had been trained in using the CAD/CAM system. In general, he moved quickly to adjust his workforce in response to new technology and the different mix of skills it utilized. For example, he found that youngsters just out of school adapted to programming as well as his skilled machinists, and could within a few months design moderately complicated dies and handle the setup of the machining centers. He therefore used his skilled workers to adapt machinery, repair tooling and assemble dies.

In sum, unlike most of his early rivals, Sembokuya not only survived but prospered. The firm's success stemmed in part from good timing, and in part from Sembokuya's own considerable business acumen. Central to this was his nurturing of personal ties, respect and trust, including his willingness to delegate work to his coworkers. Of particular note was his ability to draw on the skills and knowledge of others through interaction with both customers and equipment suppliers. This allowed him to gauge the direction in which demand was moving, and grasp technology trends despite his lack of formal training. But underneath the surface also lay his continuing ties with Jidosha Denki. It was the stability of his business relationship with them that gave him the leeway to invest in new equipment, for as long as he kept his own shop in order he did not need to fear a sudden loss of what still constituted the bulk of his business.

Conclusions

Kato Shatai illustrates vividly the interdependence of the automotive firms and their suppliers: even with bankruptcy, production continued. As Jidosha Kogyo illustrates, this could extend to secondary subcontractors. But the willingness of a parent company to assist a subcontractor did have its limits. Thus, for example, a bus body supplier of Mitsubishi Motors was allowed to go bankrupt without any attempt by the parent at rescue. Yet even there, production was shifted over a couple years to rival firms, so that younger employees could relocate (at a low cost to Mitsubishi) while older employees were able to collect a separation payment when the firm was finally liquidated. In the Kato Shatai case, Mitsubishi did not deliberately seek to bankrupt any suppliers, but when several ultimately failed, they helped Kato locate new suppliers; eleven firms were brought in after Kato's bankruptcy. This was easy because the secondary subcontractor level was used mainly for the production of small parts or custom items, and those production processes had a more widespread application than the larger machinery and production lines of the primary auto parts firms. Furthermore, the interaction of secondary suppliers with their customers in design and management was less extensive; the seconding of engineers to Jidosha Kogyo was clearly an exception for Kato.

As a consequence, rivalry was more overt at the secondary subcontractor level than with primary suppliers. Sembokuya was initially but one of fourteen similar firms, and Kato Shatai had nine rival suppliers of stampings.[17] They all lost small orders to one another, even though each firm tended to specialize in slightly different types of work. Furthermore, secondary subcontractors often found themselves in competition with their parent primary contractors. For example, Jidosha Denki (Sembokuya's parent) made small stampings, while Kato Shatai likewise shifted work in and out of the firm as the technology changed. Bringing work in-house during a business downturn was tempered by the need for cooperative suppliers should business improve. This was particularly evident in the behavior of the auto firms towards their primary subcontractors, but even a second-tier supplier such as Suzuki Bankin tried to give token orders to its subcontractors. But overall, lower-tier suppliers were less specialized and less interdependent with their parents, and this corresponded to a shorter contracting horizon.

Finally, risk and incentives stand forth in all these case studies. Both Sembokuya and Jidosha Kogyo relied on the security of their subcontractor status as they made investments in developing new process technologies. Such long-term understandings reduced the risk that an unanticipated loss of a contract would threaten the firm's existence and increased the likelihood that success would provide a financial reward. From the parent firm's perspective, lower risk slowed the pace of differentiation among suppliers and so permitted them to maintain rivalry, but it also left them with suppliers that had invested more and were more efficient. The parent firm could in addition tap the wide range of information garnered by its suppliers in their interactions with other customers. The Fukumuras and Sembokuyas of the Japanese auto industry provided far more innovation and entrepreneurship than would a vertically integrated manufacturing organization. Similarly, the use of inside contractors (as at Suzuki Bankin and Kato Shatai) provided incentives to individual workers that would be impractical in large firms with their formal and egalitarian compensation criteria. At the same time, these firms provide a reminder of the pervasiveness of the model of appropriate labor relations: Jidosha Kogyo stood out for its lack of pay norms, and was self-conscious that it was exceptional. The subcontracting system supported such diversity, and that was one of its central strengths.

The Management of Subcontracting: Innovations in Strategies and Techniques

Forty years ago, in the 1950s, the Japanese auto industry moved toward greater reliance on outside suppliers. This subcontracting strategy, however, required two sets of innovations to be workable in the long run. First, the automotive firms had to develop a mechanism to govern their relationship with suppliers. This was not as straightforward as it might seem, because interdependence was (and is) hard to manage. The "market" was inadequate: transactions were too complex to specify in contracts, and prices were hard to set when one manufacturer faced one purchaser. But by buying rather making parts, the auto companies relinquished the use of an administrative hierarchy to set prices and resolve disputes. A system of governance by trust evolved that permitted the auto firms to cope with these problems.

The term "trust" is used in part because it is the natural English term to describe the sense of the relationship. But it is also appropriate in the narrower sense, of being willing to put oneself at risk. In the U.S., the auto firms (and hence also suppliers) avoided the need for trust in two ways. First, they integrated vertically into parts production. Second, they restricted purchasing to simple items, which required little investment or other adaptation by suppliers, and which many firms could make. The Big Three could thus use the "market," pricing through competitive bids and switching orders frequently among different firms. (In practical terms, this required the purchaser to do design work and make all subassemblies in-house; see Helper 1990a, 1990c.) But in Japan, firms continued to rely upon outside suppliers even as the content of purchases evolved from the subcontracting of single manufacturing steps and simple parts to the procurement of complete subassemblies. Each side had to depend upon the other, had to put itself at risk, had to trust.

Managers in these firms responded in two ways. First, they limited the need for trust as much as possible, by developing norms for many aspects of the overall relationship, and by making the commitment of parts maker and auto firm to each other visible. The more norms there were—especially for potentially fractious issues such as pricing—the less room there was for disagreement. The greater the commitment, in plants dedicated to a given customer, and in reliance for a wide range of items upon a given supplier, the greater the incentive to seek cooperation. Their second response was to foster trust. The auto firms were careful whom they chose as suppliers, and only gradually became interdependent with them. But the auto firms also invested heavily in building up and maintaining reputation. A key tool was the supplier cooperative association, which brought individuals together in many different contexts, and which helped guarantee that untrustworthy behavior would soon be known to all.

The second major task the auto makers faced was to make purchasing itself more efficient. A car includes 10,000 or more individual parts, depending on size and options, and in Japan 5,000 or more were sourced from outside. For each, of course, not only supplier, quantity and price but also specifications and quality characteristics had to be set or clarified, and production and delivery scheduling and quality control instituted. For obvious reasons, streamlining this process was highly desirable. In the end, the Japanese auto companies were successful in developing a practical method of pricing and handling other narrowly defined purchasing tasks. Equally important, they were able to gradually extend a series of innovations used inside their firms to interfirm transactions as well. In the end, this also speeded supplier acquisition of technical and management skills, and enabled suppliers to make the single largest contribution toward lowering the cost and improving the quality and performance of Japanese vehicles.

Four such technical innovations stand out:

o pricing based on the indexing of historic costs

o just-in-time (JIT) production and inventory control

o statistical process (quality) control (SPC)

o value analysis / value engineering (VA/VE)

The first two, pricing and JIT, were largely Japanese innovations; SPC and VA/VE, however, were borrowed from the U.S. in the post-WWII era.[1] (Ironically, they began to be applied widely in Japan even as they were being forgotten here.) To use them in an interfirm context, however, required that suppliers adapt to the needs of specific customers. This was only possible in the context of a long-term purchasing relationship, and necessitated an administrative mechanism to standardize techniques and facilitate their adoption among a firms' many suppliers. Of course, firms had to trust each other to make such adaptations, the impact of which could not be predicted in advance. Again, supplier cooperative associations proved valuable, serving as a nexus for communication and coordination among subcontractors and their parent firm.

This chapter first delineates contracting practices, beginning with the legal framework and (more important) price setting. The "three jewels" of purchasing—JIT, SPC and VA/VE—are then detailed. Next, the development and function of the supplier cooperative associations are outlined. The chapter then returns to the issues of trust and governance, discussing theoretical aspects and noting parallels between theory and Japanese practice. The development of a governance mechanism was in many ways the crucial innovation, for only in the context of an ongoing, trusting relationship were firms comfortable with interdependence. This made them amenable to investing in new production technology, and to adapting to make extensive subcontracting tractable.

Contracting and Pricing

The ongoing nature of automotive subcontracting in Japan suggests that there was some form of long-term agreement to support it. In fact, there was no such formal institutional arrangement. (The concluding sections discuss whether there was instead an "implicit" or self-enforcing contract, in a game-theoretic sense.) Even though pricing was central to the smooth operation of the overall subcontracting system (and contributed to the rapid pace of technical change in the industry), it too was merely standard procedure, rather than a contractually specified rule. The following section draws heavily on research by Banri Asanuma for details of the pricing system. Here my emphasis is on facets illuminating the functioning of the overall system. For greater detail see Asanuma (1985a, 1985b) together with Ueda (1987) and U.S. International Trade Administration (1988:48–67, 74–118).

Contracts: Timing, Bidding and Volume

In the Japanese automotive industry, formal contracts and the price setting mechanism both differed from those employed by U.S. industry. Still, the purchase of a part required an agreement on price and other terms, and that specific delivery commitments be made. This commitment occurred in stages, reflected in three purchasing documents. The most general document was a *supplier agreement* formally recognizing a firm as a supplier to the automotive firm, without specifying parts or prices. It set forth only the general principles and practices for the parties to follow in purchasing transactions. (For example, it delineated the bidding process and standard payment terms.) The general supplier agreement did not, however, spell out the many coordinating mechanisms or "understandings" that were effectively part of the purchasing commitment.

Once a firm was recognized as a supplier, it could then bid on parts or agree informally to begin designing a part. An auto firm often held talks or asked for bids from several potential suppliers — Toyota, for example, always sought to approach two (but reportedly not more than two) firms at this initial stage, and typically there were three or more potential producers among a company's suppliers (Ikeda 1988a:10). Nevertheless, in practice the auto firms often informally decided on the supplier in advance. For example, when a part was to be redesigned for a model change, the supplier of the part for the previous model was typically chosen—it, after all, had the relevant manufacturing capacity already in place and available. Given the number of items to be sourced with a model change, this also economized on the number of administrative decisions. (Even where a model change resulted in a new type of part, the purchasing department took into account factors such as capacity utilization.) This process began very early—roughly three years before production commenced—when a vehicle was still in the concept stage of development, since the subcontractor was often the firm to develop the details of the unit and then do the detailed engineering and drawings. (Suppliers designed 80% of the parts Toyota bought; U.S. International Trade Administration 1988:50.) Effectively, then, an auto company made the decision to purchase a specific part from a given company well before there were detailed specifications or accurate market research on potential sales volume upon which price could be based.[2] Of course, the supplier then also had to commit engineering resources and manufacturing capacity before price was set. Suppliers were willing to do this because of the predictable manner in which prices were set, and because of their trust of the auto firms.

A formal *purchase agreement* was finally signed six to nine months before production commenced, when price negotiations were completed and the anticipated purchase quantity was fixed. (Price was, however, adjusted on a semiannual basis and *not* fixed for the duration of the contract; see below.) Engineering blueprints were incorporated into the agreement, which extended for the duration of production. Until the 1980s, model changes were less frequent in Japan than in the U.S. Minor model changes averaged once every two years, in contrast to annual changes in the U.S.; major model changes occurred only once in four years, while in the U.S. a two-year cycle was more common. Engine, transmission and drivetrain systems were changed even less frequently; a part for those could remain in production (and the purchase agreement in effect) for as long as eight years. Thus historically the formal purchasing agreement covered a longer period in Japan than the U.S. In the last decade, however, styling has become more crucial both in the domestic market and the export niches the Japanese producers targeted. Therefore on paper the obligation of the auto firms to their suppliers has now approached the one-year contract duration that was normal in Detroit.

Even this obligation was not legally binding; that occurred only with the issuing of a monthly *purchase order*. In the interim between the purchase agreement and the purchase order, however, a series of increasingly firm purchasing plans were issued, as the volume quoted in the purchase agreement was brought into line with actual production and sales. The first of these projections was a nonbinding annual forecast; it was then followed on a rolling basis by three-month production plans. When the latter was updated, the quantity for the coming month was then turned into a binding purchase order. In fact, however, production quantities varied from the purchase order; actual weekly and daily deliveries were scheduled at the factory level using just-in-time inventory procedures. (Any variance was rolled into subsequent purchase orders.) But while the legal obligation only arose on a month-to-month basis, these annual and three-month projections were in fact taken seriously; otherwise work on different parts could not be balanced to permit just-in-time production. Furthermore, as noted below, pricing for simple items was likewise made contingent on volume. At all stages of the process, therefore, the commitments on paper and in practice differed, in timing and often in detail. Again, the parties had to trust each other to countenance such a situation.

Pricing

Price, of course, was potentially a highly contentious issue. A higher price increased supplier profits, and cut those of the assembler—and vice-versa. The benefits were, however, unequal: a supplier's profits were far more sensitive, since a single part constituted a relatively large part of a supplier's business but generally an insignificant proportion for the auto maker. In addition, a new model required the auto maker to source thousands of items virtually simultaneously; it could not afford to haggle over each part. Since a single part made up a trivial portion of the final cost of a vehicle, the auto company could afford to pay too much. But if repeated across thousands of contracts, the result would be disastrous: a company would be nickeled and dimed to death, taking its suppliers with it. An efficient and fair pricing mechanism was thus critical to all parties.

To handle this task, the auto firms employed a bidding mechanism where the focus was not on comparing final unit price but on breaking costs down in detail. These line items could then in principle be compared with the bids of other firms. In fact, however, it was far simpler and virtually as effective for the primary comparison to be with previous bids of the same firm, adjusted for expected improvements in manufacturing efficiency. Furthermore, the rate of expected improvement was itself standardized across firms. Thus, as a rule of thumb, suppliers of similar parts were expected to submit bids lower than their previous one by the same fixed percentage. For more complex items or those contingent on styling or other details, design often changed significantly, and this approach could not be applied in a rigid manner. It did nevertheless provide a point of departure.

In greater detail, the components of the typical bid included the following items:

1. Material costs.
2. Purchases from secondary subcontractors of parts and processes such as anodizing and plating.
3. Direct manufacturing costs.
4. Tooling costs.
5. The gross margin (overhead plus a profit margin).

The previous bid was readily adjusted to reflect market conditions for material costs (1) and other purchasing costs (2). Direct manufacturing costs (3) were calculated as a sum of the costs for each manufacturing step, and paralleled the cost accounting system. This was thus an analog of pricing in the 1950s and earlier, discussed in chapter 3, which used the competitive (market) rate for the services of a subcontractor with a given type of machinery. Next, per unit tooling costs (4) were based on an estimate of appropriate tooling costs divided by anticipated sales. However, for simple parts the automotive purchaser effectively guaranteed to reimburse suppliers for these costs, to the extent they were judged specific to the part being purchased. Parts prices were thus adjusted downward when actual sales exceeded planned sales, while a rebate was given when sales were poor. Finally, the gross margin (5) was a standard markup set separately for each supplier rather than negotiated separately each time; it was explicitly *not* made an item of regular bargaining.

The use of target price improvements—and more generally, the indexing of costs—was one of the significant innovations of Japanese purchasing. Price adjustments were made on a semiannual basis, even within the duration of the purchase agreement. One straightforward element was to correct for changes in material prices. More important, price was lowered to reflect target improvements in productivity. Given the decades of catching-up with best practice in the U.S. and elsewhere, suppliers had long been able to improve productivity sufficiently to lower costs, despite increasing wages. In fact, labor costs did *not* enter explicitly into direct manufacturing costs (4), but were subsumed into overhead, which was fixed. A supplier with higher than average labor costs (or higher than average wage increases) therefore had to compensate through higher productivity or the provision of design or other services, which resulted in a higher gross margin (5). (This contrasts with U.S. practice, where higher labor costs provided a rationale for higher contract prices.) An automotive firm therefore set a uniform semiannual cost reduction target for its suppliers, and publicized this through its supplier cooperative association. (In the early 1980s, the targets were on the order of a 3% reduction every six months.[3]) In other words, in return for the commitment to purchase for the duration of production—and with the presumption of future contracts as well—suppliers were expected to invest in improving their own manufacturing processes, and to share a portion of those savings with their automotive customers.

The target rate of cost reduction took into account the auto maker's experience in improving its own productivity. Targets were thus chosen to be achievable, but were kept uniform across suppliers rather than being set higher for firms with a good track record or lower for firms with a poor one. Fixed targets (and hungry rivals) thus provided an incentive for firms to engage in internal process improvements. Firms that could not meet the average found their profits squeezed, while firms that exceeded the target enjoyed higher effective profit margins. Furthermore, the detailed breakdowns obtained during the bid process could be used to target engineering efforts to areas most amenable to improvement on the basis of interfirm experience. The reduction thus was intended to be fair across suppliers, and achievable in fact—even if it took the aid of the auto firm itself. Combined with a cost base that because it was historic took account of the idiosyncracies of individual suppliers, cost indexing offered a highly efficient and (almost as important) objective procedure to set target prices—even if it did not eliminate all haggling.

The "Three Jewels": JIT, SPC and VA/VE

Introduction

Innovations in production management are typically limited to application within the firm. But the Japanese auto companies were dependent on outside parties for subassemblies and other complex items that in the aggregate accounted for the majority of manufacturing costs. In addition, about half of the engineering of a new car was undertaken by suppliers. Clearly it was desirable in such a situation to extend internal management methods across firm boundaries. Firms would not have become interdependent in the first place without mutual trust; integration of management functions likewise required suppliers knowing and being willing to adapt on behalf of customers, and the auto firms taking the lead in standardizing techniques for use by their suppliers. This section focusses on three such techniques—one of which, value engineering, is not sufficiently appreciated in the U.S. The next section then concentrates on the role of supplier cooperative associations as the nexus for coordination and (tying into the final section) the locus for the creation of reputation.

Scheduling: Just-in-Time Systems

On the surface JIT functions as a production and inventory control system. That, indeed, was its genesis. When Toyota faced possible bankruptcy in 1949–1950, one of its problems was excessive inventory; in fact, contemporary descriptions of Japanese factories all noted that piles of in-process parts made it difficult to maneuver across the floor. Toyota factory managers therefore sought to balance lines, so that parts were turned out from one machine or operation only as fast as they were used in the next (Itami et al. 1988:90, 99–103). They also implemented a "pull" system in which new stock was requested only as the old approached depletion. This problem was of course not unique to Toyota (or to the automotive industry), and by 1960 many firms were implementing what they referred to as "supermarket systems," named after the inventory controls of U.S. supermarkets.

The general aim was thus to schedule small, frequent deliveries, and to have operations within a factory cycling at similar rates, so that parts could "flow" throughout. (Because of this feedback with other operations, it therefore paid to make lot sizes smaller than what setup costs alone suggested to be optimal.) In contrast, the computerized "push" methods used in the U.S., which set production in line with a master plan, often proved unwieldy and in practice led to high inventory levels. If actual demand was less than expected or the product mixed changed, excess inventory developed rapidly—and if demand was strong, production had to be expedited, with deleterious consequences elsewhere. (Material Resources Planning ["MRP II"] and similar systems are, however, appropriate for construction and other nonrepetitive scheduling situations. For an overview see Karmarkar 1989.) Furthermore, when production setups could be changed rapidly, JIT scheduling not only lessened the buildup of buffer inventories, but also permitted workers on the line to adjust production to small changes in output mix and volume. This decentralization brought administrative savings, but required adaptation of the physical manufacturing setup to match the flow of production, in line with good industrial engineering practice. (By the early 1960s, Japanese engineers also shortened the time required for a die change in stamping from 8 hours to 12 minutes; it now can take under 5 minutes. Rapid die changing only began to be widely adopted in the U.S. in the 1980s.) Note that to do this, workers had to be given the authority and training to set up dies and adjust machines, while production engineers had to design dies to common physical dimensions to facilitate rapid interchange.

There were other benefits to JIT besides decentralization. When implemented effectively, JIT lowered inventory levels dramatically, providing a large one-shot reduction of in-process inventories and in the consequent need for working capital. (It also translated into space savings, particularly critical in urban areas of Japan.) However, the long-run impact was more important, for reduced inventory levels revealed bottlenecks in the production system by pinpointing the slowest step. Engineering attention to that step or process often significantly increased the productivity of the entire operation. JIT systems also forced good maintenance habits and better attention to quality because without buffer stocks defective parts or a machine breakdown quickly affected downstream operations. JIT systems were thus effective management tools for targeting factory-level production engineering efforts. Finally, by reducing the amount of work-in-process, JIT systems made it quicker and less costly to introduce a design change into production. By shortening lead time they also facilitated producing only in response to actual orders instead of building ahead in anticipation of future sales. (In contrast, MRP systems take a lot size as a given, and depend on buffer inventories to provide leeway for minor postplan changes, machine downtime and similar problems. MRP has no internal dynamic for improvement.)

The initial efforts of Toyota and other Japanese manufacturers, however, were restricted to internal operations. But by the early 1960s, as detailed below, they began to ask suppliers to conform to their internal production scheduling system. At the initial stage of adapting to a parent firm's request for frequent, standard-sized shipments, a supplier simply built up more inventory; the piles of parts (and the associated costs) were shifted from the assembly plant to their plant. But when the parent proved reliable—and was able to schedule final assembly to limit week-to-week and day-to-day variation—a parts maker could gradually tune its own production to mesh with that of its parent. Scheduling could then be decentralized to lower levels of the firm; at present workers on the line at suppliers respond to "kanban" (inventory and work order cards) issued by assembly workers at the parent automotive plant, and even secondary subcontractors often produce and deliver to the kanban of primary suppliers.

Implementation across a supplier-purchaser interface required significant investment and adaptation of the internal operations of suppliers to the JIT standards (including, for example, the assembly line speed) of the purchaser. A supplier was only willing to do this in the context of a ongoing relationship. Thus:

Many of the U.S. and European corporations which have introduced the JIT production system, for example, have successfully used the kanban system to reduce their inventories, only to find that this system cannot be applied to their outside suppliers because close cooperative relationships of the kind seen in Japan are not maintained with these firms. Since the automotive industry is one in which division of labor is dominant and outside suppliers are depended upon for a great deal . . . benefits . . . cannot be fully realized. (Ikeda 1988a:5)

Quality Control

Bad parts are themselves costly, representing wasted effort. But if bad parts stopped the assembly line, or were built into a subassembly or vehicle that then had to be repaired or replaced, the cost was greater. Recalls and loss of reputation were potentially even more expensive. Because of this, the automotive firm faced greater losses from poor quality than the direct wastage born by a parts producer. Contracts could shift some of these costs onto suppliers, and in the early 1960s small penalties (e.g., 3%–5% of price) for late delivery or poor quality were made part of the general supplier agreement. Formal penalties increased with the spread of "just-in-time" purchasing, since the lack of buffer inventories multiplied the cost of delayed delivery or unusable parts; in principle, suppliers were expected to foot the bill for estimated losses. (See a novel by Shiroyama [1982] for a fictional account.) But in a one-time purchasing situation, a firm still inspected all incoming shipments. Precaution outweighed reliance on penalties; a firm quite naturally trusted its own inspectors more than those of a supplier. Such inspection was likely to duplicate supplier efforts, and was less effective and more costly than the upstream controls that could be installed in the context of an ongoing, trust-based relationship.

Two diametric approaches to monitoring quality exist. One was to inspect in quality; the second was to build in quality. The process of inspection is obvious; finished parts (or better, work in process) are checked against dimensional and similar specifications. But building in quality often proved less costly. Rather than checking output for faults, the production process itself was monitored. With statistical process control (SPC), the variation of individual production steps was analyzed, and the production process was then engineered so that a failure to meet final tolerances was unlikely. (For example, given the observed variation of the process, it would be controlled so that good parts would be produced with a 99.99% probability.) Machines still had to be checked and adjusted at regular intervals, but inspection per se was rendered redundant (Monden 1983:139–140). (Practical techniques for doing this in a factory environment were worked out by Dr. W. A. Shewhart at Western Electric in 1928, and were applied at U.S. military contractors during WWII. They were taught to the Japanese in management seminars under the U.S. Occupation by Juran, Deming and others.)

In the auto industry, an ongoing relationship made it practical for suppliers to build in quality. At the most trivial level, the costs of installing SPC and in-process inspection could be recouped. More important, the purchaser could directly inspect the production setup of a supplier to evaluate the adequacy of SPC and in-process inspection systems. It then could dispense with incoming checks of the output of such factories. Eventually, procedures and documentation standards for implementing and monitoring SPC and other quality control systems were standardized. Over time, the automotive firms came to rely upon the adequacy of supplier management controls, rather than detailed evaluation of supplier SPC charts and controls. (Rather than relying on contractual penalties, over time the auto firms made such management controls a precondition to remaining a supplier.) This was feasible only within the context of an ongoing relationship, where management was known to be competent and could be trusted to maintain its equipment in good operating condition.

Design Aspects: Value Analysis (VA) and Value Engineering (VE)

It is said that 80% of costs are fixed in the first 20% of the design process.[4] Certainly given the initial backward status of all facets of the Japanese automotive industry, improving vehicle and parts design was crucial. As suppliers in the 1950s and early 1960s gradually came to make first entire parts and then units and subassemblies, the number of parameters under their control increased, and hence also the potential gains from granting them autonomy in production methods and tooling design. Above all, the prospect that feedback from suppliers to engineers at the auto firms would lead to significant cost reductions or quality improvements was improved. (Shop floor productivity activities, while valuable from a labor relations standpoint, produce small benefits in comparison.)

While the stability of an ongoing relationship made it possible for supplier engineers to learn to communicate with those at their automotive customers, it did not guarantee that this interaction would be fruitful. In addition, it did not guarantee that suppliers would have any real incentive to spend money lowering costs if all the benefit were to accrue to their customers. Even within the same firm this was an issue. After all, due to extreme functional specialization, in Detroit the manufacturing engineers responsible for plant design and tooling were told nothing until after production engineering had completed the entire design process (Dertouzos et al. 1989:97). In such situations VA/VE proved particularly valuable, at least when coupled with a pricing system that provided suppliers with pecuniary benefits from their efforts.

Value analysis was initially developed in 1947 by an industrial engineer at General Electric, Lawrence Miles. He discovered that reevaluation of a design typically resulted in substantial (e.g., 30%!) reductions in cost through the use of alternative materials and imaginative design modifications. Under time constraints, engineers tend to build on previous designs or draw upon textbook approaches; engineers also take pride in an aesthetically clean design. For example, Miles found that he could often develop a "dirty" design using inexpensive, off-the-shelf components that would perform as well as a "clean" design needing expensive custom parts. But his real innovation lay in setting forth an analytic procedure to examine the cost effectiveness of a design that could be both taught and managed.

Value analysis consists of a systematic procedure for devising and analyzing alternatives to a design that will improve value (quality or function) and/or reduce cost. Miles set forth a sequence of steps that provide a framework for interaction among design engineers, manufacturing staff, quality control and purchasing staff, and finance and marketing personnel (including, where appropriate, their counterparts in suppliers). He specified three basic steps: identifying the function or "value" of a part in abstract terms ("convey energy"); evaluating the cost to deliver value as currently designed; and applying creative problem solving to suggest alternative solutions. These alternatives could then be costed out, checking for ease of manufacturing and that value as perceived by end users was preserved or enhanced. Along with developing this scheme, Miles and subsequent consultants devised exercises for developing acumen in defining function and in creative thinking, and set forth a framework for scheduling and monitoring these and subsequent steps and for evaluating the design proposals generated by VA/VE (Miles 1972).[5] The emphasis was thus on teamwork rather than individual specialization. (One value engineer, Fred Spengler, described VA as a discipline to make "white collar and technical staff work together," and to help "break down the invisible walls which surround profit centers.") But because of its cross-functional nature, VA/VE entails a commitment by senior management to permit the involvement of staff and to reward them for it.

VA/VE was first introduced into Japan circa 1960, as part of a broad effort to apply industrial engineering techniques to cost reduction that gained impetus from the publications of a 1955 Japan Productivity Center mission to the U.S. (Nihon Seisansei Honbu 1969:172). The original Miles book on VA was translated into Japanese in 1962; when the Japan Productivity Center surveyed 159 large firms in 1964, it found 87 already using VA techniques (p. 890). Nissan, for example, first used VA extensively (along with a target cost system) in 1964 for the design of its hit car the "Sunny," involving suppliers from the start. Production costs were ultimately 30% less than for the previous model, despite enhanced performance. In the initial 1964 program suppliers submitted 300 proposals, a small number compared to current efforts, but which still realized savings of "several tens of millions" of yen per month (Nissan Jidosha 1976:60). At first VA activities at Nissan and elsewhere centered around purchasing departments, and were applied primarily to selecting materials. As familiarity with VA methods increased, design and production engineering became more actively involved. But until the 1970s suppliers were seldom integrated into parent VA programs, even though many large parts firms had their own VA programs.[6]

The implementation of joint VE programs in the automotive industry entailed extensive training programs for suppliers, and the development of working teams among supplier and parent company production, design engineering and cost accounting staff. (Further details are provided in the next section.) As noted above, this made sense only in the context of an ongoing relationship, and needed to be buttressed by an incentive system. To encourage suppliers to put effort into design improvement, incentive systems were developed, but this took considerable trial and error. Toyota, for example, first introduced VA internally in 1962, and began teaching it to suppliers the following year. But only in 1965 did it set up an organizational framework or formal guidelines for VA, and a new system installed in 1969 had to be revised the following year (Matsumoto and Tsuchiya 1971).

While the details vary slightly from firm to firm, from the beginning the practice at Toyota and the other automotive firms was to split the savings generated by VA/VE 50:50 (this was also Miles' recommendation). The automotive firms assigned staff to evaluate and implement supplier proposals. If a supplier came in with a VA proposal, they checked whether it would still fulfill the relevant function and how much it would cut costs. If it was by ¥10, then the price of the part was effectively lowered ¥5, increasing a supplier's profit margin by ¥5. (In practice, price was reduced in full six months to one year after the proposal was put into effect, depending upon the relative effort of the supplier and the auto firm in developing the new design. With the typical two-year model cycle, 25%–50% of the cost reduction then accrued to the supplier in the form of an increased profit margin; Asanuma 1985a.)

The smooth functioning of VA/VE, however, was contingent not only on firms learning each other's engineering standards and developing communication channels, but also hinged on the details of the compensation mechanism and on mutual trust. For VA projects carried out after engineering was completed or the part was in production, the extent of cost reduction could be objectively measured. But for VE projects at the initial design stage, the contribution of a suggestion was harder to quantify—and the proposal might be made redundant by a later design change, or prove capable of being applied to many different parts. Finally, where design was carried out jointly by a supplier and the purchaser, assigning the relative contribution of the different parties was open to criticism. Toyota thus found in the late 1960s that even if suppliers thought of a change early in the design process, they would wait until production was about to commence to make their suggestions, to guarantee a pecuniary reward rather than leave compensation up to the discretion of the buyer for the part. In 1970 Toyota thus developed a formal checklist and tried to obtain consistency across all staff. They also moved toward using a target price system (standardized cost-down percentages) for parts designed largely by the supplier, rather than trying to adjust price separately for VA/VE efforts (Matsumoto and Tsuchiya 1971, Kawada 1972).

VA/VE programs were extensive, and received attention from senior management. The VE program at Fuji Heavy Industries (FHI) for a model designed in the mid-1980s focused on a group of 200 parts and components and involved 150 suppliers. About 450 meetings were held between design and production engineers and purchasing and sales staff from suppliers and FHI. With a 10% target, they achieved an 8% reduction (U.S. International Trade Administration 1988:59). Nippon Denso (NDK), the leading Japanese automotive electrical component manufacturer, achieved ¥10.3 billion ($70 million or 1.5% of sales) in VA/VE savings in 1984. In that year NDK put 2,000 employees through a four-hour course, and 130 through a forty-hour course, for a total of 17,000 man-hours of staff training in VE methods (SJVE 1985). Kayaba Industry, the dominant manufacturer of shock absorbers and hydraulic systems and an early adopter of VA, claimed that its VE program achieved savings of 2% of sales in 1984 (short of its target of 3%); 148 of its engineers went through a week-long of VE training program, and nine staff received certification as VE instructors. Kayaba had a VE Council comprising representatives from sales, design and production engineering, and stressed that its VE program was understood and supported by its top executives (SJVE 1985). Similarly, all the suppliers in the Soja Industrial Park had VE programs.

Summary

As with the adoption of JIT systems and the maintenance of very high quality standards, suppliers are now expected to contribute to the design process. Likewise, as with JIT and SPC, VA/VE evolved from an internal management tool to one that was applied throughout the supplier system. In the context of an ongoing relationship, it proved possible to surmount firm boundaries and integrate the design activities of parts makers with those of their automotive customers. This permitted the automotive assemblers to tap the engineering and innovative efforts of suppliers without recourse to vertical integration.

VA/VE, SPC and JIT were all taken very seriously by parts firms, as signified by formal programs and accounting measures. Ibara Seiki, a manufacturer of suspension and transmission parts and brake discs located in the Soja Industrial Park, had a formal VA/VE budget. Their goal was 140 VA/VE suggestions over five years with a target savings of ¥55 million ($370,000), or just under 1% of sales. The firm also had targets for inventory and yield, expressing its management commitment to SPC and JIT (interview at Ibara, 1984; see also Hiromoto 1988). Such efforts were representative of those elsewhere. In turn, the auto makers—from top executives on down—worked to maintain an environment conducive to supplier investment in these and similar innovations.

The Supplier Cooperative Associations

The automotive supplier associations (*kyoryoku kai*) were central to both the functioning of the governance mechanism and the diffusion and administration of systemwide management techniques. They served as a means for generating and maintaining reputation, and for the communication of norms and purchasing policy. In this manner they supported the overall relationship. But they also provided a convenient institution through which educational and consulting efforts could be organized. They thus helped the auto firms extend what were initially internal management techniques to their primary parts suppliers. (In time, primary parts firms did the same with their suppliers.) The historical development and role of supplier associations in diffusing technical and management innovations is surveyed first. The annual activities of Mitsubishi Motors' association are then described in greater detail, with an emphasis on the facets that contribute to building and maintaining reputation.

Diffusion of Technology at Toyota, Nissan and Isuzu

The Toyota supplier association, the *Kyoho Kai*, was founded in 1939 during the early years of World War II, allocating rationed materials to Toyota suppliers, at least on paper. Similar organizations were created elsewhere, including at Mitsubishi and other firms that subsequently entered the motor vehicle market. After the war, in 1946–1947, the Toyota association was reorganized into three groups, with one for the Nagoya region (where Toyota is located), one for the Osaka region and one for the Tokyo-Yokohama region. The supplier associations of Toyota and the other automotive firms initially played a passive role. They were set up as legal cooperatives, and their main function was to obtain financing (note discounts) for members through the Shoko Kumiai Chuo Kinko (a government bank for cooperatives), and to provide insurance and other services (Yokokura 1988:520–24).

Only gradually did they come to be used in a more positive manner. As in the case of Mitsubishi (chapter 2), it was undoubtedly problems with parts suppliers that led to Toyota taking a more active interest. In 1952 the Japanese government through the predecessor of the current Small and Medium Business Agency set up a consulting program for evaluating a company's suppliers (the *Kigyo Keiretsu Shindan Seido*). Given its near-bankruptcy in 1949–1950, Toyota must have had problems paying suppliers, yet needed continued deliveries by them to keep afloat. (The same thing happened at Chrysler in 1980; Smitka 1989.) In any event, Toyota availed itself of this program, and during 1952–1953 a team of consultants visited forty of its Nagoya-area suppliers, and a second team visited seventeen additional suppliers in early 1954. These consultants found Toyota's and other automotive suppliers to be far behind foreign auto parts producers, and in many cases backwards relative even to domestic firms. But they did commend Toyota for not shifting orders unusually frequently, for paying reasonable prices and for making efforts to procure materials for its suppliers. However, under the program's standard evaluation scale only eight firms rated "excellent."

Reflecting the restrained praise of the final report, Toyota's response suggested weaknesses in its prior policies, as it significantly revised (and then publicized) its supplier strategy. First, as part of the new policy Toyota agreed to share production plans with suppliers. (In particular, it promised to indicate anticipated parts requirements for each day on a monthly basis.) Second, in place of ad hoc price negotiations, Toyota began to use estimate sheets and other standardized forms for the bid and procurement process. Third, they agreed to make 80% of payment in cash with the remainder paid under 60– to 90–day notes. (In Japan interfirm payments were normally made by promissory notes payable in 60–150 days. Recipients could then have these discounted by a bank.) Given its early boom-bust cycles, the auto industry needed to attract suppliers by paying with cash and notes of short maturity. Toyota furthermore stated that, "In order to strengthen the organization of our supplier plants, we will strive to place continuing orders on a stable basis over the long run." Similarly, they "vow[ed] never to arbitrarily change suppliers." (Nikkan Kogyo 1980:140–41) These statements presumably reflected distrust by suppliers of Toyota, given its history through 1952—after narrowly avoided bankruptcy, production expanded greatly during the Korean War, only to slow when truce talks began in mid-1951. As at Toyota, supplier associations only gradually became more central at the other auto firms. The shift occurred for Nissan around 1958, for Mitsubishi Mizushima and Nissan Diesel about 1960, and for Hino and Isuzu about 1962 (Kodaira 1968:321).

While the earliest activities of the Toyota supplier association focused on supplier management, those at Nissan and the other auto firms concentrated on production technology. The first endeavor in the 1950s of the *Takara Kai*, Nissan's supplier association, was to instruct suppliers in industrial engineering and to help standardize production. About 1960, the emphasis switched to teaching statistical quality control, and in 1962 to value analysis and the reorganization of plant layouts. General management skills did not become an explicit focus until 1963, when Nissan began to tutor its suppliers in cost accounting techniques (Auto Trade Journal 1965). Finally, through its association Nissan encouraged mergers, and assisted its better-run suppliers to begin making subassemblies. Similarly, Toyo Kogyo (Mazda) began a program to train suppliers in cost accounting in 1961, while in 1964 Hino began seminars for the middle management of suppliers on topics such as industrial relations and purchasing skills (Ichikawa 1967:195ff).

Another function of the supplier associations was the centralization of purchasing to exercise countervailing power against steel and other material producers. Nissan began joint sheet steel purchases for itself and its suppliers in 1960, and expanded the coverage in 1962 and again in 1970, as outside vendors began to produce large stampings and even undertake final assembly (Nissan Jidosha 1976:75). One purpose was to have steel of uniform quality, as well as to pass volume discounts on to all its subcontractors. But Nissan could also use its bargaining power to help offset the periodic attempts by steel cartels to enforce list prices, and to lessen the impact of shortages when small firms would otherwise have found it difficult to obtain steel.[7] (Chapter 5 noted that Kato Shatai also obtained steel for its suppliers.)

The supplier associations also provided a means for teaching suppliers JIT. Toyota adopted a JIT system within its own plants by 1963; it then began to insist on JIT scheduling of incoming parts shipments. Working through its supplier association, Toyota took an active hand in helping its subcontractors implement JIT. Initially, instead of Toyota keeping inventory on its factory floors, suppliers kept inventory on theirs. But Toyota sent management consulting teams into suppliers, and took in trainees from suppliers to work temporarily alongside its own personnel. Shiomi (1985b) provides details based on a survey of eighty-nine Toyota suppliers he conducted in 1984. Half of the firms in his study reported that Toyota had sent consulting teams into their plants. As they adapted their internal production lines for rapid tooling and die changes, suppliers too began to engage in small-lot production and reduce inventories. In 1970, 60% of Toyota's vendors were scheduling shipments using kanban, the order cards used in its JIT system, but only 16 firms (18%) used kanban for their internal production control. By 1984, 76 firms (85%) had adopted kanban throughout their operations, and several were extending their use to their own (secondary) subcontractors; Shiomi documents a similar program at

Nippon Denso.[8] Toyota also had programs to help its suppliers set up QC circles and to implement statistical production control (SPC) techniques.

Nissan provides further examples of the active hand of the auto firms with their suppliers. One impetus at Nissan was its 1966 merger with Prince Motors and the consequent need to integrate former Prince suppliers into its own subcontracting system. For this purpose it established a "consulting office" in 1967 and through the Takara Kai sent out staff to work with member firms. These programs targeted the owners and managers of suppliers, especially newer suppliers. Along with helping them implement Nissan's JIT system, the consulting office provided industrial engineering assistance, helped with product planning, and provided general management consulting. One example of this was the provision to suppliers of computer facilities. Nissan began developing its proprietary COMICS (Cooperative Management Information and Control System) system in 1967. It set up a central COMICS computer center that from 1968 received trainees from Nissan suppliers. The system was built around easily modified modules, which enabled suppliers to computerize their financial, purchasing, payroll, personnel, inventory and production operations. Sixty suppliers initially joined the center (it eventually had 100 users), in part because members could use the large COMICS mainframe instead of installing their own (Nissan Jidosha 1976:62–67). In a similar vein, Nissan published how-to handbooks on quality control and industrial engineering methods, sent industrial engineering (IE) teams into supplier factories and trained 120 supplier engineers in IE.

The supplier associations at Nissan and other firms maintained permanent staff, including consulting engineers, and played an administrative role in organizing seminars and in bringing together suppliers to work on common problems. They thereby coordinated efforts to diffuse production and management technology. This was made explicit at the *Kyowa Kai* of Isuzu Motors, which was formed in 1962:

By working with each other, the members aim to improve their management and technical capabilities, and contribute thereby to their own and Isuzu's development, while at the same time fostering greater togetherness. (Isuzu Kyowa Kai 1972:2)

In particular, Isuzu intended for the association to sponsor seminars and visits by suppliers to each other's factories. Members were divided into three subcommittees: casting, forging and machining; stamping and chassis; and component manufacturers. Technical seminars were held for the companies in each group. In addition, the Kyowa Kai sponsored fifteen seminars on financial and accounting controls, personnel management, purchasing management and R&D management. (Permanent staff were assigned to a management consulting department within the Kyowa Kai from 1963.)

Each year the Kyowa Kai adopted a new theme. For example, the diffusion of value analysis (VA) began in 1963. The Kyowa Kai brought together top supplier executives for an initial seminar, and followed this up with a seminar for second-tier managers and a large number of working-level seminars. In 1964 the theme was the adoption of the "Three Jewels" of QC (quality control), VA and JIT. For VA, the association ran 27 seminars and in addition set up a basic training program for engineers. In early 1965, the staff of Kyowa Kai firms then presented successful value analysis projects in how-to demonstration sessions open to working-level personnel from all member firms. Before the end of 1965 Isuzu suppliers held 42 joint VA workshops, and during 1966 regular "VA visits" to the factories of Kyowa Kai members were scheduled. In 1967 a Value Engineer Certification Program was set up and in subsequent years formal VA/VE manuals were published and revised, awards were established and a value engineering promotion month was held. Working through the Kyowa Kai, Isuzu was thus able to mobilize its suppliers and help them to learn from each other, while leaving much of the initiative and coordination to them.

Annual Activities: Mitsubishi Motors Kashiwa-kai

The technical and engineering activities of the supplier associations were very important, but the associations also helped cement the relationship between the automotive firms and their suppliers. Mitsubishi Motors (MMC) was explicit on this point:

We depend on the outside firms which cooperate with us for items which comprise about 70% of the cost of a vehicle. As a result, it is vital for us to maintain their cooperation, to see that Mitsubishi Motors policy is fully understood and so on. . . . the purpose of the Kashiwa Kai is to contribute to the mutual development of MMC and its members by building a cooperative system in accordance with our basic policies. (Mitsubishi Motors 1982)

Technical and engineering interaction was explicitly given second place; without cooperation, the entire supplier system would be dysfunctional.

Each of the four MMC plants had its own local supplier association, dating from when the plants were part of separate firms. (That at the Tokyo plant went back to 1950, while the Nagoya one was formed in 1958 and those at Mizushima and Kyoto in 1961.) Only in 1968 was a firmwide supplier organization, the *Kashiwa Kai*, established to coordinate plant-level association activities. In 1982, of MMC's 332 suppliers, 255 belonged to one or more locals as well as to the central Kashiwa Kai association; the remaining 77 were members only of a local. While legally independent of MMC, the central and local offices of the association were located at the MMC plants, and MMC provided 10%–20% of the national and local budgets.

MMC and the other automotive firms viewed building and maintaining cooperation and coordinating the corporate strategies of their many independent suppliers as important goals for their supplier associations. At MMC, these aspects were dominant at the national association, which pulled supplier presidents and top MMC executives to its functions. In fact, there were only three annual events, all banquet-type dinner meetings at which MMC executives and association officials give speeches on the automotive industry, on MMC's business outlook, and on MMC purchasing policy. At these general meetings suppliers were made aware of changes in overall corporate policy at their parent, and of other issues of mutual interest. One function of this information was to help suppliers plan future investment, based upon a common understanding of anticipated market developments. Capacity could thus be coordinated not only within the automotive firm proper, but also with its subcontractors. (After all, there was no gain for anyone if suppliers had too much capacity, while all lost if bottlenecks kept MMC from selling cars in good times.) Similarly, top management at suppliers could be made aware of new administrative and management technologies that would be run at a lower level but would require their support and attention to be successful.

The Annual Meeting in 1982, for instance, included speeches and greetings by the chairmen, president and executive vice presidents of MMC, and the incoming and outgoing chairmen of the Kashiwa Kai, who with the other directors of the Kashiwa Kai were drawn from among the presidents of member firms. The only other formal part of the program was an hour-long presentation of Value Engineering and Sales Promotion awards to member firms. The two other annual association-wide activities were a New Year's gathering and a one-day seminar on QC (quality control) activities aimed at the top management of suppliers. In addition, the directors of the association met twice at MMC headquarters to discuss anticipated personnel rotations at MMC and future themes for local activities. Finally, the national organization published a quarterly newsletter on Mitsubishi Motors policies and activities.

The newsletter editorial meetings, however, were rotated among the four local association sites. In fact, the four locals were far more active in every aspect; while the national office had no employees, each local had two full-time employees to coordinate its functions. The 1982 activities of the MMC Mizushima Local, of which the Soja Industrial Park firms described in chapter 2 were all members, serve as an example. First, as at the national level, there were general meetings and social events. An annual meeting attended by the 25 top managers at the MMC Mizushima plant and representatives of 117 out of the 124 member firms of the Mizushima local was held at the premier hotel in the area. (The only award presented was again one for value engineering.) A similar event was held just before New Year's, and there were annual table tennis and softball tournaments. Smaller meetings were scheduled throughout the year: these included a discussion forum for fifty supplier executives and twenty MMC Mizushima mangers; three directors meetings; and a day-long retreat at a local resort followed by a tour of several supplier factories.

While there were thus many more social functions and general meetings than at the national level, seminars and working sessions on technical and specialized management topics dominated overall activities. The lead events were a series of two-day management retreats and an annual seminar. (In 1982 a nationally known expert lectured on "Japanese R&D.") There were smaller seminars on computers in management, CAD (computer aided design) systems, and the management of quality control programs. Monthly subcommittee meetings attended by one or two MMC and ten to twenty supplier representatives targeted working-level managers, with sessions rotated among the MMC Mizushima plant and the plants of different suppliers. Topics included value engineering, quality control and QC circles, tooling maintenance, rapid die changing and other specialized technical skills, and new technologies. During the course of the year over fifty such technical sessions were held.

The activities of the supplier associations thus reached far down into the staffs of both suppliers and the automotive firms. While the automotive firms commonly took the initiative in selecting topics, suppliers also found the cooperative associations valuable for sharing knowledge among themselves, and for helping each other learn about and apply new manufacturing methods and management techniques. Even in areas where they were direct rivals, suppliers through their associations could thus draw on not only the resources of their parent but also of each other.

Governance by Trust: Theoretical Perspectives

Alternative Governance Mechanisms

Ongoing transactions were desirable for automotive parts. Parts manufacturing entails significant fixed and sunk costs, while parts are highly model- and firm-specific, so that continued purchasing from the same supplier allowed costs to be amortized over a larger volume of production. These costs were not merely for plant and equipment, but also for adapting management systems and building networks among personnel to support just-in-time purchasing, value engineering and similar techniques; purchasers bore these costs as well. Hence from the standpoint of both parts maker and assembler frequent change of partners was costly—something that the Big Three and other U.S. manufacturers have only recently begun to realize.

But the real difficulty was in supporting such ongoing transactions. The principal issue was not that of administration, narrowly construed, but of governance of the overall relationship. How could disputes be resolved or avoided? How could parties adapt to new situations, without a constant fighting for advantage that would stifle any attempt at innovation? The presumption in the U.S. has been that this required vertical integration. Within a firm, transactions could be governed by hierarchy and other administrative mechanisms, rather than contracts and courts of law. Of course, even within firms factions and bureaucratic maneuvering weaken the power of managers to effect change, and they certainly increase the administrative costs of transactions. In any case, whether such skepticism is merited did not really matter in the Japanese auto industry.

Formal hierarchy simply was not present; resort to authority was not possible. This does not imply that no formal links existed between the auto firms and some suppliers, but it is not clear that they provided much leverage. In the 1950s Nissan and Toyota held large blocks of equity in their principal direct subcontractors, and even today have a network of subsidiaries and affiliates that in the aggregate employ as many workers as they do themselves. The relative weight of these two firms as shareholders, however, declined considerably over time. (Nippon Denso, for example, was spun off from Toyota as a 100% subsidiary at the time of its brush with bankruptcy in 1949; Toyota now has only a 20% stake.) Such partial shareholdings may not have provided much control, as the ongoing battle between T. Boone Pickens and Koito Seisakusho demonstrates.[9] Similarly, many observers emphasize the practice of parent firm managers "descending from heaven" to take executive positions at subcontractors. Once in such a position, however, it is not obvious why they should put the interests of their former employer above those of their current one. Thus partial shareholdings, directorships or other formal links are at best a partial remedy, and they were not extensive at the other nine automotive firms. Recourse to authority was not the solution adopted in Japanese manufacturing.

Another alternative was reliance on the market. Where there are numerous buyers and sellers—and homogeneous goods—price can be readily observed and transactions made on that basis. With many potential customers and suppliers, a firm will not be greatly inconvenienced if one or the other side reneges; an alternate customer or supplier can be quickly found. Continuity in transactions is then also a matter of convenience, not necessity. This spot market mechanism, however, was clearly not feasible for most automotive contracting. A part was normally specific to a model, and could not even be used in other vehicles produced by the same firm, while for the cost reasons noted above an automotive assembler normally procured a part from a single source. For simple parts, a partial remedy existed, because the tooling and dies used in production could be readily moved to another firm. In that case, the auto firm could purchase the dies and move them to another vendor if problems developed (Monteverde and Teece 1982a, b). But by the early 1960s, suppliers in the Japanese automotive industry were no longer producing simple parts, so this was in general not possible.

Even contracting was problematic (Williamson 1985; Holmstrom and Tirole 1989). With a single buyer interdependent with one (or two) sellers, reaching agreement on price could no longer be taken for granted. More important, even with agreement one party could hold out on the other for better terms. (For example, just before a new model commenced production a supplier could develop vague but costly problems and ask that the price be doubled. The purchaser could play similar games.) In economists' jargon, a bilateral monopoly resulted, and there was no obvious reason why rents or profits had to be distributed one way rather than another. This has led Williamson and others to argue that the costs of contracting in such situations are likely to outweigh the costs of bureaucracy and so will lead to vertical integration.

These difficulties were multiplied manifold in the Japanese auto industry, because the ideal was an ongoing transaction for complex goods with many critical characteristics. In a one-time bilateral bargaining situation, a contract could eventually be written, but this was difficult if not impossible when adaptation over time to changing conditions was important. As the time horizon lengthens the number of contingencies increases very rapidly, yet for a contract to be enforceable they must be detailed. Even worse, unanticipated events were bound to arise; long-term contracts therefore remain incomplete. Even if a court system could render judgment quickly on the terms of a simple contract, this is not possible when a contract contains ill-defined provisions.

Assuming these problems could be surmounted, one obstacle remained. Even for simple contracts, an auto firm had to trust a supplier to fulfill it, because contractual remedies would not be able to deliver the right part in the right place at the right time. Furthermore, in Japan the legal system was not well suited to contract enforcement. Only 500 lawyers a year are admitted to the bar, so that dockets are extremely crowded, resulting in years of delays. (Case law is also poorer than in the U.S.) An antagonistic environment would not only make it extremely cumbersome to write a contract, but would make dispute resolution or flexible adaptation to a constantly evolving business environment well-nigh impossible.

Two alternatives existed. One was to structure transactions in such a manner that both parties would want to cooperate, to fulfill their end. This section therefore turns next to the analysis of contracting and repeated games, to look at the potential in theory for commitments to be made credible. As might be expected, such strategies have their limits—and there still needed to be an underlying agreement. This meant that the second alternative, trust, remained necessary. The parties had to be trusted to be "fair," to not take advantage of one another as the relationship unfolded over time—and that was not easy to do. After discussing strategies of commitment, this section thus proceeds to the analysis of trust. The final portion of this section pulls these threads together; the next section then links the abstract analysis to actual automotive practice. As it turns out, the very strategies that helped limit the need for trust by making commitments credible also helped foster cooperation and trust. Ironically, then, by economizing on the need for trust, it in fact became easier for parties to trust each other.

Credible Commitments: Self-enforcing Contracts and Repeated Games

One alternative to formal contracts is to structure a transaction in such a manner that both parties will have an incentive to fulfill their end, without the threat of legal sanctions or recourse to higher authority. There is no problem, of course, if both parties expect that completing the transaction is their most profitable alternative. But in a bilateral contracting situation such as a parts purchase, the potential for holdup and other complexities meant that one or the other party could normally do better by reneging. Thus credible commitment lies in a mutual perception that both parties will gain from continuing a relationship or transaction, combined with the presence of sunk or fixed costs that would impose losses should they be overly opportunistic. In other words, both parties would need to make an investment in the relationship that could not readily be used for other purposes, and hence would be forfeited if they terminated the relationship. With the prospect of reasonable profits versus a sizable loss, an agreement would then become self-enforcing (Telser 1987; Williamson 1985:chs. 7, 8).

Automotive contracting, however, was an ongoing relationship, and that made the range of possible strategies much larger, and hence in theory made it easier to find credible cooperative strategies. In effect, a "tit-for-tat" and many other relatively arbitrary reprisal schemes appear to work (Axelrod 1984; Dasgupta 1988; Kreps 1990:chs. 15, 20). In fact, game theory shows the number of strategies in a repeated contracting situation such as was found in the automotive industry to be embarrassingly large, if not infinite. One problem thus is to pick a strategy that is sufficiently transparent for the players to understand, which may be difficult when the number of decisions to be made is very large. Furthermore, strategies would need to be stable in the face of uncertainty, since in a relationship as complex as automotive parts contracting, it would often be very hard to verify whether the other party's representations were truthful or their behavior fair. Yet reprisal strategies will tend to be all-or-nothing in nature—to buy or not to buy—and hence they may not afford a measured response to perceived unscrupulous or incompetent performance. For that matter, even a measured response could lead to ever-greater recrimination and distrust rather than a return to normalcy. In other words, to make the other party forfeit its fixed investment for a minor infraction would result in a pyrrhic victory.

There will thus typically be a range of undesirable actions which are not sufficiently bad to trigger reprisal (Kreps 1990; ch. 14). There remains the temptation to cheat just a little. In addition, unanticipated circumstances make these mechanisms even less workable, as "hostages" and strategies can lose their credibility or effectiveness (Lorenz 1988), while it becomes harder to distinguish cheating from an honest mistake from a chance occurrence. Finally, implicit in credible commitment or reprisal strategies is a long-term contract. In effect, the more times a game is repeated, the more effective the repetition of a reprisal becomes.[10] Thus parties not only have to cope with imperfect information, but the initial governance problem of how to cope with unexpected situations remains. The parties must trust each other.

The formal theory suggests several factors that will strengthen the ability of firms to rely on implicit contracts. Both sides must have a *positive incentive* to cooperate. In other words, if one party has little prospect for profit, then it will normally be wise to opt out sooner rather than later, despite any sunk investments. At the same time, if both firms have invested in the relationship and so risk to lose from cooperation breaking down, then there will be a greater readiness to cooperate; *visible commitment*, having a clear stake in the relationship, helps. In addition, *repetition* or other features that give rise to a long time horizon are important. The potential for future profits will make it easier to bear occasional unprofitable periods and hence lessen the temptation to renege. Cooperation, then, is easier to bring about when it is thought likely to be profitable, and where profits extend into the indefinite future.

Good information is valuable; the more that each party knows about the other's concerns and objectives, the less likely that responses to an unexpected situation will breed distrust and reprisal. It is better that parties share information and understand each other's costs, so that the rationale for a given action—such as a request for exceptional treatment—can be grasped. In other words, the less obvious it is that each side is holding up their end of an agreement, the more difficult it will be to reach an agreement in the first place. This is particularly true if the prospect of sanctions is stark, which can lead to undue rigidity; in general, a "forgiving" nature seems to facilitate cooperation (Axelrod 1984). Information is improved and uncertainty reduced when more aspects of a transaction are standardized or held fixed. Finally, since many possible strategies are feasible, cooperation is easier to achieve if there is a "focal point" or obvious strategy, such as "split down the middle." *Norms* for how transactions are to be carried out serve both functions, eliminating the number of choices that have to be made and making it clearer what parties are (or should be) up to.

Credible commitments and repeated game strategies played an important role in Japanese automotive subcontracting. Both parties became quite interdependent, and hence faced significant costs from a total breakdown of the relationship. The presence of this visible commitment made it clear to both parties that each viewed continuing cooperation as in principle desirable. Furthermore, since a supplier generally provided a range of parts for several models, a response short of terminating a relationship was possible. (See the discussion of reputation below.) The presence of a commitment or the ability to impose (possibly escalating) reprisals may be a necessary condition, as it makes the achievement of agreement of obvious value and places a bound on disputes. It was not sufficient. Firms had to agree to make the initial commitment, and the presence of possible reprisals did not in itself guarantee rapid and harmonious agreement. Trust was necessary.

Trust and Reputation

Without trust—the willingness to take a reasoned chance without assurance that the other party will prove trustworthy—the initial commitment will never be made. Furthermore, as argued above, a commitment can never be made fully credible; the possibility of opportunistic behavior will remain. And the more prone one is to distrust, the harder it will be to agree to cooperate. This is Othello's Dilemma: a basis can always be found for distrust, while trustworthiness can never be proven. As Gambetta (1988:234) phrases it, "Doubt is far more invidious than certainty, and distrust may become the source of its own evidence." With sufficient distrust, even simple contracts become unworkable—not to mention complex, ongoing interdependence.

As noted above, one function of markets and contracts is to eliminate the need for trust, but even in markets trust remains important. For example, in the New York Stock Exchange, who interacts with whom and in what manner is fixed. Few individuals actually make trades on the floor of an exchange, and transactions there proceed according to predetermined rules. Those making trades know and trust each other, and depend on others to transmit buy and sell orders according to other norms. At the far end of the chain the ultimate purchaser deals with a broker. The net effect of the larger institutional setting is to buffer parties remote from each other from concerns over identity and trust, in part by guaranteeing that *no* transaction is among anonymous parties. The same is true in other formal markets; Silin (1972) gives a particularly cogent analysis of the centrality of personal relationships in the wholesale vegetable market of Hong Kong.

Trust involves placing oneself at risk. If trust does not affect both parties' behavior, then it is irrelevant (or degenerates into mere loyalty or dependence). On the one hand, trust must be more than a statement of expectations about what the other party will do, where one's own actions or concerns have no influence. On the other hand, if behavior is forced—including if the only reasonable alternative for both parties is to complete a transaction—then trust is not needed; a self-centered profit motive is sufficient. Hence to be trustworthy is to be perceived as behaving properly, even when it is inconvenient to take into account the other side's welfare and expectations. Trust therefore is costly.

Several factors contribute to trust. First of all, there needs to be a *predisposition* to trust. Whether it is "old boy" ties, a letter of introduction or general good repute, a cultural or social basis is helpful, as is a widespread recognition that being "trustworthy" is important. Friendship, of course, can provide a basis, but trust is clearly more widespread than is friendship. However, ethnicity or other commonalities are not likely to be sufficient; instead, they are helpful because they make it easier to evaluate the other party (Silin 1972; cf. Dore 1983). Second, it is clearly less risky to first trust someone in small things before they are relied upon for large; *gradual commitment* makes sense. Third, clear *norms* are needed for a relationship to proceed smoothly; both sides must have the same understanding of "proper" behavior. Fourth, if trust is costly, then creating trust entails *investment in reputation*. Trust is inherently forward-looking; reputation reflects past actions. But unless one is put to the test (and passes), then trust must remain tenuous. One or the other party must take actions reflecting their trustworthiness; if it is not costly to them, then no information is revealed about how they might act when it really counts. Finally, cooperation must be taken seriously. If the transaction or relationship matters little to one party, then they may deign to be benevolent, but clearly one would rather rely on their having an *active interest*. Here again, investment specific to a transaction, the expectation of profits or expectation of future transactions, or interaction in social or other contexts improves the climate for trust.

The literature of experimental psychology provides additional insights. According to Good (1988), four threads stand out. First, the more extended the interaction of the parties, the better the cooperation. This is strengthened when an *active interest* is taken in the outcome, when the (experimental) setting is not viewed as a mere game. Second, *threats* are detrimental to cooperation—even when they are veiled threats inherent in the experimental context; Othello's Dilemma is very real. Third, trust is greatly enhanced when it can *develop gradually*. Finally, more *communication* is better. The more the participants understand about the details of the situation—the clearer the norms are—the better they can communicate about the potential for cooperation and the costs of distrust. Cooperation is then more likely to develop. The most important of these factors are the first and third, that there be an active interest, and that transactions develop gradually; these and the importance of communication overlap the above analysis.

Summary

First, the combination of mechanisms to limit the need for trust and to enhance trust both point to the importance of approaching interdependence gradually. Information is initially scarce as to what will lead to disputes, and how readily agreement can be achieved; one side or the other may not be trustworthy, or could be outright dishonest. Thus both sides will be cautious in initiating a new relationship, and will seek to build up trust first at a personal level, and then through "minor" contracts before making major commitments. Over time, these commitments add up and reinforce each other, adding to the propensity to trust and cooperate.

Second, the establishment of business norms is central. As stressed earlier, norms also lower administrative costs; fewer details must be worked out for each transaction. Given the sheer number of purchased parts in the automotive industry this aspect was important. But in terms of contracting and trust, the more aspects of a transaction that are governed by routine, the less room there is for dispute and misunderstanding and the fewer contingencies that need be specified. In this context, price setting was one of the potentially most contentious issues, so norms there were likely to be particularly useful. Cognizance of what each party views as "proper" in adapting to unexpected contingencies is also necessary. The values the other party holds need to be understood, and preferably shared.

Third, trust can be bolstered by investment in reputation. It is important for a supplier to know whether an automotive firm actually adheres to the norms it professes. And since an auto company deals with many suppliers, a small investment can potentially contribute to good repute with many. An individual supplier will in its own experience have faced only a small set of unusual circumstances, so this will also extend the range of behavior in which a company is known to have been trustworthy. Given the very crude nature of credible commitments, a supplier cannot readily determine whether a vague commitment will be held up in the future, or how a general principle will be applied to a specific situation. A supplier can at least ascertain past behavior, but it can only trust that history will be extrapolated into the future.

Finally, because trust is forward looking, personal trust remains essential. Norms may exist at the societal level, within an industry, and for a given automotive firm. But decisions are ultimately made by individuals. Corporate policy may provide guidelines, but decision making inevitably involves considerable discretion. Trust necessarily remains in part personal. Much therefore rests on personal interaction, on the managers of suppliers and purchasers knowing each other. Trust lubricates social interaction, within and outside business; socialization, properly lubricated, can help build trust as well.

All of the above can be deliberately crafted. Commitments can be visibly made, as can reprisals (though the carrot promotes cooperation better than the stick). Personal trust can be fostered, and personal and interfirm relationships deepened over time. Norms can be developed, taught, and adapted to new situations. Investments can be made in reputation. The purely business relationship can be complemented with the social. In short, a firm can consciously institute governance by trust. The next section argues that this was indeed the case in the Japanese automotive industry.

Governance by Trust: Japanese Automotive Practices

Gradual Commitment

The interdependence of an automotive purchaser and supplier makes firms naturally cautious about initiating a relationship. The difficulty of turning to the legal system for contractual enforcement, however, makes this common throughout Japanese business. Parties must size each other up, so the start of any transaction is extended socializing, typically carried out over a number of occasions. Compatibility is sought, and evidence that the other party will be committed to continuing transactions. In this context, reputation is more important in Japan than in the U.S., and hence there is a greater reliance on introductions or to membership in a community (see Yamazaki 1980; Y. Sato 1981). For strangers, desirable traits were best revealed by perseverance; the Japanese management literature is replete with anecdotes of exemplary individuals who made calls for years before their first sale (Iwata 1982; Odaka et al. 1988:147–48). Because of this slow courtship, Japanese business relationships may appear to be closed to outsiders, as Prestowitz (1988) and others argue. This, however, reflects the difficulty of developing a new relationship, rather than "unfair" practices (Smitka 1990a).

For an automotive firm, the decision to begin buying from a new supplier proceeds in stages. The first order will typically be an unimportant item, which in itself would not be worth the effort. Incremental commitment serves as a further test of the two parties' ability and willingness to work with one another. If they had misjudged each other (or, with first-hand experience found they were overly optimistic about the potential for profit), the cost of breaking off ties remained small. Beginning with small transactions also provided both sides an opportunity to learn how to deal with each other—whom to talk to for what problem—on an item that was not critical. Only after observing firsthand a potential supplier and its managers would an order for a crucial item be made.[11] In effect, significant time and money were invested to build up trust at the initial stage.

Visible Interdependence

Credible commitment lay in a mutual perception of future profits and of costs to terminating the relationship. Unlike in the U.S. auto industry, the Japanese auto firms signaled their commitment to suppliers by giving up internal manufacturing capacity, and by sourcing a specific part from only one firm. In the short run the auto company was thus dependent on a given supplier, and even in the medium run of a year often had only one or two viable alternatives. In turn, for most subcontractors an individual auto firm became their largest customer, often accounting for over half of total revenues. This was most clearly visible where a supplier had built a production line for a subassembly, had developed its own network of subcontractors, had tied this in with the final assembly line through just-in-time scheduling, and had undertaken design work jointly with its customer. Such extensive interaction could only be built up over time, but it existed for all direct suppliers to the Japanese automotive assemblers. Supplier and purchaser thus became visibly interdependent.

Positive Incentives

The emphasis in Japanese contracting, however, was not on sanctions or complicated strategies of commitment. In fact, there was virtually no discussion of such game-theoretic approaches, nor were reprisals or sanctions apparent in firm-level data. Instead the focus was on positive incentives and trust. As one American purchasing manager advised his peers (Bolton 1979:6), "There can be no room for one-sided agreement; it would ultimately result in failure."[12] Indeed, the postwar history of the Japanese auto industry provided ample evidence that both purchaser and supplier could reasonably expect gains. Most parts makers entered the industry as very small firms, and grew faster than the automotive firms themselves. This in itself was evidence that supplying parts was profitable (survey evidence also bears this out), as was the fact that firms sought to become automotive suppliers in the first place. It would have been more difficult for trust to develop in the auto industry had it had a more checkered history; continued growth helped erase the bitter memories of the early Mitsubishi and Toyota suppliers. But it was also the success of the industry that resulted in the auto firms' becoming interdependent with their suppliers in the first place, which made trust worth pursuing.

The automotive firms also expected to gain. By purchasing in a relationship governed by trust, they assured themselves access to reliable suppliers at low administrative cost. With trust, suppliers were also willing to invest in capacity and new technology. This helped the assemblers meet growing demand and survive stiff price and quality competition. Turning to an unknown supplier for an immediate price advantage would risk trading these known long-term advantages for a possible short-term gain—and would also entail managerial time to teach the new supplier the company's norms and bring it up to speed. (This reinforced the appearance of "closed" business ties noted above.)

Norms for Transactions

Norms both support trust and help make actions transparent and hence behavior more credible. On the one hand, norms represent a positive statement of the administrative procedures through which a firm handles particular tasks. It is a statement of how business is done. On the other hand, routine implicitly provides a normative statement of principles, of how business should be done. Because of the extent of the interaction between parts suppliers and the auto firms, the task of learning how business was done required attention by both parties. (At the same time, it provided a natural forum for personal interaction and socialization.)

The communication of norms was one of the ongoing functions of the supplier cooperative associations, as can be seen from the wide range of activities detailed above. Furthermore, norms were not mere general statements but took quite detailed form. Pricing was a good example. The bid process itself was quite detailed, as were the principles by which it was applied. The data employed—the previous and current bid and the prevailing target for cost reduction—were clearly set, and reasonably objective. More important, markups for a supplier were fixed over time, further reducing room for contention. Suppliers were not openly pressured to reduce their profit margins, and when indirect pressure was exerted, it was against evidence that the auto firm's profits were also suffering. Similarly, compensation for innovation through value analysis and value engineering were eventually clarified. All of this helped the auto firms to understand the cost position of suppliers, and suppliers to follow the standards applied by the purchaser, limiting disputes and better defining the object of trust.

Reputation: Well-Informed Participants

Without external enforcement mechanisms, information on how a purchaser lives up to the norms it has set is important. Here the supplier associations played the central role; proximity contributed as well (Matsubashi 1982; Sheard 1983). On the one hand, the supplier associations presented a forum in which the automotive firms communicated their expectations of suppliers. As noted, meetings included speeches by purchasing executives and others outlining policies for the coming year, and the problems they felt needed resolution. Similarly, suppliers could voice their concerns as a group. For a given firm, there would inevitably be instances when a particular outcome was unsatisfactory. However, when behavior was within acceptable norms, there would be little sense of unfairness and little consequent damage to trust.

The cooperative associations were also the locus where reputation was generated. The owners and managers of suppliers were brought together for golf, lectures and other gatherings that were only partly business. (As noted above, working-level groups meet even more frequently.) Information about the behavior of the automotive parent was thus widely and rapidly dispersed. Unfair behavior would soon be known to all. (Close interaction would also make it hard for suppliers to collude without it becoming apparent to their customer.) Reputation was (and is) consciously created—as chapter 2 noted, that was one impetus for the creation of the Mitsubishi supplier association.

Finally, the cooperative associations reinforced the pricing mechanism. On the margin, the returns to an auto firm from negotiating the best possible price on a part were at best modest; most items, on a unit basis, did not cost much. But given the thousands of purchased parts and components in the typical vehicle, systematically paying too much did make a difference. As noted earlier, suppliers (accurately) perceived that a small change in price in their favor had little effect on final vehicle costs—and had a disproportionate impact on their own profitability. It was thus critical that the automotive firms relied on a steady, incremental reduction in price for all suppliers rather than negotiating separately with each. All suppliers knew the common target and were expected to meet it. If the rate of reduction was too severe, there would be grumbling, and some firms would be able to make their demands for a higher price stick. The occasional departure from the desired norm would not be costly. But with the regular interaction of supplier managers through association functions, a systematic inability to make the target stick inevitably become known. Once known, compliance would deteriorate further. The impact on final cost of a vehicle of a total breakdown of compliance, however, was apparent to all. As long as suppliers could trust that their reduction applied to all, they could feel that their individual contribution to final competitiveness was not unreasonable.

Commitment, Trust and Rivalry

Rivalry would seem essential to keep suppliers on their toes, and yet would also seem inimical to trust. That proved not to be the case. In Japan, rivalry was important, but it was maintained through the efficient use of information rather than through cut-throat competition among suppliers. Suppliers, of course, had every incentive not to underbid. (In interviews, managers at more than one supplier stated with broad smiles that purchasers did not always know their costs.) But in turn a firm could be informed that while its bid was in general adequate, its costs on a particular step were out of line. This not only avoided direct confrontation and so made compromise easier, but because such counter-claims had to be based on evidence of other firms' costs, it helped the supplier to focus on areas where extra engineering effort might be expected to pay off. (This was far more conducive to maintaining trust than in the U.S., where buyers openly played suppliers off against each other.) There was an expectation that a supplier would continually improve or lose business, but this was tempered with a grace period —business would not be pulled suddenly—and with technical guidance to help achieve a competitive cost level.

This did not imply that rivalry was invisible. Competitors attended the same supplier association meetings—and often were located next door; on average 2.2 firms made a given part, though for different models and not the same vehicle (Ikeda 1988a:7, 10).[13] And while contracts were for the life of a part, they were not indefinite. When production of a part ceased with the introduction of a new model, the current supplier had an inside track, but was not assured the contract for the equivalent part for the new model. It was not the norm for contracts to be regularly lost, but it happened with sufficient frequency that in interviews managers consistently stressed that overconfidence led to failure. Since contracts were not lost suddenly or canceled capriciously, a marginal change in the volume of business sent a clear signal. Because a firm might supply 500 parts of varying complexity, this did not immediately threaten a firm's livelihood. But if a supplier consistently failed to match the standards of its immediate rivals, it would see its orders shrink and (eventually) be dropped altogether. Such gentle suasion normally sufficed; bald threats, with their deleterious impact on trust, were seldom needed.

Conclusions

The Japanese automotive firms adopted a strategy of subcontracting parts manufacture in the 1950s. The difficulties of managing purchasing and design led them to apply just-in-time scheduling and other techniques across firm boundaries, incorporating their suppliers into their administrative system. The combination of the indexing of process costs, the presence of a dependable cost-plus margin in the pricing formula, the implementation of a regular cost reduction target, and the explicit compensation paid to suppliers for incremental design modifications all encouraged technical change and provided the assurance that success would be duly rewarded. This was backed by the presence of the JIT system and VA/VE programs that served to focus engineering efforts. Combined with rivalry, this facilitated efficiency. Technical change at suppliers in fact matched or exceeded that at the automotive firms themselves, and was fundamental to competitiveness in the domestic and later the U.S. market.

To implement this strategy, the auto firms also had to overcome the contracting problems of transaction-specific assets and ongoing transactions; they became too dependent on suppliers to play hard and fast in the short run, while suppliers had invested too much on behalf of their customers to simply walk away from a relationship. The auto firms were ultimately successful in developing a framework for cooperation governed by trust rather than contract or hierarchy. The supplier associations contributed to this process. They served as a formal mechanism for bringing together suppliers and purchasers socially, for sharing purchaser policies and goals with suppliers, and for encouraging suppliers to adopt and improve their use of management tools and new technologies. Executives on both sides of parts transactions were then willing to devote the time of their managers and engineers to more prosaic technical interactions. Formal supplier association activities were but one facet of purchaser-supplier interactions, but by focusing on management-level personnel, they set the tone and helped both sides to monitor the overall relationship. They were thus central to the feasibility of governance by trust, and not merely to the diffusion of technology.

SEVEN

Subcontracting in
Other Industries

Previous chapters analyzed subcontracting in the automotive industry. In particular, chapter 4 argued that the use of subcontracting is in part a response to the structure of labor markets, while chapter 6 argued that specific management innovations were required to support it. Furthermore, as stressed in the more descriptive chapters, these were all outgrowths of the particular history of the Japanese automotive industry. This chapter therefore seeks to place the automotive case in perspective and to gauge the robustness of the models developed thus far. Chapter 8 then attempts to draw lessons for the U.S.

Intensive use of subcontractors is in fact prevalent throughout Japanese industry. Nevertheless, some of the facets of the supplier-parent firm relationship in the automotive industry stand out as distinctive (and there is variation even among different segments of the auto industry). After noting varying patterns within the industry, automotive subcontracting is then contrasted with that in other mass production industries (consumer electronics and watches), in producer goods industries (industrial machinery) and printing, and in skilled trades industries (shipbuilding, construction and steel). This analysis is thus limited to manufacturing.

That is a natural restriction for gaining perspective on the auto industry, and it is also appropriate from an American perspective, since it is in manufacturing that competitive problems appear greatest. However, within Japan the current policy focus is on vertical ties and contracting practices in distribution. This has also become a bilateral trade issue, and is prominently featured in the 1989–

1990 Structural Impediments Initiative. Anticompetitive strategies are more prominent there than in manufacturing, with vertical relationships used to exclude others from distribution channels (Flath 1989). Similar gains cannot be had in manufacturing, because it is harder to exclude other firms from access to suppliers.

This survey is very brief, and without more comprehensive data the conclusions presented here are therefore tentative. Nevertheless, they suggest that the labor market considerations that underlay the initial adoption of a subcontracting strategy in the automotive industry were (and still are) relevant in other industries. A case study of the watch industry not only illustrates this theme, but shows that there are many other alternatives to improving the function of pricing and other purchasing functions. At the same time, in watch manufacturing interfirm ties were far weaker; there were few or no technical or management links between the parent firm and suppliers, or among suppliers. Incentive aspects were also prominent in several industries. Finally, technical change was associated with the nature of the subcontracting relationship: where there was little need for coordination of design aspects, there was less interdependency.

Diversity in Subcontracting Within the Automotive Industry

Previous chapters presented the dominant patterns found in Japanese automotive subcontracting. There was, of course, variation within the industry itself; many examples have already been noted. One distinction was between the truck and the passenger car segments of the industry. Another is that of manufacturers of single parts and simple subassemblies (bumpers, trim) and the suppliers of components and subsystems (carburetors, braking systems, automatic steering, suspension systems). Finally, there was the distinction between primary suppliers and lower-tier subcontractors. Each of these segments of the industry differed in market characteristics, product complexity and technology.

Compared to passenger cars and light trucks, the heavy truck segment of the industry is older, produces at a far lower volume, has grown more slowly and has faced far more cyclical demand. Furthermore, a heavy truck incorporates qualitatively different components (e.g., diesel engines, air brakes, heavy-duty drivetrains and heavy-gauge stampings) and a high proportion of sales are of chassis rather than finished vehicles. Component manufacturers such as Kayaba (shock absorbers), Diesel Kiki (fuel pumps), or Akebono Brake are as old or older than the automotive firms, and hold a range of patents and foreign technology licenses that limit rivalry; in many case three firms dominate production (Dodwell 1986:part 3).[1] In turn, most component manufacturers sell to several or even all of the automotive firms, and often no single customer dominates their sales. In contrast, smaller direct suppliers (such as those in the Soja Industrial Park) are typically younger, less specialized technically, and in consequence face greater rivalry. The auto firms have considerable expertise in the metalworking and other technologies that smaller suppliers utilize; some parts are even made to drawings supplied by the automotive firms (Asanuma 1985a). Second- and lower-tier automotive suppliers, which do not sell directly to the auto firms, are on average even younger, smaller and less specialized. Unlike their parent firms, they typically concentrate on a single manufacturing process, such as simple stampings or machining (even at Sembokuya in chapter 5, most revenues were still from doing simple stampings). Their input into the design process is minimal. They face greater direct rivalry, and unlike primary suppliers, this includes rivalry from their parent firm. On the other hand, they are far more likely to have sales outside the automotive industry.

These distinctions are reflected in contracting. While all firms may submit a detailed bid, the level of detail and the ability of the purchaser to digest the detail is a function of rivalry and technology. Although bids for more complicated assemblies may be sufficient as a guideline for pricing within a cost-index framework, they do not facilitate the detailed engineering comparison that, at least in principle, can be made for smaller suppliers. In fact, the less strong the rivalry, the greater the ability of a supplier is to withhold detail —especially if price is consistently competitive. (The manager at one firm boasted that they furnished little or no detail in bids, and took the engineers of their automotive customers out to lunch, but not out to see the factory floor.)

Thus for component manufacturers the bid process approaches the American "auction" model, with designs and price quotes submitted on a competitive basis and less informal commitment that a company will receive the contract when a model is redesigned (Asanuma 1985a).[2] At the other extreme, secondary and lower-tier subcontractors are located in a loosely organized market for manufacturing services; price is based on the "going rate," varying over the business cycle, and continuity is in large part a function of inertia rather than commitment. Thus at the component manufacturer extreme of the industry the standard pricing mechanism does not work as well, while at the tertiary supplier extreme it is unnecessary.

Risk characteristics also affect contracts. While the auto manufacturer guarantees payments for tooling costs to many primary suppliers, the tooling used by secondary suppliers may be directly owned by the primary parts manufacturers. In contrast, large component manufacturers are expected to fund their own tooling. Not only does the purchaser have insufficient information to evaluate supplier claims for tooling costs, but since they produce for multiple customers and a range of models, components makers are able to diversify the risk of poor sales of a single model as much or more than the automotive firms (Asanuma 1985a, b).

The empirical picture of contracting in this study thus applies most closely to direct suppliers of simpler parts and subassemblies, which are especially prevalent in body and other stamping operations. It is these medium-sized firms that are most consciously interdependent with their automotive customers, and that undertake manufacturing activities most likely to be carried out internally at Ford or GM. Nevertheless, the difference between smaller direct and (larger) specialized component and assembly suppliers is best considered one of degree, not kind. For example, compared to the U.S. Big Three, even the large component manufacturers in Japan work more closely with their automotive customers (U.S. International Trade Administration 1988:29, quoting Dana Corporation management). And most primary suppliers have established their own subcontractor associations and are taking a more active hand in their suppliers' affairs (e.g., Ikeda 1987b). The relationship among secondary subcontractors and lower-level suppliers is still governed more by short-term market considerations, but that is no longer true for the ties of primary and secondary suppliers. The difference there, too, is one of degree, not kind.

Other Industries in Manufacturing

Watch Manufacturing: Kachikachi Corporation

Kachikachi Corporation[3] was in 1984 a watch manufacturer with 8,000 employees that was rapidly diversifying into computer printers and other "mechatronic" goods.[4] Its traditional product, purely mechanical, required the precision manufacture of gears and other parts of the movement, the assembly of the movement, the manufacture of the case, and finally the insertion of the movement into the case. Twenty years ago, assembly was purely a hand operation, but during the previous two decades it had gradually been automated, and in 1984 was carried out by hand-sized robots which inserted gears and torqued nearly-invisible screws into place. This was true not only for electronic watches, which contained relatively few parts, but also for mechanical watches.[5] In 1984 the latter were still made in huge numbers; one factory alone projected output of 15 million units, primarily for Southeast Asia and other markets where batteries were not readily available.

Despite the variety of its products, the company on the surface had an extremely simple personnel system: there was only one pay scale, for white- and blue-collar workers alike; only the eighty managers of the rank of section chief (kacho) or above were not covered. In practice some people began higher and ascended further and more quickly than others, but in principle there was no tiering of workers. A college graduate initially received the same pay as a high school graduate of the same age—though of course the latter already had four years' tenure. For that matter, title (rank) and compensation did not permit production and office workers to be distinguished; Kachikachi's personnel manager did not know the exact breakdown, because for his purposes it was not relevant. Most important, the pay system did not provide leeway for the inclusion within the firm of a group of "low-wage" employees for labor-intensive tasks: all nonmanagerial workers were members of the union, and received the union wage.

In fact, few distinctions were made in compensation during the first ten years of work. In 1984 the purely seniority component still averaged 30% of total pay, and other components were strongly correlated with age/tenure. The supplementary pay (teate) for marital status and family size made up an additional 15%, further limiting the impact of discretionary components of compensation. Finally, bonuses varied by no more than 2% within a cohort. Large pay differentials thus did not appear until nearly twenty years had passed, or about the age when promotions to middle management commenced (Koike 1988:221).

The exceptions proved the rule. For example, part-time female (*paato*) and temporary male (*rinjiko*) workers did material handling and other unskilled jobs. The union, however, had negotiated an informal agreement limiting such workers to 5% of membership and restricting them to job slots where they could not gain the skills required of regular employees. The engineers who ran the heating plants were also outside of the normal framework, as were small numbers of other tradesmen. Finally, a de facto way around a rigid wage system at many large firms throughout Japan had been to employ women, who quit (or were fired) at or soon after marriage, so that they never advanced beyond the lowest wage level. Over 40% of Kachikachi workers were women, but few of them quit upon marriage—unlike the case at an affiliate 40 kms away.[6] While on average women at Kachikachi Corporation might not move up in the hierarchy as much as men, the age and experience components of the firm's wage scale meant that they were soon far from "cheap" labor.[7]

Kachikachi itself made the movement of mechanical and quartz analog watches, for example, the *ebauche* (gears, screws, pins) and *escapement* (balance wheel and hairspring for mechanical watches or the armature, quartz crystal and controlling integrated circuit for quartz analog watches).[8] The firm used three outside suppliers of mechanical parts, but for each there was an unusual history. (One, for example, was owned and operated by the family of the founder of Kachikachi.) In controlling the mechanical aspects of watch production Kachikachi resembled other later entrants, such as Timex, but not the Swiss industry, where parts were produced by a host of independent, specialized workshops and companies with an organization similar to that of the industrial districts (*jiba sangyo*) of Japan.[9] (In contrast, for Kachikachi's printer operations, most parts were subcontracted to independent firms, and assembly to plants such as Kakaa Denka, described in chapter 4.) Prior to the automation of assembly more parts and subassemblies were subcontracted. This work was pulled in-house and placed adjacent to the assembly line. Ease of coordination and savings in material handling and inventory more than compensated for internal labor costs, and eventually most of these tasks were likewise automated. But while Kachikachi made parts, assembled the movement and did "casing" (insertion of the movement into the case) in-house, the case and associated visible parts—the watch face, numerals and hands, crystal, band and stem—were made almost exclusively by outside suppliers.

The most important of these was the case. Automation at Kachikachi had eliminated most labor-intensive tasks, but efforts to mechanize the finishing of metal watch cases had been unsuccessful. The basic shape was given by cold forging, but the surface of a case had to be ground to precise angles and sharp corners, and polished until the appearance was proper. Simple jigs and tools aided the workers, but most steps remained hand operations done at grinding and buffing wheels. In response, not only did Kachikachi subcontract all case production, but during the previous two to three years (the early 1980s) it had shifted 20% of its orders to foreign manufacturers, principally in Taiwan. Purchasing managers projected that soon all but the most expensive cases would be procured from abroad.

At 15% of total costs, the case was by far the most important single purchase. Materials and other parts accounted on average for 35% of the ex-factory price of a watch, direct labor for 15% and indirect labor (general administrative overhead) for 18%.[10] Kachikachi itself made items similar to the movement parts that were purchased, and was totally familiar with production methods and costs. In several instances, the three principle outside suppliers actually used older, Swiss-made automatic lathes leased from Kachikachi, for which there was no longer room, or (given attempts to keep total direct employment stable) workers at Kachikachi's own plants. A standard cost-plus margin could therefore be readily used to set prices.

Kachikachi had no such knowledge of case making. The watch movement was standardized by "caliber" or size, and a design might be made for a year or more, in total quantities that reached into millions. Cases were another matter. Watches are in part viewed by consumers as jewelry, and so changing the case to match current fashion, and targeting a design to specific tastes, was of the essence in marketing.[11] Kachikachi maintained an in-house team of designer-artists, who turned out 2,000 new designs a year, or about ten per working day. Prototypes were then made, but in the end the marketing arm of the firm would "buy" only about one in ten. New cases, then, were put into production at a rate of 200 a year, or one per working day. The volume of production for these varied greatly, but only one lot would be produced for most designs, in quantities from a few thousand to tens of thousands. The purchasing staff at Kachikachi therefore had to cope with ordering a large number of prototypes, and with an almost daily decision to purchase a new case design. While the logistics were changing in 1984 with the rapid shift of production offshore to Taiwan, most prototypes were still made by a domestic case maker whose operation might be suitable for the eventual production of that style case. If in the end the decision was made to go to market with the design, the prototype maker would then typically get the final order.

Until the early 1980s, however, price was set primarily by haggling. Kachikachi had simply been sufficiently profitable that little attention was paid to that facet of costs. The development of cheap plastic-case LCD (liquid crystal display) watches changed that, a change that was ironically initiated by Kachikachi's exports of inexpensive movements to Hong Kong and Taiwan.[12] Advances in the production of liquid crystal displays and the associated batteries and chips by watch and calculator manufacturers fueled a further expansion; digital "movements" (without moving parts) could be made for a fraction of a dollar. These were sold retail in the U.S. and other prime markets at the price of at most a few dollars, yet delivered all the functions (except conspicuous consumption) of the most expensive watches. The mid-range market (in between Timex and Rolex) where Kachikachi had established itself was dragged down in price. Suddenly, around 1980, the firm was actually losing money (or at least earning very little) on some designs, since the cost of producing quality cases and analog movements did not fall.

Purchasing management was therefore strengthened, with an eye to cases in particular. Using several man-years of effort (in a relatively small department), purchasing staff gradually developed an elaborate price book, composed ultimately of tables for each supplier listing the appropriate price to be paid for each standard design option. For example, the table for the watch face included about 100 options, reflecting size, surface color and texture, type of numerals, calendar options and so on. The table for the case proper included size, plating, surface finish, types of materials, and secondary parts such as bushings and seals for the crystal and stem for waterproof watches. For a given design, the amounts in these tables could then be added together, and adjusted for special features and volume to arrive at the final price.

This proved to be an effective administrative tool, simplifying the task of purchasing. More important, it helped to significantly lower prices. For the first time, Kachikachi could make systematic comparisons in the price charged by different suppliers, and it used this to drive prices down. Now a supplier could be faulted, not for being "a little bit high" on a case relative to what the purchaser *thought* he could get from another competitor, but for being higher by a specific percentage for specific options. While the method chosen differed from that used in the automotive industry, the basic idea was the same: the product was broken down into detailed features and price was then set, based on this finer-grained information.

Unlike in the automotive industry, however, this information was not combined with the provision of consulting or guidance to help suppliers in reducing costs. Kachikachi did not interact with its case makers, other than to prohibit them from working for rival watchmakers, nor did it maintain a supplier association. For that matter, Kachikachi found to its discomfiture that not only had its purchasing operation been inefficient, but its sole affiliate that manufactured cases was a high-cost producer.[13] Kachikachi was therefore looking for ways to shift the firm's facilities to other lines of business, such as floppy disk manufacture and assembly. (Its unionized workforce prevented simply closing the plant down.) But Kachikachi's other domestic suppliers of cases would have to fend for themselves.

Consumer Electronics

Consumer electronics and household appliances are physically smaller than automobiles, and in relative terms involve fewer components, face less rigorous mechanical requirements, and have a shorter product cycle. The scale of output is also different, not just because of the physical size of the typical good, but also because only a few thousand units may be made. Equally important, the underlying technology for these products has shifted with blinding speed. There have been totally new products (first TVs, then color

TVs, now VCRs), changes in the basic materials used (wood then metal then plastic for cases), and the substitution of solid state and now integrated circuits for tubes and wires. Fortunately for Japan, many of these changes to what was initially a set of labor-intensive production processes began while it was still a relatively low-wage producer. In the U.S., high labor costs had led to production being shifted offshore, including to Japan, before these technical revolutions began. This then reduced the size of the market for electrical components and (later) high-precision mechanical components, weakening the entire manufacturing base. In contrast, only in the last decade has assembly been shifted from Japan to lower-wage countries, while the relative sophistication of internal components has kept much of their production domestic.

The shifts in product and technology therefore occurred within firms, rather than primarily through the substitution of new firms for old. This was because the strength of the large, diversified electronics firms was more in their control over marketing networks rather than in the mastery of one or more production technologies. Firms integrated into manufacturing to generate new products to feed into their marketing channels. Lack of access to market channels made it risky for independent firms to venture into manufacturing and difficult for foreign manufacturers to sell in Japanese domestic markets. As with the Japanese automotive firms, manufacturers of electronic products were not highly integrated; purchases of parts and components accounted for 70% of manufacturing costs, depending on product.[14] But unlike in the automotive industry, electrical parts such as capacitors, resistors and switches approached being commodities. (Value analysis in the electronics industry was geared to finding design alternatives to use such simple off-the-shelf items.) As a result there was less technical interaction with suppliers—the auto industry used virtually no off-the-shelf parts—while the smaller size of the product reduced the importance of closely coordinating the flow of parts. Even where custom-made items were required, the investment in tooling was far lower than for autos, both because of smaller size and because of less stringent demands on mechanical performance, and far more firms had machinery that could turn out small stampings or plastic pieces than was true for the larger items used in autos. Shorter model runs (a TV model might be in production for less than a year) also militated against design-specific parts.

Supplier–parent ties were often long-standing, but interaction was more limited than in the automotive industry. A supply relationship was likely to be formalized solely by an up-front contract for the purchase of a preset quantity of parts at a fixed price, rather than through the signing of a "blanket" contract as in the automotive industry (Asanuma 1986, 1989). For technologies where the electronics firms relied on outside suppliers, such as the construction of wooden cabinets, medium-sized stampings, and printed circuit boards, there could develop a conscious interdependent relationship (Ikeda 1983b, 1984a; Sako 1988). This included feedback from suppliers to their parent firm(s) on design modifications. In general, however, short product life and (relative) engineering simplicity made it possible and necessary for firms to centralize design, so that the depth of integration found between primary auto suppliers and the assemblers was generally absent. While Japanese consumer electronics firms did have formal supplier associations, fewer firms were members, and the emphasis was on basic technical and management skills aimed at what were on average far smaller suppliers (Nishiguchi 1989:188–198, 291–96).

Alongside parts subcontracting was the contracting out of labor-intensive assembly. For example, the assembly of large capacitors (which were made in small batches) was farmed out to rural workshops run as sidelines in agricultural regions. The parent firm might not only encourage entry, but might specify capacity and process in great detail, and in turn dictate price, so that a fixed profit-cum-salary accrued to running a reliable operation. Similarly, housewives were recruited to do piecework at home or in small shops, such as placing finished capacitors on rolls of tape for feeding into automatic insertion machines.[15] In the short run, parent firms were dependent on this labor capacity, and had to be careful to maintain a steady and sufficiently remunerative flow of business, else their erstwhile subcontractors might seek other work. (To limit this and maintain its monopsonistic position over subcontractors, Hitachi reputedly lobbied local government to discourage other large electronics firms from moving into its largely rural area.)[16] As technology shifted over the long run, however, the manufacture of certain product lines changed from inside the firm, to subcontractors, and then back in-house. There were thus regular booms and busts in lines of subcontracting of an extent not seen in the auto industry, and a consequent shifting of homeworkers and the operators of farmyard sheds from one parent (or even industry) to another (Ikeda 1979, 1983b, 1984a).

The newer generation of electromechanical ("mechatronic") devices such as computer dot-matrix printers and VCRs may be changing the looseness of links, because these products are more complicated and involve a wider range of technologies.[17] The electronics firms need to work with machining, stamping, plastic forming and other specialized parts where they have little expertise. But historically design and production in Japan were decentralized to the plant level (Fruin, forthcoming). This limited staff size, and hence the amount of in-house expertise. Thus Epson turned to automotive suppliers for the design of the printer platen, as well as the case and other stampings (Imai and Itami 1984). Interdependency for such products is more explicit and is a conscious management concern. It also reflects a conscious management decision to restrict the growth of in-house engineering.

At present factories in the electronics industry are specialized by product, and hence are run relatively independent of other factories of the same firm. Each plant therefore has its own network of suppliers, with a core of firms with which it is interdependent, a set of customary suppliers of standard components, and an amorphous set of job shops or other small suppliers to which the firm turns for small stampings and items for which demand is irregular. For that matter, purchasing policy is also set at the plant level. (Nishiguchi [1989:263–271] has a fascinating case study of contrasting practices at two plants of the same firm, with one plant's supplier base eroding due to distrust and another remaining intact in the face of a business downturn.) In any case, for job shops supplying electronics plants, ties were at best discontinuous and potentially one-shot. But even with firms that made subassemblies, short-term shifts were not unknown. There was no analogous set of job shops in the automotive industry, while purchasers there worked very hard to eliminate hard-ball tactics with suppliers.

Jiba Sangyo: Machine Tools

Machine tools and industrial machinery are assembled products that come in a huge variety of models.[18] Most machine tools are made only after receiving a firm order; a stripped-down machine may be built in anticipation of future business, but the highly cyclical nature of overall demand and the variance in demand for specific models keeps the production planning horizon short. New entry into the industry in Japan was very easy, since there were large numbers of machine shops together with small suppliers of castings and other components of a typical machine tool. Thus while a small shop might exist primarily as a supplier of parts to other machine tool manufacturers, it could simultaneously assemble one or two types of machine tools, purchasing the requisite castings, motors and specialized parts. With luck, a shop could pick a product for which demand boomed, and grow quite rapidly, as happened with several (then small) firms experimenting with industrial robots.

Vertical integration was quite low in the 1960s, and since firms themselves were basically machining operations (and often continued to function as subcontractors to other firms), their knowledge of subcontracted operations was quite high. Many such firms were found in industrial districts (*jiba sangyo*) such as the machine shop district in Ota Ward in Tokyo or the Kawaguchi district for metal castings just north of Tokyo.[19] In such districts a host of small firms were located within walking distance of each other, undertaking different facets of metalworking. For specialized machinery and machine tools, marketing and afterservice were important, and the design process more complicated; large firms were more prominent for those, and for very large machines. While these industry leaders normally assembled and tested their products, and did some machining in-house, they relied on outside shops for smaller items. As important, given highly variable demand, they needed outside firms to provide additional capacity when business was good. Ties with suppliers were dominated by custom. It was easier to contract to a machinist (or broker) known to be reliable and able to make the needed item quickly and to tolerance. Steady business could result in a discount, but the need for outside machining of one firm was highly correlated with that of other firms: subcontracting, when needed, tended to be very costly (Jaikumar 1986).

During the 1980s, technological innovations increased both the strength of interfirm ties and the ability of larger firms to machine parts in-house. On the one hand, the advent of computer numerical controls (CNC) as the dominant technology made closer cooperation with electronics firms necessary, though some of the technology is now standardized and can be bought from catalogs. On the other hand, flexible manufacturing technologies made it economical to undertake a broader range of low-volume machining operations in-house. But as in the past, the cyclical nature of demand meant that even the market leaders were highly reluctant to add capacity. Subcontracting persisted, therefore, aided by ease of entry: a skilled machinist had only to lease space and a milling machine or lathe, and have garnered the personal relationships needed to find initial business. He also had to have a willingness to reduce consumption during the industry's periodic downturns.

Jiba Sangyo: Printing

The printing industry in Tokyo was also organized in an industrial district.[20] Large, integrated firms dominated the volume end of the market, printing weekly photo/news magazines and other high-volume publications. Such work had to be done to tight deadlines, and was carried out in plants that ran three shifts a day, seven days a week. Lower volume items (books, advertising brochures) were farmed out to smaller firms and brokers. Their operations were centered in Koishikawa and Otsuka, a neighborhood in Bunkyo Ward in central Tokyo, where Kyodo Insatsu (the number 3 firm) had its headquarters and the two leading firms, Dai Nippon Insatsu and Toppan Insatsu, also had plants. Located within walking distance of those firms' large factories were literally hundreds of small two- and three-floor shops. Some had only a single machine; most specialized in a single process, carried out on the ground floor with the family living above. A few did printing, others only folding and collating, some stitching or stapling, or just the trimming of edges.

However, a few larger shops—often spread out among several small buildings—were integrated operations that did complete jobs on their own. The main function of integration, however, was to back up their role as brokers. As brokers these firms subcontracted work from the large printing operations (which often arranged for all of a customer's printing), and also solicited business directly from publishers and advertising agencies. These brokers then "put out" the work, coordinating the flow among Koishikawa's myriad shops. In consequence local lanes were full of forklifts running pallets of paper and half-finished books and leaflets back and forth. Ties among firms were customary, backed by personal relationships; workers for brokers and in other larger shops often parted on friendly terms to set up their own shop. As with machine tools, market pricing prevailed; the business was both cyclical and seasonal. A new entrant saw all work disappear in a downturn; established shops would see margins fall. Sharing risk by trading business back and forth was central to survival, and one of the prime benefits of being located in a district with numerous other shops (Yamazaki 1980; Y. Sato 1981).

Shipbuilding, Steel: Inside Contracting

The predominant form of subcontracting in shipbuilding, steel and construction was inside contracting.[21] (See also the Kato Shatai case study of chapter 5.) Here, as in the U.S. construction industry, the emphasis was on hiring crews of workers. In steel mills inside contractors commonly accounted for half the workers at a site. Their crews specialized in specific processes (in the steel industry, reputedly the dirtier and heavier tasks), and thus complemented rather than substituted for direct employees. Regular employees typically had broader training and were expected to eventually fill low-level supervisory positions. With a different career track and skills, they were also on average better paid.

For shipbuilding, orders were irregular and large ships were often of a unique design. Purchased parts were relatively few, and consisted primarily of semifinished materials such as pipes and other fittings.[22] Most workers were employed by subcontractors. Crews were specialized by task, but hired separately for each job, and thus might move among different shipyards. Direct employees worked in design, supervision and other management tasks, and on the development of alternative methods. They also formed small crews that overlapped outside contractors in function. The same organization is found in large construction projects, where outside crews undertake virtually all work, as in the U.S. The emphasis, as at Kato Shatai, was on skilled-trade tasks where each job was different, and on tasks where incentives and irregular work were dominant.

Variations in Japanese Subcontracting: Analysis

Automotive industry subcontracting practices were not identical to those found in other Japanese industries. The automotive industry was distinctive in the conscious organization of subcontractors into the overall production and design process. In particular, comprehensive supplier associations (*kyoryoku kai*) were found throughout the auto industry but were less frequent elsewhere. Other differences included greater continuity among suppliers in the auto industry and greater decentralization of the design process. Little detail was available on pricing mechanisms in other industries, but there appeared to be greater reliance on administrative procedures in the auto industry, and on market or market-like prices elsewhere.

Homogeneous labor, however, was important in all industries. As with the auto industry, the structure of labor markets (and to a lesser extent that of capital markets) was central to the adoption of a strategy of intensive use of subcontracting. The electronics and watch industries historically relied on hand assembly, and were thus labor intensive; shipbuilding, construction, steel and machinery required substantial skilled labor input. However, technical, scale, volume and other factors differed more between industries than within the automotive industry alone; labor was not the whole story.

Interindustry comparisons highlight the importance of several additional factors. These include the utilization of subcontracting to diversify risk and to heighten incentives, the interaction of structure with the rate of technical change, and variation in contracting in response to transaction-specific assets. In turn, these are a function of the structure of product markets and the nature of production technology, including the stability of demand, the extent of product differentiation and the associated product cycle length, and the complexity of product. (All, of course, matter only because of the initial strategic decision to rely on subcontractors.)

First, relative to many industries, transaction-specific plant and tooling is significant in the automotive industry. One reason is that the physical size of an automobile far surpasses that of any other mass-produced good. For example, presses large enough to stamp car body panels out of sheet metal have few uses elsewhere; similarly, presses small and precise enough to stamp out watch parts in volume have few other uses. This is one reason for the unusual, pervasive interdependency exhibited in the automotive assembler-primary supplier relationship and for (in the extreme) vertical integration.

Second, an automobile is a product of complexity unequaled by any other consumer product, and probably surpassed only by commercial aircraft and other aerospace and military hardware. This makes close coordination of design and logistics with parts suppliers essential. The cost of the requisite management systems increases the asset specificity of automotive transactions, although in the form of organizational and human rather than physical capital. That technical and management consulting and coordination is less extensive in other industries is therefore understandable—but it is not totally lacking.[23]

Third, risk plays a role in subcontracting. Where assets can readily be utilized in other industries or for other customers there is little need for the purchaser to offer security of contract; at most, tools and dies are provided. Subcontractors may in fact be better able to diversify against industry-specific risk than their parent firms; procyclical pricing and especially the shifting of work in and out of a firm would be expected. This is clearly visible in the machine tool industry, among firms that operate within industrial districts and among secondary and tertiary automotive subcontractors. It may also be important for the use of inside contractors in shipbuilding and construction, as they can be cut more readily than direct employees when business is slow. (Such arrangements were also visible in the cyclical truck segment of the automotive market and among automotive tool and die suppliers.) However, inside contractors appear to complement direct employees in steel and truck manufacture, and hence cannot be readily cut, and inside contractors were noticeably absent in the passenger car segment (Koike 1988:135). Risk sharing (which appears to be much of what Piore and Sable 1984 meant by flexibility) is thus limited to particular industries, and is not always the dominant consideration for inside contracting.

This is partly because of the incentive aspects of inside subcontracting and because of egalitarian considerations. In a steel mill, inside contractors performed tasks that were more sweat intensive; in the truck industry, tasks were skill-intensive (hand welding, "bump shop" work). Within firms, piece rates and similar incentive schemes are at odds with the egalitarian wage systems of Japanese firms, and are strongly opposed by unions and (as noted in the chapter 5 case studies) even small firms; inside contractors formed a separate peer group, and so could and did ignore this pressure to conform. Inside contractors likewise took on tasks where monitoring could be used to good effect, as in janitorial services. Finally, they undertook tasks which, while of necessity carried out adjacent to those performed by "regular" workers, were lower in skill or otherwise undesirable. Along with helping diversify risk, inside contracting thus also reflected the egalitarian ethic of maintaining homogeneity among the members of a firm. This latter aspect stood out both when the skill mix required by tasks differed, and when pecuniary forms of motivation were effective.

Finally, the owner/operator of a subcontractor faced stronger incentives than did a middle manager of a large firm. Thus, for example, large firms were known to spin off poorly performing operations with a clear signal that the now-independent firm will not be bailed out. (This often did wonders, as with Kato Shatai's Sapporo plant in chapter 5.) But typically a subcontractor was a closely held corporation, so there was little separation of ownership from management and the incentives to run a tight operation were very strong. Were a small stamping operation run in one corner of a large factory, as is often done in the U.S., the compensation of the general foreman or factory manager would be only poorly correlated with performance. For one thing, internal accounting methods provide only crude measures of performance, because the allocation of overhead and investment is not very fine grained (Kaplan 1985; Hopwood 1985; Johnson and Kaplan 1987). Whatever measure is used, poor performance will at most result in dismissal, and often not even that. (Keller 1989 notes that until the late 1980s, GM virtually never fired a manager for mere incompetence.) At the same time, excellent management will at best earn a slightly larger bonus and an improved opportunity for promotion. (Performance bonuses are quite limited in Japan; what is referred to as a "bonus" is in fact a standard contractual component of compensation, negotiated in advance. And even in the U.S., management bonuses often reflect corporate rather than individual performance.) At the same time, the leeway for a middle manager to make changes is severely constrained. For the owner/operator, the gains and losses were far greater, but so was the ability to respond to problems in an entrepreneurial manner. Small lot production and other irregular work was therefore typically subcontracted (Ikeda 1983b, 1987b; Nishiguchi 1989).

Perhaps more important, subcontracting provided strong incentives for technical change, and not merely for running a "tight" ship. In the auto industry, the benefit of pushing down costs faster than rivals through incremental innovation could be substantial; the presidents of many subcontractors were visibly wealthy. Along with this implicit incentive, there was an explicit incentive in the bonus provided for value engineering. Such large pecuniary rewards are almost never provided within firms. While Japanese companies are well-known in the U.S. for their suggestion systems, neither in Japan nor in the U.S. are there more than token bonuses. In fact, the incentives internal to a firm can be perverse, since an innovation shows up the boss—or worse, may undo a project with which he was associated. Because of frequent horizontal transfers, these tensions are less in Japan. An innovative supplier brought credit to the purchasing department—and there was no limitation on a subcontractor's profits.

Finally, the importance of incremental change stood out in the auto industry; the basic design of a vehicle changed remarkably little for over seventy years (Abernathy 1978). In contrast, the need to adopt totally new technologies was critical in watches and electronic goods and other products. Historically, however, the adoption of new technology is strongly associated with vertical integration (Silver 1984). In the Japanese automotive industry in the 1930s, the initial entrants were explicit about wanting to purchase parts and components, but all were forced to integrate into their manufacture because potential suppliers did not possess the requisite technology. (This is one reason that Nissan and Toyota have an extensive network of subsidiaries and affiliated firms, while later entrants do not.) Kachikachi Corp also sought outside suppliers, but was forced for similar reasons to make its own watch parts and to begin the manufacture of integrated circuits. (No one had the technology in the former case, or thought the potential market large enough to make it worth developing low-current devices in the latter.) But where incremental change dominates, the decentralization of the design process and of control over production technology can achieve remarkable results.

Conclusions

Extensive subcontracting is found in many Japanese industries, in part as a response to rigidities in labor markets. By using outside suppliers, firms could often utilize lower-wage labor, lessen the impact of the business cycle on their unionized workforce, and provide greater pecuniary incentives. In turn, the nature of subcontracting varied with the need for an ongoing relationship. In many industries, product designs were short-lived and technology evolved rapidly. Suppliers were switched frequently, and the level of interaction was low. In other industries, specialized assets were not needed, and purchases could be made at market rates. Where there was continuity, subcontracting provided strong incentives for technical change and for running an efficient manufacturing operation.

Subcontracting lowered current costs, through the more efficient allocation and motivation of labor. But while using suppliers improved static efficiency, the real benefits were achieved in the long run, through improved incentives for innovation. The organization of activity within firms dulls the incentives to bear risks and to make changes; both the downside costs of failure are lower, resulting in more bad choices, and the returns to success are less, resulting in fewer choices being made (Sah and Stiglitz 1986). Historically, Detroit discouraged supplier initiative (Wright 1979; Helper 1990a). The Japanese automotive firms, however, showed that suppliers could be made into a central source for technical and design change. Over time, this dynamic aspect helped the auto firms and other manufacturers of assembled goods to become world-class competitors.

Conclusion

Summary

Subcontracting was integral to the achievement of international competitiveness in the automotive and other industries. It allowed suppliers and purchasers to obtain the best of both worlds: the incentives of the market, and the coordination of hierarchy. Japanese manufacturers used outside suppliers of parts and components to lower costs by permitting them to work around labor market rigidities imposed by unions and by an egalitarian social ethic. But the ongoing nature of parts purchasing gave suppliers the confidence to invest heavily in modern plant and equipment. It also provided the auto companies with a framework through which they could extend just-in-time and other management techniques across firm boundaries. Finally, in the Japanese subcontracting environment, independent suppliers faced stronger incentives to innovate, and had greater freedom to undertake entrepreneurial activities than did middle managers in large firms. With purchases constituting 70% of total manufacturing costs, incremental improvements in supplier operations—and supplier contributions to better parts design through value engineering and other interfirm coordination—were critical to the success of the Japanese automotive industry.

Manufacturers in the automotive industry were initially vertically integrated. This changed rapidly in the 1950s, however, as output expanded at a time when unions made it costly to produce parts in-house. Small manufacturers also held substantial machinery and other real assets, so through subcontracting parts production was expanded without the need for much new capital. When in the late 1950s the automotive firms began building specialized assembly plants, they already had the beginnings of a dependable network of suppliers, and chose to rely on them rather that invest in building parts facilities. Indeed, they actually shifted parts manufacture from in-house shops to subcontractors. By the middle to late 1960s, each of the Japanese automotive assemblers had developed a stable group of between 200 and 300 direct suppliers. These firms made and eventually came to design many of the parts and subassemblies for the completed vehicle.

Managing this network of suppliers required innovations in the governance of contracts and the administration of purchasing. Subcontracting was not initially a problem because only single manufacturing steps and simple parts were purchased; if problems arose, work could be switched to alternate suppliers. But as the Japanese auto firms sought to limit their internal expansion in the 1950s and early 1960s, purchases were no longer restricted to simple items. Due to this strategy, parts firms had to make substantial investments in plant and organization. Alternate suppliers could no longer be found in the short run, and the auto firms became locked into buying a particular part or component from two or three suppliers. The extraordinary growth of automotive demand in turn meant that the automotive firms became their suppliers' dominant customers. Parts firms and auto companies became interdependent. With their mutual investments, they desired an ongoing, cooperative relationship. That was not easy to achieve.

The core innovation for that purpose was the development of trust as a governance mechanism. Trust was initially required for firms to be willing to invest in interdependency. (Similarly, over time some parts would no longer be needed, so parties had to trust that terminating a relationship would not be approached rapaciously, else they would be reluctant to initiate one.) Second, investments in specialized equipment and adaptations to a specific auto firm's management system made purchasing on an ongoing basis desirable. But because of the inherent complexity of such a long-term relationship, this could be handled only in part by (informal) contracts. Firms still had to trust each other not to take advantage of unforseen circumstances.

Once initiated, both parts firms and the auto companies gradually built up an investment in the relationship, and this helped make their commitment to future cooperation credible. In addition, the establishment of well-understood business norms lessened the room for disputes. Finally, investments could be and were made to develop and maintain reputation by the automotive firms, through the formation of supplier associations (*kyoryoku kai*). Through frequent interaction with each other and with their "parent" firm, suppliers could at least verify past behavior; they had to trust that it would be repeated in the future.

Administrative innovations contributed to the viability of subcontracting. The most important was the evolution of traditional cost accounting as a basis for pricing. Unlike in the U.S., where the ideal in purchasing is a competitive bidding situation, in Japan direct rivalry for a new contract was typically limited to two or three firms, and there was often an informal understanding that the previous supplier would get the new order when a model was changed. Despite this apparently stunted competition, the Japanese auto firms were able to use the rich set of information generated by the cost breakdowns that were part of their bidding system—together with the visible presence of at least one rival—to keep suppliers on their toes. Purchasers used their detailed cost breakdowns to push suppliers to remain competitive for individual production steps and material costs. This was less threatening than the "take it or leave it" bargaining used in Detroit. At the same time, discussion of individual costs helped direct the engineering efforts of suppliers to potentially solvable problems—and if needed, purchaser engineers were there to serve as consultants. This pricing norm significantly lessened the potential for opportunism by one or the other party, and decreased the room for honest disputes as well. Both helped the auto companies foster a competitive purchasing environment without sacrificing trust.

Supplier cooperation associations contributed to the efficiency of the subcontracting system, and not just to the maintenance of trust. Through the supplier associations, the auto firms were able to extend the implementation of JIT (just-in-time purchasing), SPC (statistical process/quality control) and VA/VE (value analysis/value engineering) across firm boundaries. They also provided a convenient route for the auto firms to help suppliers improve their production methods and management capabilities. But the associations also became the organizational nexus for jointly coordinating the entire subcontracting system, serving as a forum for discussing corporate strategy and coordinating investment. All of this, however, required not only adaptation among firms, but also the sharing of detailed business strategy, engineering and cost information. This, too, required trust.

Lessons for the U.S.

This study provides two lessons for the U.S. The first is that a subcontracting strategy is more beneficial than widely thought. The second is that a subcontracting strategy is more feasible than widely thought. In other words, both interdependency and trust are valuable, and both can be deliberately developed.

Benefits

The initial benefits from subcontracting in the Japanese automotive industry were reduced labor and capital costs. Turning to outside parts suppliers lessened the power of labor unions; Japanese auto firms avoided being locked into a common job classification and wage structure. Subcontracting also made new entry easier, which militated against the formation of an oligopoly that preferred the status quo. In contrast, the U.S. automotive industry faced the curses of a tight oligopoly, rigid union rules and sluggish management.

More important were the benefits of faster technical change. Subcontracting permitted the Japanese auto firms to tap the entrepreneurial abilities of suppliers, and this was central to how the Japanese "did it," how they caught up with their Western rivals. The mechanism through which prices were set gave an impetus for improving process technology; keeping ahead of rivals earned substantial profits. (At the same time, keeping up with the increases in productivity of rival firms was necessary to remain a supplier.) In the 1970s and 1980s, subcontractors were gradually integrated into the new car design process; value engineering drew upon supplier acumen to help improve design. This—rather than factory management—became central, as Japanese parts firms reached the state of the art in manufacturing technology.

Would increased utilization of subcontracting bring similar benefits for U.S. firms? If so, then why was a subcontracting strategy not adopted in the past? In Japan, historical circumstances clearly motivated the initial adoption of a subcontracting strategy.

In the U.S., the merger wave following World War I left GM vertically integrated. As argued in Chandler (1962), GM and similar
firms met the challenge of running very large organizations by
developing a multidivisional structure and financial accounting systems. But the Big Three were less successful in managing outside
suppliers, which were reluctant to have the majority of their sales
to GM or another single customer (Helper 1990c). Finally, integration into parts manufacturing allowed the auto firms to capture the
high margins available in the repair parts market for themselves
(Crandall 1968).[1]

A second aspect is that, at least until 1970, the constraints
U.S. automotive firms faced in their utilization of labor differed
from those of the Japanese firms. In the U.S., industrywide labor
unions could not be readily circumvented through subcontracting.
Furthermore, the differential between union and nonunion pay scales
was initially smaller than in Japan, while geographic variations in
wage rates in the U.S. had narrowed over time. However, wages in
the U.S. automotive industry diverged from those of the economy
as a whole in the 1970s, driven by the cost of living adjustments
(COLA clauses) and generous benefits packages negotiated during
the 1960s. During the 1950s automotive wages averaged 18%–19%
above those of manufacturing as a whole; the gap expanded to
21%–23% during the 1960s. But during the 1970s the automotive
gap rose to 24%–28%, and automotive wages were a full 33%
higher by 1984.[2] Furthermore, this understates the differential, because during the 1970s benefits made up an ever increasing share of
total compensation; those provided to the auto workers became
particularly generous. The total differential may have been as high
as 60% in the early 1980s (Halberstam 1986:621). It is surely greater
now: including benefits, Chrysler's labor costs now average $33 per
hour. (In contrast, in April 1991 the minimum wage will increase
to $4.25, and the cost of labor inclusive of Social Security and other
items will be roughly $4.70 per hour—one-seventh Chrysler's av-
erage.) Until the last fifteen years, therefore, the advantages of circumventing the union wage structure may have been perceived as
small. That is certainly not the case now.

But as with Japan, unions are not the entire story. While an
egalitarian ethic may be more visible in Japan, is not totally absent
in the U.S. The popular perception here is that one is hired to do a
job, and that compensation thus reflects job rather than individual

characteristics; in Japan, the individual and not the job is perceived as the focus. But in the large firm studied by Rosenbaum (1984), many job changes were to newly created positions; the individual was in fact the focus, and it was the job title that was adjusted. For that matter, far more Americans than Japanese work in very large firms, where rigid bureaucratic norms are typically used to maintain control in an environment in which "permanent employment" is actually more prevalent than in Japan (Sterling 1984). Thus while a large firm would potentially face much lower costs at a rural Southern plant than at an urban Northern one, they in fact still pay far more than the minimum wage (Doeringer 1984; Cain 1976). Recent attempts in the U.S. to implement two-tier wage systems provide additional evidence of an egalitarian ethic. The *Wall Street Journal* (June 16, 1987:A1) observed that "Once seen as an equitable way to control wages, two-tier systems now are thought by many to be too damaging to morale." They have foundered in the face of worker dissatisfaction, just as in the 1960s Japanese firms were forced to limit their use of temporary workers (*rinjiko*).

It should therefore not be surprising that the Big Three are increasing their outsourcing, even though this has led to skirmishes between the auto firms and the UAW (Helper 1990b). Ironically, Big Three parts imports increased during the early 1980s, even as Ford and Chrysler pleaded for protection from vehicle imports. But increased demand for parts has encouraged new entry within the U.S. as well, with approximately 160 Japanese automotive parts firms setting up manufacturing operations by 1986, together with probably an equal number of European firms (U.S. International Trade Commission 1987:Appendix G), and 40 more since then.

Finally, good design is becoming more critical. The tight grip of the Big Three on the U.S. market has ended. More foreign manufacturers have more dealerships in more parts of the country than was true a decade ago; over 600 models of cars are now marketed in the U.S. But as noted in chapter 1, Detroit has been slow to respond to changes in tastes because their design process is sluggish and costly. In addition, automotive design is changing more rapidly than at any time in the last fifty years, as electronics, ceramics, plastics and other nontraditional technologies are being applied in the industry. Turning to outside suppliers will likely improve the access of American firms to the requisite expertise, while cutting their need to undertake costly investment in new factories. And through "systems contracting" and cooperative engineering, turning to outside suppliers should also lead to better design.

Because of the historic purchasing practices in Detroit, suppliers have poorer engineering capabilities than their Japanese counterparts, and less experience with designing entire systems; in 1980, Ford found few American suppliers when it sought to use "co-engineering" for the development of the Taurus/Sable (Burt 1989). Furthermore, the Big Three have less experience with value engineering and other techniques for coordinating operations across corporate boundaries. (GM finds it hard to work across division boundaries; Keller 1989.) Nevertheless, there are many capable companies, particularly among firms with experience in heavy truck manufacture—and among the 300 suppliers from Europe and Japan that have set up transplant factories here. If Detroit is able to countenance interdependence with suppliers—and suppliers with Detroit—then they, too, are likely to reap the benefits of better designs obtained faster and at lower cost. This process will be traumatic for many locales, as less efficient producers lose out. In the short-run, shifting work to outside suppliers will also exacerbate the tensions in labor relations caused by declining sales (Brown and Reich 1989; Helper 1990b). But with greater competition, the Big Three—and existing suppliers—must change if they are to survive. We as an economy will ultimately benefit from the increase in competitiveness (Smitka 1989, 1990a).

Trust

This book should provide food for thought as American executives search for structures that will support a viable subcontracting relationship or other "strategic alliances," because U.S. manufacturers will face the same problems that confronted Japanese firms thirty-five years ago if they choose to implement cooperative strategies. In the past, Japanese industry benefited in many ways from being followers. Now American industry has an opportunity to learn supplier management techniques from Japan. Even with the greater ability to rely on legal contracts in the U.S., an interdependent supplier-purchaser relationship is simply too complex for contracting to be sufficient. Instead, the parties will need to consciously set forth business norms, and develop the personal and organizational trust that make an ongoing relationship possible. For the auto industry, it will also be important to stress that commitments must be made credible, including through visibly forsaking internal manufacture where it competes with outside suppliers. They will also have to make deliberate investments in reputation by foregoing excessively short-term price considerations, particularly given the legacy of distrust from the strong-arm tactics they have long used with suppliers. Here supplier associations would provide a formal means for the exercising of "voice" among the auto companies and their suppliers; at present complaints merely lead one side or the other to "exit" (Helper 1990a, 1990c; Hirschman 1986).

Greater interdependence with suppliers will also require better integration of purchasing with other corporate functions. U.S. firms are quickly learning the mechanics of just-in-time production control systems and statistical quality control techniques (Hall 1981, 1982; Productivity Press, numerous titles). But as firms implementing such systems are discovering, they only function smoothly in an ongoing relationship. This is equally true of value analysis, which because it is little known in the U.S. merits particular attention. All of these programs require extensive sharing of information, and careful administrative coordination. Again, supplier associations provide a potentially useful tool.

Trust, of course, can build on a cultural foundation—in fact, no society could function without trust. Many have viewed trust as an expression of Japanese culture, and hence subcontracting as inherently limited to Japan. This study argues that is not the case. The Japanese auto firms deliberately built up trust among their suppliers, and subsequently worked hard to maintain their reputation. This included the creation of social ties among the management of suppliers and the auto firms. It was further aided by the organization of supplier associations. Americans need to be careful not to launch complex ventures on a handshake; we are, if anything, too trusting, and mergers and acquisitions have meant increased difficulties because continuity in management cannot be relied upon (Galante 1987; cf. Larson 1988, 1990). It will take careful experimentation—and the gradual weeding out of inappropriate partners—to make trust work. But there is no inherent reason why in the long run we cannot also learn to develop strategic alliances with suppliers in a systematic and orderly manner. Given the potential benefits of cooperation, failure to learn to trust would clearly be costly.

Lessons for Economists

This study adds to the literature on the theory of the firm and on contracting, pointing out that our dichotomy into "firm" and "market" is unduly limiting. It also suggests that greater attention needs to be paid to sociological features in labor markets. Finally, it suggests we ought to work more on the economics of cooperation, and less on short-term optimization.

Economists have typically assumed the firm to be an atomistic agent in a market economy. Interactions among firms were thus relegated to an arms-length spot market. When economists have chosen to open the black box of the firm, they have typically assumed it operates via command in a hierarchy. This research shows that these clear-cut divisions are inappropriate. On the one hand, Chandler (1962) and others have argued that large corporations succeeded in part because they were able to replicate some of the functions of a market internally. But in the Japanese auto industry quite complex coordination extends across firm boundaries. Thus, in the real world, it is very hard to disentangle organization and market. In particular, while some market features may be replicated within firms, corporate boundaries are even less of a barrier to developing formal and informal organization. As economists, we must therefore be more cautious in seeing the advantage of the firm as providing organization.

When economists explicitly model human behavior, they typically presume that self-seeking pecuniary motives are dominant, downplaying social constraints and nonmonetary incentives. Part of this is a mere analytic simplification, since other variables can readily be substituted for "money" in formal models. But in practice such variables are very difficult to utilize in empirical work, and because it is so easy to show that money matters, it is all too easy to drift into thinking and teaching that money is *all* that matters. Instead, greater attention must be given to take into account social constraints and nonpecuniary incentives.

In subcontracting, profit was clearly important. Both parties ᴨad to expect to receive profits for a relationship to be initiated, while if conditions changed and indefinite losses appeared likely, then a relationship would be terminated. But economic models focus on the short-run aspects of contracting problems (in part to remain tractable), and ignore the long-run tradeoffs of an ongoing relationship. In addition, by limiting themselves to pecuniary goals, principal-agent and other formal contracting models unduly restrict the range of feasible outcomes; they predict a level of antagonism and opportunism, of paranoia and unrestrained aggression, that is not observed in practice. One of the functions of institutions is surely to restrict the realm in which decisions must be made, economizing on our limited ability to think and communicate and protecting us from our own fallibility. But organization also restricts the realm within which our baser motives are brought into play, and makes it easier to develop trust and cooperation. The case of the Japanese auto industry suggests some of the ways in which this can occur.

Prospects

American firms are currently rethinking their vertical integration strategies, and adopting a more Japanese-like policy toward suppliers. A number of firms have apparently succeeded. Like the U.S. automotive firms, Xerox was buffeted by Japanese competition. It therefore was willing to learn from the success of its joint venture, Fuji Xerox, in the Japanese copier market. In the early 1980s Xerox reduced the total number of its vendors from 5,000 to less than 300, while increasing the integration of suppliers into the design process for new copiers. A feature of the new relationship, and one signifying improved trust, was the elimination of prior price quotes. The result has been a shorter product development cycle and greater design efficiency; development costs have been cut to one third of previous levels. The ultimate benefit has been improved market performance and profitability (Hillkirk and Jacobson 1986:232–36).[3] To date the U.S. auto firms have been laggards. But with the arrival of Honda, Nissan, Toyota and the other Japanese transplant operations in the U.S., they, too, are now being forced to change.

Notes

O N E / Overview

1. Calculated from *Automotive News*, January 8, 1990, including Japanese-built vehicles sold by the Big Three. Imports are limited by a Voluntary Export Restraint ceiling to 2.3 million vehicles (though with the stronger yen, the Japanese are unlikely to sell that many), while production capacity in the U.S. is roughly 2.1 million vehicles, including vans and light pickup trucks. This gives a maximum share of 29% (4.4 million vehicles in a 15–million vehicle market). The share in the passenger car market, however, is already higher.

2. Helper argues that suppliers were bought out during the earlier decades of this century to obtain their organizational skills. Suppliers were at the time generally older and more technically proficient than the auto firms proper. Thus, for example, Sloan of GM, among others later prominent at Ford and GM, had been a supplier executive. See also Coase (1988).

3. As long as the Big Three did not compete on the basis of quality or price, it was potentially more profitable to simply beat down parts prices. Furthermore, vertical integration permitted the auto firms to control sales to the lucrative repair parts market. See Helper (1987) and Crandall (1968), respectively. Demsetz (1988) summarizes an ongoing debate over the initial adoption of the integration strategy by GM.

4. Many have coined terms, including quasi-integration (Blois 1978), relational contracting (Williamson 1985), interpenetration of market and hierarchy (Imai and Itami 1984), PALs (Kanter 1989) and strategic alliances.

5. See Gambetta (1988) on the definition of "trust."

6. Herein I maintain the fiction that these requirements are automatically met for transactions internal to firms.

7. The number of direct ("primary") suppliers is taken from *Nihon no Jidosha Buhin Kogyo* (Japan Automotive Parts Industry Yearbook), which

attempts to systematically list all such firms. The number of secondary suppliers here is equal to the number of firms reported in the *Census of Manufactures* after excluding direct suppliers. Since at least 300 primary firms have supplier cooperation associations with 20 or more firms, this number could be considerably higher (Sheard [1983] found an average of 25 secondary suppliers per direct supplier). The number of tertiary firms is derived by assuming that each secondary supplier on average maintains several suppliers of its own (Sheard found 4.5 tertiary per secondary firm). Note that in my own field work, I found that many smaller firms were not listed in the *Census*, and that when they were, it was often under technology-related classifications ("rubber parts," "machining") rather than automotive parts.

8. Recent studies on Japanese small business include Wood (1984), Patrick and Rohlen (1987) and Sterling (1984). Two-thirds of the Japanese labor force are in establishments of under 300 workers, while in the U.S. two-thirds are in establishments of over 300 workers.

9. Teikoku Data and Tosho Research are the two leading compilers of commercial credit reports. Unfortunately their published data are unsuitable for statistical analysis; though a large number of firms are covered, only cursory information is presented, and their directories are extraordinarily cumbersome to use. To my knowledge, researchers have not been granted access to the far more extensive computer databases these firms maintain. Other directories include the annual *Nihon no Jidosha Buhin Kogyo* (Japan Automotive Parts Industry Yearbook) and miscellaneous compilations by marketing consultants such as Yano Keizai Kenkyusho and the Nagoya-based Industrial Research Center. An English-language recompilation of these is published periodically by Dodwell Marketing Consultants, *The Structure of the Japanese Auto Parts Industry*.

10. The Market-Oriented, Sector-Specific (MOSS) trade talks focused on two industries or issues, in the hope of marshaling our government's limited negotiating resources in a fruitful manner. The Structural Impediments Initiative, completed in June 1990, addressed broader bilateral issues. In addition, the locus of parts production is reappearing as a trade issue with Europe, as it will determine whether cars made by Japanese-owned plants in the U.S. are "American" and can be exported to Europe.

11. This includes Chandler (1962), who traces management innovations, which he argues facilitated organizing additional transactions within firms, and much of Williamson (1985). (Williamson, however, also developed some of the earliest formal models of diseconomies of vertical integration.) All along, of course, the benefits of size have been the prime focus of the antitrust literature.

TWO / A Case Study: The Soja Industrial Park

1. This chapter is based on (1) interviews in 1984 with the management of the Mizushima Industrial Park and four of its member firms, with Nippon Eagle Wings Industries in the U.S. in 1989, and with purchasing personnel at Mitsubishi Motors Corporation in Japan and the U.S. in 1984 and 1989, (2) brochures and other unpublished materials on the park and its member firms, (3) three articles on the park, by Takizawa (1966, 1983) and Takeshita (1967), and (4) two books on Mitsubishi Motors, Yoshii (1980) and Ikari (1988).

2. An additional member provided trucking services to the other firms; the park also employed 400 workers directly. As pointed out later in the chapter, the park initially had more members.

3. Takizawa (1983:13–14). Data on Mizushima vehicle exports were not given, but knock-down (CKD kits) alone accounted for 16% of Mizushima output in 1980 and 19% in 1981.

4. This section is based primarily on Yoshii (1980).

5. It thus followed the other three-wheel vehicle producers, Toyo Kogyo (Mazda), Daihatsu and Fuji Heavy Industries (Subaru).

6. This did not continue long, as Kaiser-Fraser ceased passenger car production in 1954.

7. Chrysler held about 12.5% of MMC in October 1989. Its stake rose briefly to 24% after the listing of MMC on the Tokyo Stock Exchange in December 1988, but a large block of shares was sold during the fall of 1989.

8. Yoshii (1980:appendix, pp. 4, 6, 11); Ikari (1988:chapter 6) and the June 1989 MMC financial statements (*Yuka Shoken Hokoku Sho*) are the data sources. Detailed historic information was not readily available, as Mitsubishi was not required to file public financial statements prior to its listing in December 1988 on the Tokyo Stock Exchange.

9. Engines and drivetrain are procured in large part from MMC Kyoto, so (internal) Kyoto sales were probably larger.

10. This does not include engine purchases from MMC Kyoto.

11. MMC launched a light three-wheel car in 1959, selling 3,140 vehicles the first year and 16,283 in 1960.

12. Professor Kikutaro Takizawa returned to MMC Mizushima about once every three years during the succeeding twenty years, and also undertook similar consulting for MMC Nagoya and for Toyota. He was successful in part because of the personal backing of top management at the two firms. (Takizawa, personal communication.) Shozo Takeshita (1967) was also a consultant. In interviews, the president of the Soja Park venture in Illinois stressed the contribution of these consultants in general, and of Professor Takizawa in particular. Takizawa subsequently was an advisor to the Japanese government in the drafting of the 1970 Small and Medium

Subcontractor Promotion Law, and since 1986 has headed the Subcontractor Committee of the Small and Medium Business Modernization Advisory Council, the key government group dealing with small business policy.

13. Workers aged 35 and older dropped from 53% to 28% of the Mizushima labor force.

14. The other twelve firms continued to operate at least one other establishment. This placed a burden on the manager(s) of what at the time were still small firms.

15. Government subsidy programs ended shortly after the industrial park opened in 1965, so that subsequently the firms were forced to borrow on commercial terms. MMC also reached its credit limits, and so could not guarantee additional loans for the park (Takeshita 1967:302).

16. Sales rose even more rapidly because firms switched from using steel and other materials supplied by MMC (with the cost therefore not reflected in sales) to purchasing materials directly (and hence sales reflected materials purchases). Value added, which is sales less purchases, corrects for this change.

17. Four small machining firms merged to form one jointly owned firm. As independent "one-man" firms they had been unable to expand as rapidly as MMC production required. By pooling their resources they sought, apparently successfully, to remain viable. Of the various firms that exited, none, apparently, did so due to outright bankruptcy. (Interview with Eagle Wings Industries.)

18. Other than the joint brake venture, Mitsubishi held equity in one other firm. Details were unavailable, but presumably at some point Mitsubishi had supplied capital to finance the resuscitation or takeover of a weak supplier.

19. MMC was able to hire and retain new school leavers, but most of the park firms employed mid-career workers (chuto saiyo). After 1974, park firms were increasingly able to hire and keep young workers, including newly minted engineers.

20. Thus, while contemporary reports emphasized high turnover, it seems likely that the Soja firms also had a core group of employees who stayed or who were experienced when hired.

21. Interviewees did not define "virtually." I took it to mean perhaps 10% lower than a similar MMC worker. Since the Soja firms employed more women, average wages were probably more than 10% lower than at MMC, with its largely male workforce.

22. Akebono Brake, MMC and Hiruta each owned one-third of Sanyo Brake. In 1983, the president of Hiruta was the president of both Sanyo Brake and Sanyo Hydric firms. Akebono Brake licensed technology from Bendix (U.S.) in 1961, which gave it an initial monopoly on the domestic

brake market. It gradually lost this position. Along with Sanyo Brake, Toyota set up a similar joint venture in 1968, Hosei Brake. Meanwhile other domestic firms (e.g., Nisshin Kogyo) licensed brake technology from European rivals of Bendix. (See Akebono Brake 1979:139–40.)

23. Takeshita (1967) reported that some firms were founded by or had former MMC personnel in management, but provided no details.

24. Value analysis (VA) and value engineering (VE) were developed by industrial engineers as tools for analyzing function and design characteristics in order to reduce costs without sacrificing value as perceived by the ultimate customer. Through a specific sequence of steps, VA serves to stimulate and coordinate this effort across engineering, marketing, finance and other middle-management functions. While developed in the U.S., American firms have been poor in applying VA/VE to their design and R&D activities. (See chapter 7 for more details. Professor Fred Spengler of Virginia Tech provided me with an overview of value analysis and commented on an early version of my discussion of VA/VE.)

25. Staff engineers in one supplier proudly pointed to their Value Engineer certifications, prominently framed on the wall of the conference room of their head office. The first dated from 1980.

26. One MMC supplier in Tokyo claimed to have never had a customer's engineer on its factory floor; they were treated to a business lunch, not a plant tour. The firm claimed to be unusually low in cost in its specialty, and in addition gave Mitsubishi a better price than rival auto firms. The suggestion was that MMC knew this and saw no gain from forcing the issue.

27. There is apparently variation across firms in this regard. Toshihiro Nishiguchi has told me that he observed frequent rotations into and out of the purchasing function at Toyota and at Pioneer, an electronics manufacturer.

28. The president of one Soja firm was a former MMC manager, who used his retirement bonus to purchase a 20% stake from the firm's owners. The founder's family retained 80%.

29. Nissan and Toyota claim not to face this problem. Their suppliers are larger, and hence have a corps of professional managers. They are also older, so most have already weathered the separation of ownership and management. In the case of Mitsubishi, most of their Nagoya suppliers were involved in fighter aircraft production during WWII and so were old firms. However, only one-third in the Mizushima area had made the generational transition, while most Tokyo-area suppliers were yet young.

30. This American firm, along with a German firm, dominated world markets for such products in the 1930s. I could not determine its identity from its Japanese name.

31. Two Soja firms made textiles in the 1930s, but during the war

were forced to make airplane parts. This provided a base for their post-WWII entry into the auto parts market. Their founders had technical training, like Mr. Namba.

32. In 1984, 14% of sales were to Mazda and 7% to agricultural machinery firms. Hiruta Kogyo and three other firms had 40% or more of sales to non-MMC customers. Many firms were increasing their Mazda sales.

33. Parts purchases and subcontracting by Soja Park suppliers generally accounted for under 20% and often for under 10% of costs (calculated from Takizawa 1966:tables 7, 26 and Takizawa 1983:table 17).

34. Thus while plating is only 10% of sales at OM Kogyo, it nevertheless remains important to the OM group as a whole.

35. There might be inheritance or other tax aspects that would create opportunities for tax avoidance (e.g., firms in Japan are not required to consolidate their tax filings).

36. This section draws upon a newspaper series, "Tobe Iigurusu" (Fly, Eagle!), Sarariiman Series No. 241, *Nihon Keizai Shimbun*, 1987 and interviews with Mr. Isamu Kawasaki, Eagle Wings Industries and others at Diamond-Star Motors and its suppliers, August 1989.

37. Calculated from Yoshii (1980:47). I do not have specific data on U.S. export shares. Note that Chrysler prevented Mitsubishi from opening its own U.S. dealerships until 1981.

38. *Yuka Shoken Hokokusho* (Financial Statements), Mitsubishi Motors Corporation, fiscal year 1988 (ending March 31, 1989), p. 54. It appears that this was for U.S. dollar-denominated loans, presumably borrowed from banks in the U.S. to finance construction of the plant.

39. Indeed, a number of the members of the original park have now built plants in a new and larger industrial park near Mizushima that commenced operations in the fall of 1990.

THREE / The Evolution of the Automotive Parts Industry

1. Recent historiography stresses that this shift stemmed from fears that the Japanese economy was not recovering, and hence Congress might have to be approached about appropriating more money for the 24cupation. Schonberger (1989).

2. While Toyoda family members remain active at Toyota—one is currently president—this is not due to family ownership. In contrast, Henry Ford's descendants remain the dominant vote holders of Ford Motor Company. See S. Nakamura (1957:110–12, 114) and Genther (1990:57–59) on the Toyota bailout. There was widespread sentiment among end-users that imports were preferable and the domestic auto industry should be allowed to fail. The famous April 1950 statement of Bank of Japan Governor Ichi-

mada that it was better to import automobiles preceded by a few days the wage concessions at Toyota, which were a prerequisite to the reorganization of the firm. His statement therefore cannot be taken at face value, and in fact Ichimada apparently supported easy loans by the Bank of Japan to counteract the Dodge Line fiscal policy. Schonberger (1989:224).

3. Tobata sought to ease entry into auto production. It set up Nissan as a subsidiary in 1934, while Hitachi was part of the same conglomerate (Cusumano 1985:38–39). Odaka et al. (1988:198) note that in the 1920s Teikoku Spring sold springs, bumpers and spare wheel carriers to Ford and GM, but was unable to sell wheel rims to the American auto firms until 1935.

4. In 1931 Ministry of Commerce and Industry data showed tires as 60% of the 14.8 million of auto parts output. In 1936, tires were 50% of the 53.5 million output of parts. Other data are drawn from the advertising section of *Nihon no Jidosha Buhin Kogyo*, 1965.

5. There were 60,000 cars in Japan in 1952, most quite old and hence in frequent need of spare parts. New production was under 6,000 vehicles a year. See Genther (1990:73–79).

6. The role of monitoring and evaluating customers and providing insurance resembles that played by trading firms. Hence it is interesting to note that an early controversy in the Japanese small business literature was whether subcontracting reflected "merchant capital" (putting-out) or "industrial capital" ("true" subcontracting). In English, see Shinohara (1968).

7. Most reports are of Toyota and Nissan. However, contemporary observers, such as Okumura et al. (1965), were careful to label these as "examples," explicitly noting similar efforts elsewhere. Concepts such as JIT were widely discussed; Toyota was ultimately the most successful, but its efforts were by no means unique.

8. Several likely biases exist in the data. First, the changes in ratios may reflect a shift in product mix and not strategy. During the 1950s and early 1960s output shifted from trucks to passenger vehicles; trucks were sold without bodies, and cars with bodies and extensive trim, so that purchases would likely increase with car output. Second, initially the auto industry was small, and the *Census of Manufactures* probably counted many suppliers under nonautomotive classifications. Even in the 1982 Census, most Kato Shatai suppliers were not classed as automotive parts firms (census classification 3613), and inside contractors were not even counted. (See chapter 5.)

9. Hino tied up with Renault, Isuzu with the British Rootes Motor, Nissan with Austin and Mitsubishi with Willys-Overland. MITI nixed a Chrysler tie-up with Fuji Heavy Industries (Subaru), while through bad luck two attempts at a Toyota-Ford venture failed. Nissan ended CKD assembly in 1959, while production at the other firms peaked in 1960–1961, and ceased by the end of 1964.

10. Calculated from table 3.5 and Nissan Jidosha Chosabu (1983:4–5). Ministry of Transport regulations inhibited the development of independent repair shops. Dealerships were (and are) thus the main source of repair services and the auto firms have thereby been able to control the aftermarket. The same was true in U.S. aftermarket in the 1930s; see Crandall (1968).

11. In Japan, purchases were 65.5% of manufacturing costs, including 13% for steel purchases. Note also that taxes, profits and depreciation were 24%–25% at GM and Renault, but only 14% for Japanese firms.

12. For example, one small firm, Yamagata Seisakusho, machined nozzles and fit them on brake tubes. The "factory" was a work shed adjacent to the owner's house, in which a dozen or so neighborhood women and older men worked. Data from interviews at Bendix (Japan), Akebono, and Yamagata.

13. The pre-WWII component manufacturers had multiple customers all along, and technical expertise (combined in many cases with the licensing of U.S. and European patents) often gave them considerable market power. When in the 1960s Akebono Brake raised capital by selling stock, it was able to place 25% of the new shares with Nissan and Toyota. Other firms were likewise able to preserve their independence by getting two or more auto firms to invest on an equal basis.

14. This is familiar to economists as the Averch-Johnson effect, named after their observation of incremental but over time very sizable improvements of efficiency among electric utilities in the stable rate environment of the 1960s.

15. Note that NUMMI, the Toyota-GM joint venture based in GM's idle Freemont, California assembly plant, quickly surpassed the productivity of other GM-affiliated plants without resort to high levels of automation. In contrast, productivity was particularly low at GM's Hamtramack, Michigan plant, with its state-of-the-art automation.

16. Suppliers have relied on this advantage when they have followed their automotive customers overseas. While in the long run Honda, Mazda and the other auto makers will set up design operations in the U.S., most engineering functions remain in Japan. In the interim, few foreign suppliers have been willing to set up engineering liaison offices in Japan. See Smitka (1990a) and Mair et al. (1988).

17. For specialized producers long-standing ties are not unknown in the U.S.; the Budd Company, for example, has probably supplied Chrysler since the latter's formation in the 1920s, while Bendix has long supplied braking systems to Ford.

18. A few existing suppliers of Toyota from the Tokyo area joined the association when they built plants in the Toyota vicinity. In addition, it is likely that some firms changed their names or merged with other firms. While I was able to make some corrections for such changes, these data undoubtedly slightly exaggerate the extent of exit and entry. Further-

more, the names of some of the new members suggest that they were affiliates of Toyota Shatai, itself a subsidiary of Toyota, and hence might have been supplying Toyota all along.

FOUR / Labor Markets and Subcontracting

1. In fact, the pay scales in the Japanese "transplant" car factories in the U.S. suggest that workers here are more willing to accept flat pay scales than those in Japan. See Taira (1989).

2. There is no nationwide minimum wage system in Japan. Instead, minimum wages are set by prefecture based on actual wages, so that they are not a binding constraint on employers but rather serve as a signal as to what *ought* to be paid. The 1989 national average minimum wage for part-time workers was ¥492 per hour (*Japan Economic Journal*, October 7, 1989, p. 15).

3. This is for salary plus bonus. There are substantial fringe benefits, such as subsidized mortgages, but even then senior executives are not highly paid by U.S. standards. The top twenty to thiry-five executives typically are directors, and their cash compensation is reported in financial statements. The data used here are drawn from Kyoikusha (1980:136). On the U.S., see Pucik (1986).

4. Most *paato* were women returning to the labor force after their children entered school who found a seven-hour workday ideal. At the same time, from the firm's standpoint a longer workweek required provision of benefits mandated for full-time workers. See *Wall Street Journal*, May 8, 1989:A12 on these roughly eight million workers.

5. Data are from *Rodo Jiho*, June 1985, p. 58, figure 6, adjusted for a 180–hour workmonth and a bonus of four months' basic pay. Regular workers receive benefits as well.

6. Nissan Diesel produces engines and mid-size trucks and chassis. The firm originally was part of Minsei Sangyo, but the truck division performed poorly and was spun off into a separate firm in the late 1940s. It became a subsidiary of Nissan in the 1950s (Kodaira 1968:330ff).

7. A similar analysis for Mitsubishi Motors using 1989 data shows labor costs a full one-third higher, at ¥472,650 per month, and 45% more than MMC's average base pay of ¥324,698. MMC employed 25,300 workers, who averaged 38.5 years old.

8. The data on bonuses and hours worked are drawn from *Rodo Tokei Chosa Geppo* (Monthly Labor Statistics), May 1984.

9. This name is a pseudonym.

10. In the 1980s, as road transport improved and the town became suburban, the proportion of farm wives declined to 60%.

11. Odaka et al (1988:188). Recent information is from scattered news reports and interviews with end-users.

12. Kato obtained volume discounts on sheet metal, of which Ma-

ruzen used small quantities. Maruzen would have had to go to small distributors, who got their sheet metal from the cheapest source and so did not maintain consistent quality.

13. *Chusho Kigyo Hakusho* (1983:136, figure 1.2.2) for data on female workers. The underlying source is Sorifu, *Rodo Ryoku Chosa*. Data on age and education is from *Chusho Kigyo Hakusho*, 138–39, Figure 1.2.4; the underlying source is the Wage Census. See too Patrick and Rohlen (1987).

14. See the section entitled "Egalitarian Mentality" in Iwata (1982), esp. p. 72.

15. Doeringer (1984) presents a case study that demonstrates this is also true for the rural U.S. Local considerations also appear important for employers in the rural Virginia county where I reside.

16. See also Odaka (1984) and Taira (1970).

17. See also Fruin (1978, 1983) on the management model in the soy sauce brewing industry. Trading firms are discussed in various sources as a model. The bureaucracy, the military and railroads may have provided alternative models.

18. Gordon (1985). The seminal description of "the" Japanese employment system is Abegglen (1958). Okayama (1987) notes that management also pressed for the inclusion of white-collar workers in unions, to help hold radical elements in check.

19. During the war indexing in principle was to keep pay sufficient to procure rations, but premia (*teate*) systems also enabled firms to circumvent wage controls in a tight labor market.

20. Miyashita (1971), a small business management handbook, shows how to calculate a wage that will provide a "standard" level of living for a given age and family size. His tables are based on econometric estimates of the elasticity of expenditure by age and family size on a standard basket of consumption goods.

21. Cusumano (1985) and Halberstam (1986). They were replaced by compliant "second unions" facilitated by the "open shop" provisions of Japanese labor law. See Gould (1984).

22. Personal communication with Kazuo Koike and seminar comments of Haruo Shimada, two leading Japanese labor economists.

23. *Chingin Jittai Chosa*, now the *Chingin Kozo Kihon Tokei Chosa*, published by the Ministry of Labor (Japan. Rodosho). The first, in 1954, surveyed over 2 million employees.

24. Mori (1978), a handbook for small firm management, lists "model wage" surveys by prefectural and local employers' associations and government bodies as sources for wage comparisons. These surveys, undertaken to assist small businessmen, uniformly use as their main categories industry, education, sex, age-cum-tenure and white- versus blue-collar. That these are drawn up separately by so many localities and place a heavy

emphasis on industry-by-industry collation suggests that, relative to large firms, small firms must pay greater reference to interfirm markets.

25. He appears to draw on a 1966 Ministry of Labor survey; similar surveys are cited in T. Ono (1980).

26. He provides sample evaluation forms on pp. 185–198, and details the "model" wage on pp. 278–285. The new evaluation system required each worker to set the standards and targets he or she would seek to achieve. The performance rating reflected past assessments and not just the current evaluation, while the evaluation itself drew upon input from the worker and others, lessening the weight of the immediate supervisor.

27. Honda: See Sakiya (1982). Rodosha Chosa Kenkyu Kai (1983:170) notes some individuals were promoted after only five years, suggesting divergence has since become more rapid. The tightening of labor markets after 1960 led to rapid hikes in entry-level wages, but firms did not make comparable raises in the wages of older workers. Instead they held fixed the absolute increment between different-aged workers, while increasing base pay.

Daihatsu: See Rodosha Chosa Kenkyu Kai (1983:106–10). A group leader system was introduced in 1957 and a rank system in 1962 (replacing an "incentive" pay system that in fact gave the same increment to all workers). Actual practice did not reflect the paper criteria until 1970, when Daihatsu entered into a tie-up with Toyota.

Isuzu: See Nihon Seisansei Honbu (1965, 1969) and Miyashita (1971:292–99). Isuzu, whose workforce was initially composed of skilled workers, replaced a "Densan" system with an ability pay system in 1960 when it began hiring large numbers of unskilled workers. A conversion table was drawn up to help fit workers with relevant outside experience into the pay scale at a rank above unskilled hires.

Nissan: See Yamamoto (1978, 1981).

Toyota Shatai: See Cole (1979).

Toyota: See Nishiguchi (1989, chapter 4).

Suzuki: See Suzuki (1970:440ff).

Mazda: See *Chuo Koron Keiei Mondai* (Summer 1966) 5(2):209–216.

28. *Chuo Koron Keiei Mondai* (Summer 1963), 2(2):344, 209–216, and the June 1989 Annual Report (*Yuka Shoken Hokokusho*) of Mitsubishi Motors.

29. Kamata (1982) is an exposé of the life of Toyota seasonal workers during 1973, a boom year when as a college student I was also employed during the summer at Chrysler. Unlike Kamata, I received the same UAW wage as veteran workers, and could not be automatically fired at summer's end.

30. "Now from around this time [1955], in order to supplement their workforce, firms began to implement policies of systematically and stra-

tegically utilizing 'temporary' workers in parallel to the use of subcontractors." Nihon Seisansei Honbu (1969:250).

31. For Nissan see Cusumano (1985:415, n. 43) and Yamamoto (1981:tables 6, 7). For Toyota see Okayama (1987:181–86), Nishiguchi (1989, chapter 4) and Allinson (1975:178–79). Gordon (1985:401–7) presents data on temporary workers at Toshiba for 1958–1983, where temporary workers peaked at a third of the workforce in 1960, but were less than 10% after 1964, and under 3% after 1970.

32. Gordon (1985: 410–17). The differential of *rinji-ko* to average pay was 1:3 in 1959 and 1:2 in 1963. Given the sharp age/wage gradient at that time the average wage of regular workers would be much more than the starting wage, so they were probably paid at least as much as new school-leavers, and if they were on average young, their pay then differed little from that of their regular worker peers. Experience conversion tables for Isuzu suggest the *rinji-ko* entry route did not imply permanently lower wages. Finally, the average compensation of *rinji-ko* at Nissan increased 60% from 1959 to 1963, a more rapid increase than that of regular workers.

33. Data from interviews with union and personnel officials. See also Koike (1988:135).

34. For example, see the cover story of *Fortune*, "Who Needs a Boss," May 7, 1990, and Smitka (1990b). More generally, the business press is now trumpeting the benefits of "focused" organizations, in other words, that groups of workers pursuing well-defined tasks perform better.

F I V E / Case Studies: Kato Shatai Group
and Sembokuya

1. Data are drawn from (1) interviews at Kato Shatai and four suppliers, including multiple interviews at Suzuki Bankin, (2) unpublished material and brochures on Kato Shatai and its products, (3) a privately published company history, Kato Shatai (1971) and (4) Wood (1982). My particular thanks to Robert Chapman Wood for suggesting I contact Suzuki Bankin and to Mr. Yuzo Ohkawa of Suzuki Bankin, who gave of his time on multiple occasions, and arranged and participated in all the interviews.

2. Like many firms, Kato at war's end proved to have been hording rationed materials.

3. Cusumano (1985:256) notes that one body supplier, Shin-Nikkoku, shifted from working for both Toyota and Nissan to working only for Nissan c. 1951. Nissan subsequently purchased shares; the firm is now known as Nissan Auto Body.

4. Press Kogyo (1975:85). Isuzu was the largest shareholder, and tried to convince it to make cabs; Press Kogyo, however, refused. Instead it was

able to push Isuzu to finance a joint venture, Shatai Kogyo. While 50% of the capital was from Isuzu, management and directors were from Press Kogyo.

5. While the interest rate charged by government small business banks was typically below market rates, as owner/manager he could not afford the time needed to meet documentation requirements. Moreover, each government loan had to be applied for separately, while with local banks he could roll over a loan or renew a credit line with a single visit.

6. Suzuki had investigated purchasing steel directly. He would have realized a substantial one-time savings, as wholesalers could be paid under promissory notes of up to five months' duration. However, Suzuki would have had to bear any price fluctuations and might face availability problems and fluctuations in steel quality as wholesalers bought from several producers. He thus adjudged the benefit not worth the risk.

7. Kato had sent *shukko* to only one other supplier, and then only one person. As noted in the Soja Park case study of chapter 2, the reassignment of technical or other personnel to customers or suppliers was not unusual in the auto industry.

8. An NC (numerically controlled) turret punch substituted for a cutting torch. It had a single punch that could be moved rapidly across a sheet of steel, knocking out holes 5 to 10 mm in diameter several times a second. These could be slightly overlapped to make accurate, irregular-shaped blanks, and once the programming was done, setup costs were minimal—although the edges had then to be smoothed.

9. Data are from an extended interview with Mr. Sembokuya and two other top managers at his firm, a tour of his facilities, press clippings, and brochures and other unpublished materials.

10. He had little capital and was unable to borrow from local financial institutions or obtain credit with local wholesalers, so for materials he had to go to the supplier of Jidosha Denki in Tokyo.

11. Aoyama finished only junior high and so was passed over for promotion at Hitachi and eventually "loaned" (*shukko*) to Jidosha Denki. Going to a smaller firm offered him better prospects.

12. Jidosha Denki had a thirty-member supplier association, but data were not available to corroborate or qualify Sembokuya's statements.

13. EDMs use electric current in a very fine wire to cut metal. Because there were no tools to be abraded, they permitted dies to be machined with a dimensional accuracy of 3–4 microns (thousands of a millimeter).

14. He regularly shipped complicated dies or prototype parts within a few days, while a traditional tool-and-die manufacturer might require a month or more. If his advertising brochures are to be believed, his prices were one-seventh those of firms using the older, manual techniques.

15. While some employees held shares, he had no outside investors.

His new financial director was looking into venture capital and other means of raising equity. At ¥60 million ($500,000), the firm's capitalization was less than annual depreciation, and only 10% of the anticipated cost of the new factory.

16. For a brief English-language reference to such programs see U.S. Congress, Office of Technology Assessment (1990:chap. 6).

17. From data on the Kato Shatai Kyoryoku Kai (supplier association), which in 1984 encompassed 39 parts firms and 7 inside contractors.

SIX / The Management of Subcontracting:
Innovations in Strategies and Techniques

1. Many other techniques are being paraded in the U.S. but are less important. For example, in Japan QC circles were largely a tool for improving shop-floor labor relations, and resembled techniques that have long been employed in the U.S. and Europe (Walton 1985).

2. Asanuma (1985b) notes that uncertainty over the identity of the eventual supplier was greatest for items such as batteries, tires and other discrete components made with technologies divergent from that of the auto makers. Such purchases are much closer to the American "auction" model than to the Japanese "cost-index" model emphasized here.

3. For Mazda, the targets for the semiannual adjustments following the first oil crisis (1974–1975) were 5%, 3%, 2%, and 2%, or 12% over two years. The 1988 target was 10% over six months, and a total of 50% over the succeeding five semiannual periods (Ikeda 1988a:18–19).

4. I thank Professor Fred Spengler of Virginia Polytechnic Institute for taking time to discuss VA/VE with me and to help place it in context with other industrial engineering techniques.

5. Along with "the" book by Miles see the annual conference volumes of the Society of American Value Engineers (SAVE) and (in Japanese) the Society of Japanese Value Engineers (SJVE).

6. See, for example, SJVE (1985:2, 9) and Isuzu Kyowa Kai (1972:5). Interfirm VA programs began at Isuzu in 1969, with the establishment of standard procedures for coordinating with Isuzu, and the collation of a manual. At Mitsubishi, interfirm VA programs dated from 1980.

7. Corey (1978) notes that in 1973 GM intervened on behalf of suppliers to obtain specific types of steel. Japanese efforts, however, were not limited to times of crisis. This was possible in part because Japan has no analog to the Robinson-Patman Act, which in the U.S. restricted the ability of firms to price-discriminate by offering volume discounts to large customers, and hence made attempts by the auto firms to obtain discounts less fruitful.

8. Note that seven firms (8%) reported *no* use of kanban. Toyota

sources consistently claim greater rates of diffusion than Shiomi found, and probably otherwise overstate the uniqueness of their kanban system.

9. During 1989–1990, T. Boone Pickens, an American investor active in corporate mergers and acquisitions, bought over 20% of the stock of Koito, which supplies Toyota with headlamps and similar fixtures. Despite now being the largest shareholder, Pickens has to date been unable to obtain a seat on the board or otherwise exert much influence.

10. The obvious end-game strategy to a limited series of transactions is to take advantage of the other party; there is no future reprisal or loss of business to worry about. But if I am going to be betrayed tomorrow, should I not betray today?—and so on, back to the first step. One saving aspect is that, if there is uncertainty about when the last transaction will occur, cooperation may then again become rational.

11. Thus U.S. auto parts manufacturers have been offered orders for insignificant items or products they do not routinely make. Yet the Japanese auto companies may have viewed this as a necessary initial step before a major order, rather than being a polite rejection.

12. He continues, noting that "The objective of systems contracting [his approach] is to develop long-term associations with selected suppliers so that they become even more efficient in their ability to provide needed supplies with a high degree of reliability." This contrasts with classic purchasing, "the art of buying the right material at the right price. Is this [appropriate]? What about inventory control, delivery times, points of delivery, cost versus price, and so on?"

13. In the U.S. dual sourcing of the identical part was prevalent, and there were on average ten suppliers companywide. Contracts were also shifted more readily. (Anecdotes in Detroit suggest that on occasion a contract was shifted merely to "keep suppliers on their toes," or even out of sheer nastiness.)

SEVEN / Subcontracting in Other Industries

1. These include: automatic transmissions, piston rings, timing belts, engine bearings, engine valves, carburetors, fuel pumps, distributors, alternators, starters, spark plugs, air conditioners, headlights, gauges, speedometers, automatic transmissions, clutch housings, disc brake assemblies, shock absorbers and leaf and coil springs.

2. But several component manufacturers have factories adjacent to plants of Toyota, Mitsubishi Motors and Mazda, which are remote from other customers, so this is not uniformly true.

3. As with Kakaa Denka, this name is suitably anonymous. To preserve anonymity, data from published materials are not cited. For background on the watch industry see Knickerbocker (1976), Chusho Kigyo

Chosa Kyokai (1978), Uchihashi (1978), R. Ono (1980), (Takugin) Chosa Geppo (1983), Hattori (1985), Landes (1985), Hoff (1987) and Porter (1989).

4. See Hattori (1985) on diversification at Daini Seikosha, another watch manufacturer. He noted that the watch market was not expanding, and diversification was needed to maintain permanent employment.

5. Kachikachi did not produce digital watches; all its electronic ones were "analog," encompassing small motors to drive the hands, together with the associated battery, quartz crystal and integrated circuit.

6. In the commercially oriented former castle town where the affiliate was located, factory work was looked down upon. Kachikachi was in an old silk and textile region, and it was socially acceptable for women to work in factories, and to continue working after marriage. Women who quit because of marriage in their fifth through tenth year in the firm could collect a separation allowance of a month's base pay for each year of work. Otherwise (including for male employees) voluntary separation resulted in a low allowance relative to that received upon involuntary separation or retirement. The voluntary separation payment increased in stages, and reached parity with retirement bonuses at twenty-five years' tenure—when a worker would still be young enough to try starting his own firm.

7. At the parent factory of Kachikachi Corp the average tenure of women was seven years (eleven years for men) and average pay was ¥146,000 a month (¥242,000 for men). However sharp the contrast with other locales, relative to men, women still tended to quit early in their careers.

8. In 1984 it also made integrated circuits and liquid crystal displays for computers and for Taiwanese and Hong Kong makers of inexpensive watches.

9. See Knickerbocker (1976), Landes (1985) and OECD (1988:181–202) on the Swiss industry and on Timex, a U.S. firm that adopted an integrated manufacturing approach in 1950, with great success.

10. Breakdowns for the remaining 17%, which included depreciation and profits, were not provided. Value added in watch manufacture was of the same magnitude as total purchases, while most purchases were of materials. In the automotive industry value added was but half of purchases, and most purchases were of parts. Finally, note that manufacturing costs were a fraction of final retail price. Distribution costs averaged 80% of the $60 retail price of Daini Seiko watches, which occupied a similar market niche to Kachikachi watches (Hattori 1985:108).

11. There were three broad segments to the mid-priced market in 1984: thin watches with clean lines for the domestic, the U.S., and European markets; watches with gadgetry for Southeast Asia; and heavy, gaudy watches for less developed countries elsewhere.

12. Kachikachi's distribution network and marketing strategy were not geared to the low end of the market, and so they made no "cheap"

LCD watches themselves, to avoid muddying their several upscale brand names.

13. Kachikachi had purchased various assets of a near-bankrupt firm, and had not deliberately sought to have its own case-making operation.

14. See Asanuma (1989) for detailed data from one firm he studied. For 1982, the broad census class of electrical machinery included 1.5 million workers in 30,000 establishments (versus 0.9 million in 12,000 establishments for transport equipment). Only 52% worked in establishments with over 200 employees (versus 67% in medium and large establishment for transport equipment).

15. At a Kachikachi supplier, homeworkers put masking tape on watch hands for two-tone plating. The use of homeworkers is legal in Japan but generally illegal in the U.S. New England wholesalers of home-knit sweaters had to go to Congress to ask for an exemption.

16. Data are from Chuo Daigaku Keizai Kenkyusho (1976) and conversations with Professor Masayoshi Ikeda on Hitachi and other consumer electronics firms.

17. Changes in manufacturing technology could have a similar impact; when and if flexible manufacturing becomes more feasible, interaction from the design stage and closer coordination of capacity may increase in importance. See Jaikumar (1986, 1988) and Piore and Sable (1984).

18. For machining, this section draws upon interviews with Sumitomo Machinery and several small firms, upon Jaikumar (1986, 1988) in English and upon Kikai Shinko Kyokai (1966), Hoshino and Kosaka (1960), and Y. Sato (1981) in Japanese. See Friedman (1988) for an excellent recent study.

19. The Ota district took shape in the 1930s, but the Kawaguchi district had its roots in traditional iron foundries, and dated back over two centuries.

20. Data on printing are drawn from interviews in the Koishikawa neighborhood, where I lived, and from Sugita (1982). The printing district began to form early in this century.

21. This section draws upon interviews with small construction contractors in both the U.S. and Japan, and for steel, personal communication with Professor Kazuo Koike. See also Itozono (1978).

22. I presume that marine engines were ordered by the purchaser directly from the manufacturer and then installed by the shipbuilder, as is the case in the U.S. even with diesel engines for trucks.

23. See Imai and Itami (1984) on Epson printers, Hillkirk and Jacobson (1986) on Fuji Xerox copiers, Sako (1988) on printed circuit board suppliers for consumer electronics and Nishiguchi (1989:chs. 5, 6) on household consumer electronics.

EIGHT / Conclusion

1. In Japan, the auto firms have been relatively successful in forcing dealerships to carry only "genuine" parts. Since there is only a weak system of independent car repair shops, it was sufficient for the auto companies to control distribution and not manufacturing.

2. I thank Banri Asanuma for suggesting that the wage gap was smaller. See Gavin Wright (1987) on geographical change. Data on relative wages are from the U.S. *Monthly Labor Survey.*

3. They describe design practices that suggest the use of VA by Fuji Xerox and Xerox, though they do not refer to value engineering by name (Hillkirk and Jacobson 1986:108, 179, 235).

Bibliography

The following bibliography includes several types of items. First, it incorporates all items cited in the book. However, unpublished materials such as financial statements and corporate brochures are not included, nor (to maintain confidentiality) are interviews. Second, writings useful as references or that influenced my research are also included. I have tried to be more thorough in this regard with the Japanese than the English language literature, but have avoided providing extensive citations to the general economics literature on the theory of the firm, on efficient contracting and antitrust. The interested reader should instead refer to the bibliographies in Holmstrom and Tirole (1989), Katz (1989), Kreps (1990), Perry (1989) and Williamson (1985).

Serials and Statistical Compilations

(Aichi) Keizai Kenkyu (Economic Studies), Nagoya: Aichi Prefecture.

Automotive News, weekly.

Census of Manufactures. See *Kogyo Tokei Hyo.*

Chosa Daijesuto (Research Digest), Tokyo: Chusho Kigyo Jigyodan and Chusho Kigyo Joho Sentaa, monthly.

Chosa Geppo (Monthly Research Report), Tokyo: Kokumin Kinyu Koko, monthly.

Chosa Jiho (Research News), Tokyo: Chusho Kigyo Kinyu Koko, monthly.

Chuo Koron Keiei Mondai (Chuo Koron Management Issues), Tokyo: Chuo Koron Sha, quarterly. (Superseded by *Will*, monthly.)

Chusho Kigyo Kiho (Small Business Quarterly Report), Osaka: Osaka Keizai Daigaku Chusho Kigyo Keiei Kenkyusho.

Chusho Kigyo Hakusho (Small Business White Paper). Japan. Chusho Kigyo Cho (Small and Medium Enterprise Agency), annual.

Engineering Industries of Japan, Tokyo: Kikai Shinko Kyokai (Machine Industries Promotion Association), irregular.

Fortune, biweekly.

Japan. Rodosho. 1954. *Shokushu-betsu To Chingin Jittai Chosa/Kojin-betsu Chingin Chosa: Kekka Hokoku Sho* (Report on the Survey of Individual and Craft Wages: "Wage Census"). Tokyo: Rodo Horei Kyokai.

———— 1964. *Chingin Sensasu: Chingin Kozo Kihon Tokei Chosa* (Wage Census). Tokyo: Rodo Horei Kyokai.

———— 1974. *Chingin Kozo Kihon Tokei Chosa Hokoku* (Wage Census). Tokyo: Rodo Horei Kyokai.

Japan Economic Journal, weekly.

Japanese Economic Studies, quarterly.

Harvard Business Review, bimonthly.

Kaisha Shiki Ho (Quarterly Handbook of Listed Companies). Tokyo: Toyo Keizai Shimpo Sha, quarterly.

Keiken Shiryo. Osaka: Osaka Furitsu Shoko Keizai Kenkyusho (Economic Institute Reports) (Osaka Prefecture Research Center on Commerce and Economics), irregular.

Keizai Hakusho (Economic White Paper). Japan. Keizai Kikaku Cho (Economic Planning Agency), annual.

Kikai Keizai Kenkyu. Tokyo: Kikai Shinko Kyokai (Machine Industries Economic Studies Promotion Associations), irregular.

Kikan Gendai Keizai, (Modern Economics) quarterly.

Kogyo Jittai Kihon Chosa Hokokusho: Sokatsu Hen (Dai 6–kai) (Sixth Basic Survey of Manufacturing: Summary Volume). 1984. Japan. Chusho Kigyo Cho and Tsusho Sangyosho (MITI), survey of year-end 1981.

———— *Kogyo Jittai Kihon Chosa Hokokusho: Sokatsu Hen (Dai 5–kai)* (Fifth Basic Survey of Manufacturing: Summary Volume). 1979. Survey of year-end 1976.

Kogyo Tokei Hyo (Census of Manufactures). Japan Ministry of International Trade and Industry, annual.

Nenpo Nihon no Rodo Kankei (Yearbook of Japanese Labour Relations). Tokyo: Nihon Rodo Kyokai, annual.

Nihon Keizai Shimbun (Japan Economic Journal), daily newspaper.

Nihon Kogyo Shimbun (Japan Industrial Journal) daily newspaper.

Nihon no Jidosha Buhin Kogyo (Japan Automotive Parts Industry Yearbook). Tokyo: Auto Trade Journal, annual.

Nikkan Kogyo Shimbun, daily newspaper (Daily Industrial Journal).

Nihon Rodo Kyokai Zasshi. Tokyo: Nihon Rodo Kyokai (Japan Labour Association Magazine), monthly.

Purchasing. Boston: Cahners Publications, monthly.

Reports, Kikai Shinko Kyokai, irregular monograph series.

Rodo Jiho (Labor Report). Ministry of Labor, monthly.

Rodo Keizai no Bunseki ("Rodo Hakusho") (White Paper on Labor). Japan Ministry of Labor, annual.

Rodo Tokei Chosa Geppo Japan Ministry of Labor, monthly (Monthly Labor Statistics).

Shakai Seisaku Jiho, monthly, (pre-1945).

Shoko Kinyu. Tokyo: Shoko Kumiai Chuo Kinko, monthly, Comercial and Industrial Cooperatives Finance.

Yuka Shoken Hokoku Sho (Semi-annual financial statements), published for all companies listed on Japanese stock exchanges, Tokyo: Okurasho Insatsu Kyoku.

Articles and Monographs

Abegglen, James C. 1958. *The Japanese Factory: Aspects of its Social Organization.* Glencoe, Ill: Free Press. Updated as *Management and Worker: The Japanese Solution.* Tokyo: Sophia University and Kodansha International, 1973.

Abernathy, William J. 1978. *The Productivity Dilemma: Roadblock to Innovation in the Automobile Industry.* Baltimore: Johns Hopkins University Press.

Acheson, James M. 1985. "The Maine Lobster Market: Between Market and Hierarchy." *Journal of Law, Economics and Organization* 1(2):385–98.

Aichi Ken Keizai Kenkyusho. 1967. *Tokai Chiku ni okeru Jidosha Buhin Kogyo no Kozo Henka to Saihensei* (The Changing Structure of the Automotive Parts Industry in the Tokai Region). Nagoya, Japan: Aichi Ken Keizai Kenkyusho.

——— 1970. *Jidosha Buhin Kogyo no Jittai: Niji Meekaa no Henbo wo chushin to shite* (The Automotive Parts Industry: Second-Tier Suppliers). Report No. 93, Nagoya, Japan: Aichi Ken Keizai Kenkyusho.

——— 1978. "Jidosha Kanren Chusho Kogyo no Jittai to Mondaiten" (Status and Problems of Small and Medium Automotive Ancillary Firms). *(Aichi) Keizai Kenkyu* (January), no. 120, pp. 1–69. Nagoya, Japan: Aichi Ken Keizai Kenkyusho.

——— 1982. "Jidosha Kanren Chusho Kogyo Jittai Chosa Kekka (Dai 2 Ho): Nishi Mikawa Chiku wo chushin to shite" (Report on the Survey of Small and Medium Automotive Ancillary Firms [Second Report]: Firms in the West Mikawa District). *(Aichi) Keizai Jiho* (January), no. 135, pp. 63–166. Nagoya, Japan: Aichi Ken Keizai Kenkyusho.

Akebono Brake. 1979. *Akebono Brake 40–Nen Shi* (40 Year History of Akebono Brake). Tokyo: Akebono Brake.

Akerlof, George A. and Janet L. Yellen. 1990. "The Fair Wage-Effort Hypothesis and Unemployment," *Quarterly Journal of Economics* (May), 105(2):255–83.

Alchian, Armen A. and H. Demsetz. 1972. "Production. Information Costs, and Economic Organization," *American Economic Review* (December), pp. 777–95.

Alchian, Armen A. and Susan Woodward. 1988. "The Firm is Dead; Long Live the Firm: A Review of Oliver E. Williamson's *The Economic Institutions of Capitalism.*" *Journal of Economic Literature* (March), 26(1):65–79.

Allinson, Gary Dean. 1975. "The Moderation of Organized Labor in Postwar Japan." *Journal of Japanese Studies* (Spring), 1(2):409–36.

——— 1975. *Japanese Urbanism: Industry and Politics in Kariya.* Berkeley: University of California Press.

Amagai, Shogo. 1982. *Nihon Jidosha Kogyo no Shiteki Tenkai* (Historical Perspectives on the Japanese Automotive Industry). Tokyo: Aki Shobo.

Aoki, Masahiko. 1984. "Aspects of the Japanese Firm." In Masahiko Aoki, ed., *The Economic Analysis of the Japanese Firm.* Amsterdam: Elsevier/North-Holland.

——— 1984. *The Cooperative Game Theory of the Firm.* London: Clarenden Press of Oxford University Press.

——— 1986. "Horizontal vs. Vertical Information Structure of the Firm." *American Economic Review* (December), 76(5):971–83.

——— 1987. "The Japanese Firm in Transition." In Kozo Yamamura and Yasukichi Yasuba, eds., *The Political Economy of Japan.* Volume 1: *The Domestic Transformation.* Stanford: Stanford University Press.

Arnesen, Peter J., ed. 1987. *The Japanese Competition: Phase 2.* Michigan Papers in Japanese Studies No. 15. Ann Arbor: Center for Japanese Studies, University of Michigan.

——— 1987. *Is There Enough Business to Go Around?—Overcapacity in the Auto Industry.* Michigan Papers in Japanese Studies No. 16. Ann Arbor: Center for Japanese Studies, University of Michigan.

Arrow, Kenneth J. 1974. *The Limits of Organization.* New York: Norton.

Asanuma Banri. 1985a. "The Organization of Parts Purchases in the Japanese Automotive Industry." *Japanese Economic Studies* (Summer), 13(4):32–53.

——— 1985b. "The Contractual Framework for Parts Supply in the Japanese Automotive Industry." *Japanese Economic Studies* (Summer), 13(4):54–78.

——— 1986. "Transactional Structure of Parts Supply in the Japanese Automobile and Electric Machinery Industries: A Comparative Analysis." Technical Report No. 3, Socio-Economic Systems Research Project, Kyoto University.

——— 1989. "Manufacturer-Supplier Relationships in Japan and the Concept of Relation-Specific Skill." *Journal of the Japanese and International Economies* 3:1 (March), 1–30.

Asao, Boichi. 1983. "Jidosha Kogyo ni okeru Rodo Ryoku Ruigata" (Job Structures in the Automotive Industry). *Kenkyu Kiyo*, Nihon Fukushi Daigaku, (September), no. 57, pp. 63–131.

Axelrod, Robert. 1984. *The Evolution of Cooperation.* New York: Basic Books.

Benke, Ralph L., Jr. and James Don Edwards. 1980. *Transfer Pricing: Techniques and Uses.* New York: National Association of Accountants.

Bhote, Keki R. 1987. *Supply Management: How to Make U.S. Suppliers Competitive.* AMA Management Briefing. New York: American Management Association.

Blois, K. J. 1978. "A Pricing Model of Vertical Quasi-Integration." *European Economic Review* 11(2):291–303.

Bolton, Ralph A. 1979. *Systems Contracting: A New Look.* American Management Associations Management Briefing. New York: AMA-COM.

Brown, Clair and Michael Reich. 1989. "When Does Union-Management Cooperation Work? A Look at NUMMI and GM-Van Nuys." *California Management Review* (Summer), 31(4):26–44.

Burt, David N. 1989. "Managing Suppliers Up to Speed." *Harvard Business Review* (July-August), pp. 127–35.

Buttrick, John. 1952. "The Inside Contract System." *Journal of Economic History* 12(3):205–21.

Cable, John and Hirohiko Yasuki. 1985. "International Organization, Business Groups and Corporate Performance: An Empirical Test of the Multidivisional Hypothesis in Japan." *International Journal of Industrial Organization* 3(3):401–20.

Cain, Glen G. 1976. "The Challenge of Segmented Labor Market Theories to Orthodox Theory: A Survey." *Journal of Economic Literature* (December), 14(4):1215–57.

Chandler, Alfred. 1962. *Strategy and Structure.* Cambridge: MIT Press.

—— 1964. *Giant Enterprise: Ford, G.M. and the Automobile Industry.* Boston: Harcourt, Brace & World.

—— 1977. *The Visible Hand: The Managerial Revolution in American Business.* Cambridge: Harvard University Press/Belknap Books.

—— 1982. "The M-Form: Industrial Groups, American Style." *European Economic Review* 19(1):3–23.

Chosa Daijesto. 1980. "Kokusai Bungyo ga Shitauke Kigyo ni ataeru Eikyo: Jidosha Sangyo" (The Impact of the International Division of Labor on Subcontractors: The Automotive Industry). *Chosa Daijesuto,* no. 461.

—— 1982. "Kikai Kogyo 4 Gyoshu no Gijutsu Kakushin to Seisan Kozo no Henka: Kosaku Kikai, Minseiyo Denshi Kikai, Jidosha, Kamera" (Technical Change and the Organization of Production in 4 Machinery Industries: Machine Tools, Consumer Electronics, Automobiles and Cameras). *Chosa Daijesuto,* no. 545.

Chosa Jiho. 1955. "Jidosha Kogyo ni okeru Shitauke Kigyo no Mondai" (Problems of Subcontractors in the Auto Industry). *Chosa Jiho* (Chusho Kigyo Kinyu Koko) (August), pp. 7–11.

—— 1960. "Kigyo Keiretsu to Chusho Kigyo no Kaizo Bunseki" (Manufacturing Keiretsu and the Vertical Structure of Small and Medium Firms). *Chosa Jiho* (Chusho Kigyo Kinyu Koko) (August), pp. 1–11.

Chuo Daigaku Keizai Kenkyusho. 1976. *Chusho Kigyo No Kaizo Kenkyu* (Hierarchy In Small Business). Tokyo: Chuo Daigaku Shuppanbu.

Chusho Kigyo Cho (Small and Medium Business Agency). 1965. *Kigyo Kan Shinyo no Gyoshu Betsu Jittai: Kigyokan Shinyo Jittai Chosa Hokoku* (Status of Interfirm Credit by Industry: A Report on the Survey of Interfirm Credit).

Chusho Kigyo Chosa Kyokai. 1977. *Shitauke Keiretsu Kozo Chosa Hokoku Sho* (Report on the Subcontracting Structure Survey). Tokyo: Chusho Kigyo Chosa Kyokai.

—— 1978. *Tokei Kogyo ni okeru Shitauke Keiretsu Kozo Chosa Hokokusho* (Report on the Survey of Subcontracting Structure in the Watch and Clock Industries). Tokyo: Chusho Kigyo Chosa Kyokai.

Chusho Kigyo Kenkyu Sentaa. 1968a. *Jidosha Buhin Kogyo no Genjo to Mondaiten: Jidosha Buhin Kogyo Jittai Chosa Hokokusho* (Status and Issues of the Automotive Parts Industry: Report on a Survey of the Automotive Parts Industry). Chosa Kenkyu Series 2. Tokyo: Chusho Kigyo Kenkyu Sentaa.

—— 1968b. *Jidosha Buhin Kogyo Jittai Chosa Shukei Hokokusho* (Report on the Survey of the Automotive Parts Industry: Statistical Appendix). Chosa Kenkyu Series 2. Tokyo: Chusho Kigyo Kenkyu Sentaa.

—— 1977. *Wagakuni ni okeru Gaichu, Shitauke Kanri no Tomen suru Kadai to sono Tenbo: Kikai Kogyo wo chushin to shite* (Current and Future Issues in the Management of Purchasing and Subcontracting in Japan: The Machinery Industries). Survey Report No. 19. Tokyo: Chusho Kigyo Kenkyu Sentaa.

—— 1979. *Jidosha Sangyo Ni Okeru Gaichu Kanri no Arata na Doko: Seisan Taisei tono Kanrensei wo Megutte* (New Developments in Subcontractor Management in the Automotive Industry: How They Relate to the Production System). Survey Report No. 24. Chusho Kigyo Kenkyu Sentaa.

Clark, Kim B., Bruce W. Chew and Takahiro Fujimoto. 1987. "Product Development in the World Auto Industry." *Brookings Papers on Economic Activity* Special Issue on Microeconomics. 3:729–81.

Clark, Robert C. 1985. "Agency Costs versus Fiduciary Duties." In John Pratt and Richard Zeckhauser, eds., *Principles and Agents: The Structure of Business.* Boston: Harvard Business School Press.

Clark, Rodney C. 1979. *The Japanese Company.* New Haven: Yale University Press.

Coase, Ronald H. 1937. "The Nature of the Firm." *Economica* (November), 4:397–405.

———— 1988. "The Nature of the Firm: Origin, Meaning, Influence." *Journal of Law, Economics, and Organization* (Spring), 4(1):3–47.

Cohen, Jerome B. 1949. *Japan's Economy in War and Reconstruction*. Minneapolis: University of Minnesota Press.

Cole, Robert E. 1971. *Japanese Blue Collar: The Changing Tradition*. Berkeley: University of California Press.

———— 1979. *Work, Mobility and Participation: A Comparison of Yokohama and Detroit Workers*. Berkeley: University of California Press.

Cole, Robert E. and Taizo Yakushiji, eds. 1984. *The American and Japanese Auto Industries in Transition*. Ann Arbor: Center for Japanese Studies, University of Michigan.

Corey, Raymond E. 1978. *Procurement Management: Strategy, Organization, and Decision-Making*. Boston: CBI Publishing Company.

Crandall, Robert 1968. "Vertical Integration and the Market for Repair Parts in the United States Automobile Industry." *Journal of Industrial Economics* (July), pp. 212–234.

Cremer, Jacques 1986. "Cooperation in Ongoing Organizations." *The Quarterly Journal of Economics* (February), 101(1):33–49.

Cusumano, Michael A. 1985. *The Japanese Automobile Industry, Technology and Management at Nissan and Toyota*. Cambridge: Harvard University Press.

Cyert, R. M. and J. G. March. 1963. *A Behavioral Theory of the Firm*. Englewood Cliffs, N.J.: Prentice-Hall.

Dasgupta, Partha. 1988. "Trust as a Commodity." In Diego Gambetta, ed., *Trust*. London: Blackwell.

Demsetz, Harold. 1988. "The Theory of the Firm Revisited." *Journal of Law, Economics and Organization* 4(1):141–161.

Dertouzos, Michael L. et al. 1989. *Made in America: Regaining the Productive Edge*. Cambridge: MIT Press.

Diesel Kiki Co., Ltd. 1981. *Diesel Kiki 40–Nen Shi* (40 Year History of Diesel Kiki).

Dodwell Marketing Consultants. 1986. *The Structure of the Japanese Auto Parts Industry*. Tokyo: Dodwell.

Doeringer, Peter B. 1984. "Internal Labor Markets and Paternalism in Rural Areas." In Paul Osterman, ed., *Internal Labor Markets*. Cambridge: MIT Press.

Dore, Ronald P. 1983. "Goodwill and the Spirit of Market Capitalism." *British Journal of Sociology* 34(4):459–82.

———— 1986. *Flexible Rigidities*. Stanford University Press.

Dowst, Somerby. 1982. "Xerox Centralizes Buys for Cost Fight." *Purchasing* 93(7):56–59.

Eccles, Robert G. 1985. *The Transfer Pricing Problem: A Theory for Practice*. Lexington, Mass.: Lexington Books.

Ehrenberg, Ronald and Robert Smith. 1985. *Modern Labor Economics.* 2d ed. New York: Scott, Foresman.

Flath, David. 1989. "Vertical Restraints in Japan." *Japan and the World Economy* 1(2):187–203.

Foulkes, Fred K. 1980. *Personnel Policies in Large Nonunion Companies.* Englewood Cliffs, N.J.: Prentice-Hall.

Friedman, David 1988. *The Misunderstood Miracle: Industrial Development and Political Change in Japan.* Ithaca: Cornell University Press.

Fruin, W. Mark. 1978. "The Japanese Company Controversy: Ideology and Organization in a Historical Perspective." *Journal of Japanese Studies* 4(2):267–300.

——— 1983. *Kikkoman: Company, Clan, Community.* Cambridge: Harvard University Press.

——— forthcoming. *The Japanese Enterprise System: Competitive Strategies and Corporate Structures.* New York: Oxford University Press.

Fujita, Keizo. 1965. *Nihon Sangyo Kozo to Chusho Kigyo* (Japanese Industrial Structure and Small and Medium Enterprises). Tokyo: Iwanami Shoten.

Funahashi, Naomichi. 1974. "The Industrial Reward System: Wages and Benefits." In Kazuo Okochi, Bernard Karsh and Solomon B. Levine, eds., *Workers and Employers in Japan: The Japanese Employment Relations System.* Princeton: Princeton University Press and University of Tokyo Press.

Galante, Steven P. "Merger of Two Bakers Teaches Distributors a Costly Lesson." *Wall Street Journal* September 14, 1987.

Gambetta, Diego. 1988. "Can We Trust Trust?" In Diego Gambetta, ed., *Trust.* London: Blackwell.

Genther, Phyllis. 1990. *A History of Japan's Government-Business Relationship: The Passenger Car Industry.* Michigan Papers in Japanese Studies No. 20. Ann Arbor: Center for Japanese Studies, University of Michigan.

——— 1986. "The Changing Government-Business Relationship: Japan's Passenger Car Industry." Ph.D. dissertation, George Washington University.

Good, David. 1988. "Individuals, Interpersonal Relations, and Trust." In Diego Gambetta, ed., *Trust.* London: Blackwell.

Gordon, Andrew. 1985. *The Evolution of Labor Relations in Japan: Heavy Industry, 1853–1955.* Cambridge: Harvard University Press.

Goto, Akira. 1982. "Business Groups in a Market Economy." *European Economic Review* 19(1):53–70.

Gould, William B. 1984. *Japan's Reshaping of American Labor Laws.* Cambridge: MIT Press.

Halberstam, David. 1986. *The Reckoning.* Paperback ed. New York: William Morrow.

Haley, John O. 1988. "Introduction: Legal vs. Social Controls." In John O. Haley, ed., *Law and Society in Contemporary Japan: American Perspectives.* Dubuque, Iowa: Kendall/Hunt.

Hall, Robert W. 1981. *Driving the Productivity Machine: Production Planning and Control in Japan.* Falls Church, Va.: American Production and Inventory Control Society.

———— 1982. *Kawasaki U.S.A.: Transferring Japanese Production Methods to the United States, A Case Study.* Falls Church, Va.: American Production and Inventory Control Society.

Harrigan, Kathryn R. 1983. *Strategies for Vertical Integration.* Lexington, Mass.: Lexington Books.

Hattori, Ichiro. 1985. "Product Diversification." In Lester C. Thurow, ed., *The Management Challenge: Japanese Views.* Cambridge: MIT Press.

Hayes, Edward J. 1984. "Evolving Manufacturer-Supplier Relationships." In Robert E. Cole, ed., *The American Automobile Industry: Rebirth or Requiem?* Michigan Papers in Japanese Studies No. 13. Ann Arbor: Center for Japanese Studies, University of Michigan.

HBS Case Services. 1982. "Toyo Kogyo Co. Ltd. (A)." Case #682–092. Boston: HBS Case Services.

———— 1982. "Toyo Kogyo Co. Ltd. (B)." Case #682–093. Boston: HBS Case Services.

Helper, Susan. 1987. "Supplier Relations and Technical Change: Theory and Application to the US Automobile Industry." Ph.D. dissertation, Harvard University.

———— 1990a. "Strategy and Irreversibility in Supplier Relations: The Case of the US Automobile Industry." *Business History Review,* forthcoming.

———— 1990b. "Subcontracting: Innovative Labor Strategies." *Labor Research Review* (April), no. 15, pp. 89–99.

———— 1990c. "Comparative Supplier Relations in the US and Japanese Auto Industries: An Exit/Voice Approach." *Business and Economic History* 2nd series, 19:153–162.

Hill, Hal. 1981. "Subcontracting and Technological Diffusion in Philippine Manufacturing." Discussion Paper No. 81–12. Quezon City: School of Economics, University of the Philippines.

Hillkirk, John and Gary Jacobson. 1986. *Xerox: American Samurai.* New York: Macmillan.

Hirao, Koji 1964. "Shitauke Keiretsu Kigyo ni miru Kozo Henka" (Structural Change Among *Keiretsu* Subcontractors). *Keizai Hyoron* 13(4):40–52.

Hiromoto, Toshiro. 1988. "Another Hidden Edge—Japanese Management Accounting." *Harvard Business Review* (July-Aug), 88(4):22–26.

Hirosaki, Shinhachiro. 1941. *Nihon no Romu Kanri* (Personnel Management for Japan). Tokyo: Toyo Shokan.

Hirschman, Albert O. 1986. "Exit and Voice: An Expanding Sphere of Influence" (reprinted from *The New Palgrave*). In *Rival Views of Market Society*. New York: Viking.

Hoff, Edward J. 1987. "Hattori-Seiko and the World Watch Industry in 1980." Case Study No. 9-385-300. Boston: Harvard Business School.

Holmstrom, Bengt and Joan Ricart i Costa. 1986. "Managerial Incentives and Capital Management." *Quarterly Journal of Economics* (November), pp. 837-60.

Holmstrom, Bengt R. and Jean Tirole. 1989. "The Theory of the Firm." In Richard Schmalensee and Robert D. Willig, eds., *Handbook of Industrial Organization*. vol. 1/ Amsterdam: North-Holland.

Hopwood, Anthony G. 1985. "The Growth of Worrying About Management Accounting," commentary on Robert S. Kaplan, "Accounting Lag." In Kim B. Clark, Robert H. Hayes and Christopher Lorenz, eds., *The Uneasy Alliance: Managing the Productivity-Technology Dilemma*. Boston: Harvard Business School Press.

Hoshino, Yoshiro and Masao Kosaka. 1960. "Kikai Kogyo no Shiteki Tenkai" (A Historical Perspective on the Machinery Industries). In Masao Kosaka, ed., *Kikai Kogyo* (Machinery Industries); vol. 5, part 1 of Hiromi Arisawa, general editor, *Gendai Nihon Sangyo Koza* (Studies on Modern Japanese Industry). Tokyo: Iwanami Shoten.

Ichikawa, Hirokatsu. 1965. "Jidosha Buhin" (Automotive Parts). *Chosa Jiho* (Chusho Kigyo Kinyu Koko) (January), 6(4):20-31.

——— 1965. "Jidosha Buhin Kogyo ni okeru Senmonka no Doko to Keiretsu Kigyo Saihensei no Mondaiten" (Specialization in the Automotive Parts Industry and the Reorganization of Supplier Keiretsu). *Chosa Jiho* (Chusho Kigyo Kinyu Koko) (September), 7(2):61-84.

Ichikawa, Shin. 1967. "Kanto Chiku Buhin Kogyo no Doko to Mondaiten" (Trends and Issues: Parts Suppliers in the Kanto Region). In Auto Trade Journal, ed., *Nihon no Jidosha Buhin Kogyo*.

Ijiro, Katsumi. 1981. "Kogyo Kikai Gyokai ni okeru Shitauke Kigyo no Genjo to Kadai" (Subcontractors in the Industrial Machinery Industry: Current Status and Issues). *Shoko Kinyu* (June), 31(6):46-59.

Ikari, Yoshiro. 1988. *Mitsubishi Jidosha Zenkai: Seme ni Tenjita Global Senryaku* (Mitsubishi Motors: Shifting to an Aggressive Global Strategy). Tokyo: Diamond Sha.

Ikeda, Masayoshi 1979. "The Subcontracting System in the Japanese Electronic Industry." *Engineering Industries of Japan* no. 19, pp. 43-71.

——— 1982. "Nichiei Jidosha Sangyo ni okeru Shitauke Kigyo no Kikaku Bunseki" (A Comparative Analysis of Subcontractors in the British and Japanese Automotive Industries). *Chosa Jiho* (Chusho Kigyo Kinyu Koko) (January), no. 249, pp. 41-57.

——— 1983a. "Shitauke Seisan Kozo to Nihon-teki Keiei" (The Structure of Subcontracting and Japanese-Style Management). *Nihon no Kagakusha* (June), 18(6):9–14.

———— 1983b. "Karaa Tereebi no Seisan Kozo to Shitauke Kigyo: Nagano-ken Nosanson Chiiki no Purinto Kiban Kumitate Shitauke Kigyo no Jittai Bunseki" (Subcontractors and the Organization of Color TV Production: A Study of Printed Circuit Subcontractors in Mountain Villages in Nagano). *Chuo Daigaku Keizai Kenkyu Nenpo* no. 13.

———— 1984a. "Rationalization After the Oil Shock: Production and Supplier Systems in the Electric Appliance and Automotive Industries." Draft Paper, Tokyo: Chuo University.

———— 1984b. "Haiteku ga Toyo no Suisu wo Nurikaeta" (High Technology is Repainting the Face of the Switzerland of Asia). *Economisuto* December 3.

———— 1984c. "Shoreisai Kigyo no ME-ka" (The Introduction of Mechatronics by Very Small Manufacturers). *Chosa Geppo (Kokumin Kinyu Koko)* (November).

———— 1987a. "An International Comparison of Subcontracting Systems in the Automobile Component Manufacturing Industry." Working Paper, First Policy Forum, MIT International Motor Vehicle Program.

———— 1987b. "The Japanese Auto Component Manufacturers' System for the Division of Production." Working Paper, First Policy Forum, MIT International Motor Vehicle Program.

———— 1988a. "Series: JIT Enters a New Phase in the Japanese Auto Industry (part 2)—An Approach to Japan's Subcontracting System." *InSite* (February), pp. 3–21.

———— 1988b. "A Comparative Study of International Subcontracting Systems: The Automotive Parts Industries of the United States, Great Britain, France and Japan." *InSite* (May), 3–15.

Imai, Kenichi and Hiroyuki Itami. 1984. "Interpenetration of Organization and Market: Japan's Firm and Market in Comparison with the U.S." *International Journal of Industrial Organization* 2(4):285–310.

Imai, Kenichi, Ikujiro Nonaka and Hirotaka Takeuchi. 1985. "Managing the New Product Development Process: How Japanese Companies Learn and Unlearn." In Kim Clark, Robert Hayes and Christopher Lorenz, eds., *The Uneasy Alliance: Managing the Productivity-Technology Dilemma*. Boston: Harvard Business School Press.

Inoue, Kazue. 1975. "Noson Kogyoka to Fujin Rodo" (Industrialization of Farm Villages and Married Female Workers). In Toshio Sakayori and Tadao Takagi, eds., *Gendai Nihon no Rodosha* (Workers in Modern Japan). Tokyo: Nihon Hyoron Sha.

Ishida, Hideto. 1983. "Anticompetitive Practices in the Distribution of Goods and Services in Japan: The Problem of Distribution Keiretsu." *Journal of Japanese Studies* (Summer), 9(2):317–34.

Isobe, Zoichi. 1964. "Jidosha Kogyo ni okeru Keiretsu" (Vertical Firm Groupings in the Automotive Industry). *Chosa Jiho* (Chusho Kigyo Kinyu Koko) (August), 6(3):20–31.

Isuzu Kyowa Kai. 1972. "Nenpyo: Isuzu Kyowa Kai 10–Nen Shi to Sono Haikei" (Chronology: Background and Ten Year History of the Isuzu Kyowa Kai). *Isuzu Kyowa Kai Kaiho* (Kyowa Kai Journal), Supplement.

Itami, Hiroyuki, et al. 1988. *Kyoso to Kakushin: Jidosha Sangyo no Kigyo Seicho* (Competition and Revolution: Corporate Growth in the Automotive Industry). Tokyo: Toyo Keizai Shimpo Sha.

Ito, Taikichi and Yasutaka Sakai 1967. *Jidosha Sangyo to Kigyo Keiretsu: Jidosha Buhin Kogyo no Kozo, Jittai, Tenbo* (Keiretsu and the Auto Industry: The Structure, Status and Prospects of the Auto Parts Industry). Tokyo: Keio Gijuku Daigaku Sangyo Kenkyusho.

Itozono, Tatsuo. 1978. *Nihon no Shagaiko Seido* (The Japanese Inside Contractor System). Tokyo: Minerva Shobo.

Iwata, Ryushi. 1982. *Japanese-Style Management: Its Foundations and Prospects.* Tokyo: Asian Productivity Organization.

Jacoby, Sanford M. 1985. *Employing Bureaucracy.* New York: Columbia University Press.

Jaikumar, Ramchandran. 1986. "Yamazaki Mazak (C)." Case Study #9–686–085. Boston: HBS Case Services.

———— 1988. "Yamazaki Mazak (A)." Case Study #9–686–083, revised version of 1986 case. Boston: HBS Case Services.

Japan. Tsusho Sangyo Sho, Jukogyo Kyoku. 1971. "Jidosha Buhin Kogyo Jittai Chosa" (Survey of the Automotive Parts Industry). Ministry of International Trade and Industry, Heavy Industry Division.

Jidosha Buhin Kogyokai and Nihon Kikai Kogyo Rengokai. 1957. *Jidosha Buhin Kogyo no Jittai.* Tokyo: Jidosha Buhin Kogyokai and Nihon Kikai Kogyo Rengokai.

Johnson, H. Thomas and Robert S. Kaplan. 1987. "The Rise and (Fall) of Management Accounting." *Management Accounting* (January), pp. 22–30.

Joskow, Paul L. 1985. "Vertical Integration and Long-Term Contracts: The Case of Coal-Burning Electric Generating Plants." *Journal of Law, Economics and Organization* (Spring), 1(1):33–80.

Kamata, Satoshi. 1982. *Japan in the Passing Lane: An Insider's Account of Life in a Japanese Auto Factory.* New York: Pantheon.

Kanagawa Ken (Kanagawa Prefecture). 1961. *Keihin Kogyo Jitai ni okeru Kanren Chusho Kogyo* (Ancillary Small and Medium Manufacturers in the Keihin [Tokyo-Yokohama] Region). vol. 1. Yokohama: Kanagawa Prefecture.

———— 1964. *Keihin Kogyo Jitai ni okeru Kanren Chusho Kogyo* (Ancillary Small and Medium Manufacturers in the Keihin [Tokyo-Yokohama]

Region). vol. 2: Tokei Hen (Statistics). Yokohama: Kanagawa Prefecture.

———— 1964. *Keihin Kogyo Jitai ni okeru Kanren Chusho Kogyo* (Ancillary Small and Medium Manufacturers in the Keihin Tokyo-Yokohama Region). vol. 3: Keesu Recoodo Hen (Case Studies). Yokohama: Kanagawa Prefecture.

Kanter, Rosabeth Moss. 1989. "Becoming PALs: Pooling, Allying and Linking Across Companies." *Academy of Management EXECUTIVE* 3(3):183–93.

Kaplan, Robert S. 1985. "Accounting Lag: The Obsolescence of Cost Accounting Systems." In Kim B. Clark, Robert H. Hayes and Christopher Lorenz, eds., *The Uneasy Alliance: Managing the Productivity-Technology Dilemma*. Boston: Harvard Business School Press.

———— 1984. "The Evolution of Management Accounting." *Accounting Review* (July), 59(3):390–418.

Karmarkar, Uday. 1989. "Getting Control of Just-in-Time." *Harvard Business Review* (September-October), 89:5.

Kato Shatai Kogyo 1971. *Michi: Kato Shatai Kogyo 70 Nen no Ayumi* (Paths: The 70–Year Journey of Kato Auto Body). Ebina City, Kanagawa Prefecture: Kato Shatai Kogyo.

Katz, Michael L. 1989. "Vertical Contractual Relations." Chapter 11 in Richard Schmalensee and Robert D. Willig, eds., *Handbook of Industrial Organization*, vol. 1. Amsterdam: North-Holland.

Kawada, Yoshio. 1972. "Kyoryoku Kojo e no VE Fukyu Tichaku-ka no tame no Ichi Kosatsu." *SJVE Nenkan* (Society of Japanese Value Engineers Yearbook), vol. 3.

Kawasaki, Seiichi and John McMillan. 1987. "The Design of Contracts: Evidence from Japanese Subcontracting." *Journal of the Japanese and International Economies* (September), 1(3):327–349.

Keller, Maryann. 1989. *Rude Awakening: The Rise, (Fall) and Struggle for Recovery of General Motors*. New York: William Morrow.

Kikai Shinko Kyokai Keizai Kenkyusho. 1981. *Jidosha Sangyo ni okeru Kokusai Bungyo no Hatten to Shitake Kigyo* (The Impact of Advancing International Division of Labor in the Automotive Industry on Subcontractors). Report No. 55–9. Tokyo: Kikai Shinko Kyokai.

———— 1980. *Kikai Kanren Shitauke Kigyo no Kokusai Kyosoryoku ni kansuru Chosa Kenkyu* (A Study on the International Competitiveness of Machinery Subcontractors). Report No. 54–5. Tokyo: Kikai Shinko Kyokai.

———— 1966. *Kikai Kogyo ni okeru Shitauke Kozo no Henbo Chosa* (A Study on the Changing Structure of Subcontracting in the Machinery Industries). Report No. 40–K161. Tokyo: Kikai Shinko Kyokai.

Kikan Chosa to Kenkyu. 1964. "Buhin Kogyo no Hatten wo Unagasu mono to Kobamu mono" (Factors Which Inhibit and Accelerate the Development of Parts Manufacturers). *Kikan Chosa to Kenkyu (Mitsubishi Keizai Kenkyusho)* 3(1):66–71.

Kikuchi, Hideyuki. 1976. *Wagakuni ni okeru Gaichu, Shitauke Kanri no Tenkai: Kikai Kogyo wo chushin ni shite* (The Evolution of Management of Subcontractors and Suppliers in Japan: Focusing on the Machinery Industries). Chosa Kenkyu Hokoku No. 18. Tokyo: Chusho Kigyo Kenyu Sentaa.

———— 1977. *Wagakuni ni okeru Gaichu, Shitauke Kanri no Tomen suru Kadai to sono Tenbo* (Current Issues and Prospects in the Management of Subcontractors and Suppliers in Japan). Chosa Kenkyu Hokoku No. 19. Tokyo: Chusho Kigyo Kenkyu Sentaa.

Kishigawa, Tadayoshi. 1956. "Shitauke Kigyo no Jittai to Shitauke Kigyo Daikin Chiharai Mondai" (Status of Subcontractors and the Issue of Payment Delays to Them). *Kotori* (February), pp. 30–39.

Klein, Benjamin. 1988. "Vertical Integration as Organizational Ownership: The Fisher Body—General Motors Relationship Revisited." *Journal of Law, Economics, and Organization* 4(1):199–213.

Klein, Benjamin, R.A. Crawford and Armen A. Alchian. 1978. "Vertical Integration, Appropriable Rents, and the Competitive Contracting Process." *Journal of Law and Economics* (October), pp. 297–326.

Klein, Benjamin and K.B. Leffler. 1981. "The Role of Market Forces in Assuring Contractual Performance." *Journal of Political Economy* (August), pp. 615–41.

Knickerbocker, Frederick. 1976. "Note on the Watch Industries in Switzerland, Japan, and the United States." Case Note #9–373–090, revised September 1976. Boston: Harvard Business School Cases.

Kobayashi, Yoshio. 1969. "Chusho Kigyo Jiritsuka Mondai to sono Genjitsu" (Issues and Reality of the Independence of Small and Medium Scale Firms). *Chosa Jiho* (Chusho Kigyo Kinyu Koko) (September), pp. 53–60.

Kodaira, Katsumi. 1968. *Jidosha* (Automobiles). Tokyo: Aki Shobo.

Koike, Kazuo. 1981. *Chusho Kigyo no Jukuren—Jinzai Keisei no Shikumi* (Training in Small and Medium Scale Enterprises: Patterns of Human Capital Formation). Tokyo: Dobunsha.

———— 1983. "Internal Labor Markets: Workers in Large Firms." In Taishiro Shirai, ed., *Contemporary Industrial Relations in Japan*. Madison: University of Wisconsin Press.

———— 1983. "Workers in Small Firms and Women in Industry." In Taishiro Shirai, ed., *Contemporary Industrial Relations in Japan*. Madison: University of Wisconsin Press.

———— 1983. "The Formation of Worker Skill in Small Japanese Firms." *Japanese Economic Studies* (Summer), pp. 3–57.

———— 1988. *Understanding Industrial Relations in Modern Japan*. New York: St. Martin's Press.

Kokumin Kinyu Koko Chosabu. 1982. *Nihon no Chusho Kikai Kogyo.* Gyoshu-betsu Chusho Kigyo Series No. 10. Tokyo: Chusho Kigyo Research Center.

Komiya, Ryutaro, Masahiro Okuno and Kotaro Suzumura, eds. 1984. *Nihon no Sangyo Seisaku* (Japanese Industrial Policy). Tokyo: University of Tokyo Press. Translated as *Industrial Policy of Japan.* Tokyo: Academic Press, 1988.

Komiyama, Takuji. 1941. *Nihon Chusho Kigyo Kenyu* (Studies of Japanese Small and Medium Scale Manufacturers). Tokyo: Chuo Koron Sha.

Kosei Torihiki Iinkai (Fair Trade Commission). 1959. *Jidosha Kogyo no Keizairyoku Shuchu no Jittai* (An Analysis of the Concentration of Economic Power in the Automotive Industry). Tokyo: Kosei Torihiki Kyokai.

Krafcik, John. 1988a. "Comparative Analysis of Performance Indicators at World Auto Assembly Plants." MSc dissertation, Sloan School of Management, MIT.

—— 1988b. "A Summary of Findings and Future Research in Manufacturing Practice." MIT International Motor Vehicle Program.

—— 1988c. "Triumph of the Lean Production System." *Sloan Management Review* (Fall), pp. 41–52.

Kreps, David M. 1990. *A Course in Microeconomic Theory.* Princeton: Princeton University Press.

Kyoikusha. 1980. *Jidosha Gyokai Joi 9–Sha no Keiei Hikaku* (Comparative Financial Results of the Nine Largest Listed Automotive Firms). Tokyo: Kyoikusha.

Kyushu Keizai Chosa Kyokai. 1974. *Jidosha Kogyo no Chiiki Bunsan to Chusho Kigyo no Taio: Hokubu Kyushu ni okeru Jiba Chusho Kikai Kinzoku wo chushin ni* (Geographic Diversification in the Automotive Industry and the Response of Small and Medium Scale Firms: A Case Study of Local Small and Medium Machinery and Metal-working Firms in Northern Kyushu). Kenkyu Hokoku No. 167. Fukuoka: Kyushu Keizai Chosa Kyokai.

Lall, Sanjaya. 1980. "Vertical Inter-Firm Linkages in LDCs: An Empirical Study." *Bulletin of the Oxford Institute of Economics and Statistics* (August), 42(3):203–26.

Landes, David S. 1985. *Revolution in Time: Clocks and the Making of the Modern World.* Cambridge: Harvard University Press.

Larson, Andrea L. 1988. "Cooperative Alliances: A Study of Entrepreneurship." Ph.D. dissertation, Harvard University.

—— 1990. "Partner Networks: Leveraging External Ties to Improve Entrepreneurial Performance." Draft paper, Darden School, University of Virginia.

Lorenz, Edward H. 1988. "Neither Friends nor Strangers: Informal Networks of Subcontracting in French Industry." In Diego Gambetta, ed., *Trust.* London: Blackwell.

Macauley, Stewart. 1963. "Non-Contractual Relations in Business." *American Sociological Review* 28:55–70.

Mair, Andrew, Richard Florida, and Martin Kenney. 1988. "The New Geography of Automobile Production: Japanese Transplants in North America." *Economic Geography* (October), 64(4):352–73.

Marsh, Robert M. and Hiroshi Mannari. 1976. *Modernization and the Japanese Factory*. Princeton: Princeton University Press.

Matsubashi, Koji. 1982. "Ryomo Chiku Jidosha Kanren Shitauke Kogyo no Zonritsu Kozo: Nissan Kei Niji Shitauke Kigyozo wo chushin ni" (The Economic Basis for Auto-related Subcontractors in the Ryomo District: A Study Primarily of Secondary Subcontractors to Nissan). *Keizai Chirigaku Nenpo* (Annals of the Association of Economic Geographers), 28(2):59–91.

Matsui, Toshiji. 1973. "Jidosha Kogyo ni okeru Shitauke Keiretsuka no Jittai (Jo)(Ge): Motokata Fukusuka Dankai no Kigyo Keiretsu ni tsuite" (An Empirical Study of Subcontracting Keiretsu in the Automotive Industry: On Keiretsu in an Era of Multiple Parent Firms, Parts I & II). *Ritsumeikan Keieigaku* 12(2):117–166, 12(4):369–404.

———— 1976. "Jidosha Kogyo ni okeru Keiretsuka no Shinten to 'Chuken Kigyo': Chuken Kigyo Hihan." *Ritsumeikan Keieigaku* (January), 14(6):75–106.

Matsumoto, Hisao and Takahiro Tsuchiya. 1971. "Shiirisaki kara no VE Teian ni taisuru Hoshu Seido no arikata ni tsuite" (Compensating Suppliers for their VE Proposals). *SJVE Nenkan* (Society of Japanese Value Engineers Yearbook), vol. 2.

Miles, Lawrence D. 1972. *Techniques of Value Analysis and Engineering*. 2d ed. New York: McGraw-Hill.

Minato, Tetsuo. 1982. "Nihon no Gijutsu Tokusei to Shitauke Seisan Shisutemu" (Distinctive Aspects of Technology in Japan and the Subcontracting Production System), *Shoko Kinyu* (July), 32(7):43–16.

Mito, Seiichi. 1982. *Kobai/Gaichu no Kosuto-daun* (Reducing Costs Through Purchasing). Tokyo: Chuo Keizai Sha.

Mitsubishi Keizai Kenkyusho and Nihon Kikai Kogyo Rengokai. 1965. *Buhin Meika Senmonka no Jittai Bunseki: Jidosha, Mishin, Jitensha, Kamera* (The Specialization of Parts Manufacturers in the Auto. Sewing Machine. Bicycle and Camera Industries), 1963–nendo Kikai Kogyo Kiso Chosa Hokokusho (FY1963 Report on the Basic Survey of the Machinery Industry), Tokyo: Nihon Kikai Kogyo Rengokai.

Mitsubishi Motors Corporation. 1982. "Mitsubishi Jidosha Kashiwa Kai ni tsuite" (The Mitsubishi Motors Kashiwa Kai). unpublished memo. Tokyo: Kobai Kanri Bu.

Miyashita, Kenji. 1971. *Nihon Teki Kyuyo Seido—Sono Koso to Sekkei & Unyo* (Japanese-Style Compensation Systems: Their Principles, Design and Operation). Tokyo: Nihon Noritsu Kyokai.

Monden, Yasuhiro. 1983. *Toyota Production System—Practical Approach to Production Management.* Atlanta: Industrial Engineering and Management Press.

Monteverde, Kirk and David Teece. 1982a. "Supplier Switching Costs and Vertical Integration in the Automobile Industry." *Bell Journal of Economics* (Spring), 13(1):206–213.

——— 1982b. "Appropriable Rents and Quasi Integration." *Journal of Law and Economics* (October), 25:321–28.

Mori, Goro, ed. 1978. *Shin Chusho Kigyo no Chingin Kanri* (Employee Compensation for Small Businesses: Revised). Tokyo: Nihon Rodo Kyokai.

Muto, Hiromichi. 1988. "The Automotive Industry." In Ryutaro Komiya, Masahiro Okuno and Kotaro Suzumura, eds., *Industrial Policy of Japan.* Tokyo: Academic Press.

Nakamura, Hideichiro. 1981. "Shitauke Kigyo no Saihyoka: Nihon-gata Sangyo Soshiki to Kanren sasete" (A Reevaluation of Subcontractors: Implications for Japanese-Style Industrial Organization Theory). *Chosa Jiho* (Chusho Kigyo Kinyu Koko) (July), pp. 11–23.

Nakamura, Hideichiro et al. 1981. *Gendai Chusho Kigyo Shi* (The History of Modern Small and Medium Scale Enterprises). Tokyo: Nihon Keizai Shimbun Sha.

Nakamura, Sei. 1981. "Shitauke Sei no Jun Suichoku Togoteki Seikaku" (Quasi-Vertical Integration Aspects of the Subcontracting System). *Shoko Kinyu* (November), 31(11):3–15.

Nakamura, Seiji. 1983. *Gendai Jidosha Kogyo Ron* (A Study of the Contemporary Automotive Industry). Tokyo: Yuhikaku.

——— 1953. *Nihon Jidosha Kogyo Hattenshi Ron* (An Essay on the Development of the Japanese Automotive Industry). Tokyo: Keiso Shobo.

——— 1957. *Nihon no Jidosha Kogyo* (The Japanese Automotive Industry). Tokyo: Nihon Hyoron Sha.

Nakamura, Tsutomu. 1983. *Chusho Kigyo to Daikigyo: Nihon no Sangyo Hatten to Jun Suichokuteki Toto* (Small and Large Firms: The Development of Japanese Industry and Vertical Quasi-Integration). Toyo Keizai Shimpo Sha.

Nakane, Chie. 1970. *Japanese Society.* Berkeley: University of California Press.

National Productivity Council (India). 1966. *Ancillary Industries for Automobile Manufacturing in Japan.* Study Mission No. 1. New Delhi: Asian Productivity Organization.

Nihon Jidosha Buhin Kogyo Kai 1969. *Nihon Jidosha Buhin Koshi* (A Brief History of the Development of the Auto Parts Industry). Tokyo: Nihon Jidosha Buhin Kogyo Kai.

Nihon Keiesha Dantai Renmei (Japan Employers Federation). 1975. *Kigyo ni okeru Chingin Taikei no Jitsurei* (Handbook of Firm Compensation Systems). Tokyo: Nihon Keiesha Dantai Renmei.

Nihon Seisansei Honbu (Japan Productivity Organization). 1957. *Jidosha*

Buhin Kogyo: Jidosha Buhin Kogyo Seisansei Shisatsudan Hokoku-sho (The Auto Parts Industry: The Report of the Auto Parts Industry Productivity Study Tour). Productivity Report 5. Tokyo: Nihon Seisansei Honbu.

———— 1959. *Kikai Kogyo no Kindaika to Koyo Kozo* (Employment Structure and the Modernization of the Machine Industries). Tokyo: Nihon Seisansei Honbu.

———— 1965. *Nihon Keieishi* (Japanese Management History), vol. 3. Tokyo: Nihon Seisansei Honbu.

———— 1969. *Nihon Keieishi* (Japanese Management History), vol. 4. Tokyo: Nihon Seisansei Honbu.

Nikkan Kogyo Shimbun. 1980. *Toyota wo Sasaeru Kigyogun* (Toyota's Suppliers: Its Foundation for Success). Tokyo: Nikkan Kogyo Shimbun.

Nishiguchi, Toshihiro. 1989. "Japanese Subcontracting: Evolution Towards Flexibility." Ph.D. dissertation, Oxford University.

Nissan Jidosha. 1976. *Nissan Jidosha Shashi: 1964–1973* (History of Nissan, 1964–73). Tokyo: Nissan Jidosha.

Nissan Jidosha Chosabu. 1983. *Jidosha Kogyo Handobukku 1983 Nenpan* (Automotive Industry Handbook, 1983 edition). Tokyo: Nissan Jidosha.

Odaka, Konosuke. 1978. "The Place of Medium- and Small-Scale Firms in the Development of the Automobile Industry—A Study of Japan's Experience." CA Conference Paper. Tokyo: International Development Center of Japan.

———— 1981. "Senkanki ni Okeru Shitauke Kikai Buhin Kogyo Hattatsu no Sho Yoin" (Sources of the Development of Parts Subcontractors in the Interwar Period). In Takafusa Nakamura, ed., *Senkanki no Nihon Keizai Bunseki* (Analysis of Japan's Interwar Economy). Tokyo: Yamakawa Shuppansha.

———— 1984. *Rodo Shijo Bunseki* (An Analysis of the Labor Market), Tokyo: Iwanami Shoten.

———— 1985. "Is the Division of Labor Determined by the Extent of the Market?: A Study of Automobile Parts Production in East and Southeast Asia." In Kazushi Ohkawa and Gustav Ranis, eds., *Japan and the Developing Countries: A Comparative Analysis.* Oxford: Basil Blackwell for the International Development Center of Japan and the Economic Growth Center of Yale.

Odaka, Konosuke, ed. 1983. *The Motor Vehicle Industry in Asia.* Singapore: University of Singapore for the Council on Asian Manpower Studies.

Odaka, Konosuke, Keinosuke Ono and Fumihiko Adachi. 1988. *The Automobile Industry in Japan: A Study in Ancillary Firm Development.* Tokyo: Kinokuniya Company and Oxford University Press.

OECD. 1988. *Industrial Revival Through Technology*. Paris: Organization for Economic Cooperation and Development.

Ogawa, Eiji. 1983. "Jidosha Kogyo ni okeru Shitauke Keiretsu Kozo (Ka)" (The Changing Structure of Subcontracting in the Automotive Industry, Part III). *Shoko Kinyu* (June), pp. 27–41.

Ogawa, Eiji and Yoshio Sato. 1979. "Kankyo Henka to Chusho Kigyo: Kikai Kogyo ni miru Zonritsu Kiban no Henka to Tenbo" (Small Business, the Changing Environment: The Shifting Economic Basis and Prospects for the Machinery Industry). *Shoko Kinyu* (July), 29(7):3–40.

Ojiro, Taromaru. 1970. *Nihon Chusho Kogyo Shiron* (Essays on the History of Japanese Small and Medium Scale Manufacturing). Keio Gijuku Keizai Gakkai Keizaigaku Kenkyu Sosho 11. Tokyo: Nihon Hyoron Sha.

Okamura, Hajime. 1974. *Yume to Wakasa to Sozo to—Honda no Jinji Kanri* (Creativity, Youth and Vision: Personnel Management at Honda). Tokyo: Kaihatsu Sha.

Okayama, Reiko. 1987. "Industrial Relations in the Japanese Automobile Industry 1945–70: The Case of Toyota." In Steven Tolliday and Jonathan Zeitlin, eds., *The Automobile Industry and Its Workers*. New York: St. Martin's Press.

Okazaki, Keiko. 1984. "Gendai Shitauke Kigyo no Jissho Bunseki" (An Empirical Study of Contemporary Subcontractors). *Kikan Gendai Keizai* (Summer), pp. 49–58.

Okochi, Kazuo, Bernard Karsh and Solomon B. Levine. 1974. *Workers and Employers in Japan*. Princeton: Princeton University Press.

Okochi, Kazuo and H. Shimokawa, eds. 1980. *Development of Mass Marketing in the Automobile Industry*. Tokyo: University of Tokyo Press.

Okumura, Hikaru. 1960. "Jidosha Buhin Kogyo: Shoreisai Saishitauke Kigyo wo Chushin ni" (Auto Parts Industry: Small-Scale and Household Sub-Subcontractors). In Ichiro Oshikawa et al., eds., *Chusho Kogyo ni okeru Gijitsu Shimpo no Jittai* (Studies of Technical Progress in Small- and Medium-Scale Manufacturing). Chusho Kigyo Kenkyu, vol. 5. Tokyo: Toyo Keizai Shimpo Sha.

———— 1962. "Jidosha Buhin Kogyo to Kozo Henka" (Changes in Industrial Structure: The Auto Parts Industry). In Ichiro Oshikawa et al., eds., *Kodo Seicho Katei ni okeru Chusho Kigyo no Kozo Henka* (Structural Changes of Smaller Firms under the Impact of Rapid Growth). Dainiji Chusho Kigyo Kenkyu, vol. 1. Tokyo: Toyo Keizai Shimpo Sha.

Okumura, Hiroshi, Junichi Hoshikawa and Kazuo Matsui. 1965. *Jidosha Kogyo* (The Automotive Industry). Gendai no Sangyo (Contemporary Industry) Series. Tokyo: Toyo Keizai Shimpo Sha.

Okumura, Shoji. 1960. "Jidosha Kogyo no Hatten Dankai to Kozo" (The Level of Development and Structure of the Automotive Industry). In Masao Kosaka, ed., *Kikai Kogyo* (Machinery Industries); vol. 5, part 1 of Hiromi Arisawa, general editor, *Gendai Nihon Sangyo Koza* (Studies on Modern Japanese Industry). Tokyo: Iwanami Shoten.

Ono, Akira. 1981. *Nihon no Rodo Shijo* (Japanese Labor Markets). Tokyo: Toyo Keizai Shimpo Sha.

Ono, Rei. 1980. *Gijutsu no Kyokugen ni Idomu Seiko Group* (The Seiko Group: Pushing the Limits of Technology). "Za Kaisha" (The Company) Series No. 15. Tokyo: Asahi Sonorama.

Ono, Toshio. 1980. "Nenko Chingin Sei-ka no Kojin-Kan Kakusa" (Interpersonal Pay Variation Under the Seniority Wage System). *Nihon Rodo Kyokai Zasshi* no. 2, pp. 2–12.

Ono, Tsuneo. 1980. "Postwar Changes in the Japanese Wage System." In Shunsaku Nishikawa, ed., *The Labor Market in Japan: Selected Readings.* Tokyo: University of Tokyo Press.

Ono, Yoshiyasu. 1986. "Subcontracting and Monopsony in Parts Acquisition." Discussion Paper #105 in Economics. Princeton: Woodrow Wilson School, Princeton University.

Osaka Furitsu Shoko Keizai Kenkyusho. 1968. "Purasuchikku Seihin no Kaihatsu niyoru Jidosha Kanren Chushokogyo no Eikyo: Aichi Chiku no Jittai" (The Impact of the Change to Plastics on Smaller Scale Auto Parts Firms). *Keiken Shiryo* no. 464.

Osaka Keizai Daigaku Chusho Kigyo Keiei Kenkyusho. 1978. *Chusho Kigyo Kenkyu—Choryu to Tenbo* (Small and Medium Enterprise Studies—Past Currents and Current Directions). Tokyo: Nichigai Asoshietsu.

Ouchi, Hyoe, ed. 1969. *Chiiki to Sangyo* (Industry to Regional Economies). Tokyo: Shin Hyoron.

Ozaki, Masahisa. 1955. *Jidosha Nihon Shi* (A History of Automobiles in Japan), vol. 1. Tokyo: Jikensha.

Paine, Susan. 1971. "Lessons for LDC's from Japan's Experience with Labour Commitment and Subcontracting in the Manufacturing Sector." *Bulletin of the Oxford Institute of Economics and Statistics* (May), 33(2):115–33.

Pascale, Richard Tanner and Anthony G. Athos. 1981. *The Art of Japanese Management: Applications for American Executives.* New York: Warner Books.

Pascale, Richard Tanner and Thomas P. Rohlen. 1983. "The Mazda Turnaround." *Journal of Japanese Studies* (Summer), 9(2):219–63.

Patrick, Hugh and Thomas P. Rohlen. 1987. "Japan's Small-Scale Family Enterprises." In Kozo Yamamura and Yasukichi Yasuba, eds., The Political Economy of Japan. Volume I: *The Domestic Transformation.*

Perry, Martin K. 1989. "Vertical Integration: Determinants and Effects." In Richard Schmalensee and Robert D. Willig, eds., *Handbook of Industrial Organization*, vol. 1. Amsterdam: North-Holland.

Piore, Michael and Charles F. Sabel. 1983. "Italian Small Business Development: Lessons for U.S. Industrial Policy." In John Zysman and Laura Tyson, eds., *American Industry in International Competition: Government Policies and Corporate Strategies*. Ithaca: Cornell University Press.

———— 1984. *The Second Industrial Divide: Possibilities for Prosperity*. New York: Basic Books.

Porter, Michael E. 1989. "Hattori-Seiko and the World Watch Industry in 1980: Teaching Note." Harvard Business School Case Study No. 5–390–074. Boston: Harvard Business School Publishing.

Press Kogyo. 1975. *Press Kogyo Goju-nen Shi* (50-year History). Kawasaki: Press Kogyo.

Prestowitz, Clyde. 1988. *Trading Places: How We Allowed Japan to Take the Lead*. New York: Basic Books.

Pucik, Vladimir. 1986. "White Collar Human Resource Management: A Comparison of the U.S. and Japanese Automobile Industries." In John Creighton Campbell, ed., *Entrepreneurship in a "Mature Industry."* Michigan Papers in Japanese Studies No. 14. Ann Arbor: Center for Japanese Studies, University of Michigan. Published originally in *Columbia Journal of World Business* (Fall 1984), pp. 87–94.

Radner, Roy. 1981. "Monitoring Cooperative Agreements in a Repeated Principal-Agent Relationship." *Econometrica* 49(5).

———— 1986. "The Internal Economy of Large Firms." *Economic Journal* 96(supplement):1–22.

Richardson, G. B. 1972. "The Organization of Industry." *Economic Journal* (September), 82(4):883–96.

Rodosha Chosa Kenkyu Kai (Laborer's Research Institute). 1983. *Jidosha: Shiriizu Rodosha no Jotai (3)* (The Automotive Industry: The Condition of the Laborer Series No. 3). Tokyo: Shinnihon Shuppan.

Rohlen, Thomas P. 1974. *For Harmony and Strength: Japanese White Collar Organization*. Berkeley: University of California Press.

Rosenbaum, James E. 1984. *Career Mobility in a Corporate Hierarchy*. Orlando, Fla.: Academic Press, Inc. (Harcourt Brace Jovanovich, publishers).

Sah, Raaj Kumar and Joseph Stiglitz. 1986. "The Architecture of Economic Systems: Hierarchies and Polyarchies." *American Economic Review* (September), 76(4):716–27.

Sakai, Yasutaka. 1965. *Kigyo Keiretsu to Sangyo Kozo* (Industrial Organization: Vertical Firm Groupings). Tokyo: Nihon Hyoron Sha.

Sakamoto, Kazuichi. 1985. *Gijutsu Kakushin to Kigyo Kozo* (Enterprise Structure and the Technological Revolution). Tokyo: Minerva Shobo.

Sakayori, Toshio and Tadao Takagi, eds. 1975. *Gendai Nihon no Rodosha* (Labor in Contemporary Japan). Tokyo: Nihon Hyoron Sha.

Sakiya, Tetsuo. 1982. *Honda Motor: The Men, The Management, The Machines.* Tokyo: Kodansha International.

Sako, Mari. 1988. "Neither Markets nor Hierarchies: A Comparative Study of Informal Networks in the Printed Circuit Board Industry." Madison, Wisc.: Conference on Comparing Capitalist Economies.

Sakurabayashi, Makoto. 1979. "Kigyo-betsu Rodo Shijo Kiban wo Chushin to shite" (On the Foundation of Firm-Specific Labor Markets). *Nihon Rodo Kyokai Zasshi* no. 11, pp. 14–25.

Sasawara, Senzuru. 1934. "Chusho Kogyo to Kogyo Kaikei Nitsuite" (Small Industry and Cost Accounting). *Shakai Seisaku Jiho* (December), no. 171, pp. 136–51.

Sato, Yoshio. 1983. "Jidosha Kogyo ni okeru Shitauke Keiretsu Kozo (Jo)" (The Structure of Subcontracting in the Automotive Industry, part 1), *Shoko Kinyu* (May), pp. 3–21.

Sato, Yoshio, ed. 1981. *Kyodai Toshi no Reisai Kogyo: Toshi-gata Mattan Sangyo no Kozo Henka* (Small-Scale Enterprises in a Giant Metropolis: Changes in the Structure of Urban Industrial Districts). Tokyo: Nihon Keizai Hyoron Sha.

Schonberger, Howard B. 1989. *Aftermath of War: Americans and the Remaking of Japan, 1945–1952.* Kent, Ohio: Kent State University Press.

Sei, Shoichiro. 1977. "Jidosha Sangyo ni okeru Seisan Gorika to Shitauke Fukyo no Jittai" (The Influence of Rationalization in the Auto Industry and the Business Downturn Among Subcontractors). *Kikai Keizai Kenkyu* (June), 10:53–75.

———— 1982. "Japanese Automotive Parts Industry and Its Progress of Selection." *Engineering Industries of Japan* (June), no. 22, pp. 1–54.

———— 1983. "Japanese Automotive Parts Industry and Its Progress of Selection." *Engineering Industries of Japan* (June), no. 23, pp. 41–52.

———— 1984. "Jidosha Sangyo ni okeru Juzoteki Seisan Kozo no Keisei to Hatten" (The Formation and Development of the Vertical Structure of the Automotive Industry). In Kanagawa-ken, ed., *Kanagawa-ken Shi Kakuron Hen 2: Sangyo, Keizai Nukizuri* (Miscellaneous Essays on the History of Kanagawa Prefecture: vol. 2, Industry and Economics). Yokohama: Kanagawa Prefecture.

———— 1987. "The Electronic JIT System and Production Technology." Working Paper, First Policy Forum. Cambridge: MIT International Motor Vehicle Program.

Sei, Shoichiro, Harunobu Ohmori and Naohiko Nakajima. 1976. "Jidosha Buhin Kogyo ni okeru Seisan Kozo no Kenkyu" (A Study of the Structure of Production in the Auto Parts Industry). *Kikai Keizai Kenkyu* (August 1975 and June 1976), nos. 8 and 9.

Sheard, Paul. 1983. "Auto-production systems in Japan: organizational and locational features." *Australian Geographical Studies* 21(1): 49–68.

Sheriff, Antony. 1988. "The Competitive Product Position of Automobile Manufacturers: Performance and Strategies." Cambrdige: MIT International Motor Vehicle Program.

Shimokawa, Koichi. 1982a. "Development of the Supplier Relationship in Japan: Its Innovation and Production Flexibility." International Policy Forum, Hakone, Japan.

——— 1982b. "The Structure of the Auto Parts Industry and Its Contribution to Automotive Process Innovation." International Policy Forum, Hakone, Japan.

——— 1982c. "Nihon ni okeru Jidosha Meika: Buhin Meika Kankei to sono Bungyo Kozo no Rekishiteki Hatten to Gendaiteki Igi" (The Relationship Between Auto and Auto Part Manufacturers in Japan: The Historical Development of the Division of Labor and Its Contemporary Significance). *Keiei Shirin* (Hosei Daigaku) 19(2):23–47.

——— 1983a. "Sengo Nihon Jidosha Sangyo Keieishi ni tsuite" (Management History of the Postwar Japanese Auto Industry). *Bijinesu Rebyu* 31(2):53–66.

——— 1983b. "Nihon no Keiretsu Soshiki: Nihon Jidosha Sangyo no Jirei wo Chushin ni" (The Organization of Japanese Keiretsu: The Case of the Japanese Automotive Industry). *Soshiki Kagaku* (March), 17(1):25–36.

——— 1985. "Keiretsu and Subcontracting in Japan's Automobile Industry." *Japanese Economic Studies* (Summer), 13(4):3–31.

Shinohara, Miyohei. 1968. "A Survey of the Japanese Literature on Small Industry." In Bert F. Hoselitz, ed., *The Role of Small Industry in the Process of Economic Growth*. The Hague: Mouton.

Shiomi, Haruhito. 1985a. "Seisan Rogisutikkusu no Kozo: Toyota Jidosha no Keisu" (Production Logistics: The Case of Toyota Motors). In Kazuichi Sakamoto, ed., *Gijutsu Kakushin to Kigyo Kozo* (Enterprise Structure and Technological Revolution). Tokyo: Minerva Shobo.

——— 1985b. "Kigyo Gruupu no Kanriteki Togo: Nihon Jidosha Sangyo ni okeru Buhin Torihiki no Jissh Bunseki" (Centralization of Management in Firm Groups: An Empirical Analysis of Parts Transactions in the Japanese Automotive Industry). *Oikonomika (Nagoya Shiritsu Daigaku Keizai Gakkai)* (June), 22(1):1–36.

Shirai, Taishiro, ed. 1983. *Contemporary Industrial Relations in Japan*. Madison: University of Wisconsin Press.

Shiroyama, Saburo. 1982. *Yusha wa Katarazu* (The Brave Remain Silent). Tokyo: Shinchosha.

Shirozawa, Teruo. 1975. *Jidosha Sangyo* (The Automotive Industry). Sangyokai Shirizu 3. Tokyo: Kyoikusha Shinsho.

Shizuoka-Ken Chusho Kigyo Seisaku Kenkyukai (Shizuoka Prefecture Small and Medium Scale Enterprise Policy Research Committee). 1979. *Gekido-ka no Chusho Kigyo* (Small and Medium Scale Enterprises Under Rapid Economic Change). Tokyo: Gyosei.

Shoko Kumiai Chuo Kinko. 1971. *Shitauke Chusho Kigyo no Jittai: Shitauke Kigyo 4363–sha wo taisho ni shita Jittai Chosa Hokokusho* (The Status of Small- and Medium-Scale Subcontractors: A Report on a Survey of 4.363 Firms), Tokyo: Yaesu Shoko.

——— 1977. *Shitauke Chusho Kigyo no Genkyo: Antei Seicho Keizaika ni ikiru Michi* (The Status of Small- and Medium-Scale Subcontractors). Tokyo: Yaesu Shoko.

Silin, Robert H. 1972. "Marketing and Credit in a Hong Kong Wholesale Market." In W.E. Willmott, ed., *Economic Organization in China.* Stanford: Stanford University Press.

Silver, Morris. 1984. *Enterprise and the Scope of the Firm.* London: Blackwell.

SJVE. 1985. *Part I, Value Analysis Study Tour and Part II, Value Analysis / Value Engineering in Japan, A 1985 Overview.* Tokyo: Society of Japanese Value Engineering.

Smith, Robert J. 1989. "Presidential Address: Something Old, Something New—Tradition and Culture in the Study of Japan." *Journal of Asian Studies* (November), 48(4):715–723.

Smitka, Michael. 1989. "American Management: Reformation or Revolution? The Transfer of Japanese Management Technology to the US." Working Paper No. 37, Center for Japanese Economy and Business, Graduate School of Business, Columbia University.

——— 1990a. "Business-Business Relations: Auto Parts Sourcing in Japan." *Japan's Economic Challenge* Joint Economic Committee, U.S. Congress.

——— 1990b. "The Invisible Handshake: The Development of the Japanese Automotive Parts Industry." *Economic and Business History,* 2nd series, 19:163–171.

Spengler, Manfred L. 1988. "Value Analysis / Value Engineering / Value Management." *Proceedings, Spring 1988 International Conference of the Institute of Industrial Engineers,* Orlando, Fla: Institute of Industrial Engineers.

Stein, Guenther. 1935. *Made in Japan.* London: Methuen.

Sterling, William. 1984. *Comparative Studies of American and Japanese Labor Markets.* Ph.D. dissertation, Harvard University.

Stigler, George. 1951. "The Division of Labor is Limited by the Extent of the Market." *Journal of Political Economy* (June), 59(3): 185–93.

Stoll, Henry W. 1988. "Design for Manufacture." *Manufacturing Engineering* (January), pp. 67–73.

Stuckey, John A. 1983. *Vertical Integration and Joint Ventures in the Alu-*

minum Industry. Harvard Economic Studies, vol. 152. Cambridge: Harvard University Press.

Sugita, Toshio. 1982. *Insatsu, Seihan Gyokai* (The Printing and Bookmaking Industry). Sangyokai Series No. 340. Tokyo: Kyoikusha Shinsho.

Sumiya, Mikio. 1976. *Nihon Chinrodo no Shiteki Kenkyu* (Historical Studies of Wage Labor in Japan). Tokyo: Ochanomizu Shobo.

———— 1980. "Teinen Sei no Keisei to Shushin Koyo" (Permanent Employment and the Development of the Retirement System). *Nenpo: Nihon no Roshi Kankei* (Yearbook of Japanese Labor Relations). Tokyo: Nihon Rodo Kyokai.

Suzuki, Haruo. 1969. *Chusho Kigyo ni Hataraku Hitobito* (Those Who Work in Small Businesses). JIL Bunko 49. Tokyo: Nihon Rodo Kyokai.

Suzuki Motors. 1970. *50–Nen Shi: Suzuki Jidosha Kogyo* (50–Year History, Suzuki Motors). Shizuoka: Suzuki Motors.

Taira, Koji. 1970. *Economic Development and the Labor Market in Japan.* New York: Columbia University Press.

———— 1989. "Human Resource Management and Industrial Relations in the United States: Japanization of America or Americanization of Japanese Techniques?" presented to the Association of Japanese Business Studies meeting.

Takagi, Tadao and Kaneyoshi Fukami. 1974. *Chingin Taikei to Rodo Kumiai: Jokan* (Labor Unions and the Wage Structure: vol. 1). Tokyo: Rodo Junpo Sha.

Takanashi, Sho. 1980. "Rinji & Shagaiko Rodo Shijo no Henbo to Koyo Seisaku" (Changes in Labor Policy and the Changes in the Labor Market for Temporary Workers and Inside Subcontractors). ch. 3, sect. 2. In *Nenpo: Nihon no Roshi Kankei* (Yearbook of Japanese Labor Relations). Tokyo: Nihon Rodo Kyokai.

Takeshita, Shozo. 1967. "Mizushima Chiku Buhin Kogyo no Doko to Mondaiten" Trends and Issues for Parts Firms in Mizushima. ch. 2, sect. 3. In *Nihon no Jidosha Buhin Kogyo.* Tokyo: Auto Trade Journal.

Takeuchi, Hiroshi. 1974. "Kosaku Kikai" (Machine Tools), in Miyohei Shinohara and Masao Baba, eds., *Gendai Sangyo Ron 2: Sangyo Soshiki* (Studies on Modern Industry: vol. 2, Industrial Organization). Tokyo: Nihon Keizai Shimpo Sha.

Takeuchi, Masami. 1962. "Sosetsu" (General Introduction). In Ichiro Oshikawa et al., eds., *Kodo Seicho Katei ni okeru Chusho Kigyo no Kozo Henka* (Structural Changes of Smaller Firms under the Impact of Rapid Growth). Dainiji Chusho Kigyo Kenkyu, vol. 3. Tokyo: Toyo Keizai Shimpo Sha.

Takizawa, Kikutaro. 1965. *Nihon Kogyo no Kozo Bunseki* (Analysis of the Structure of Japanese Industry). Tokyo: Shunju Sha.

———— 1966. "Kozo Hendo Katei ni okeru Chusho Kikai Kogyo no Zonritsu Kiban" (The Economic Base of Small Scale Manufacturing in the Face of Structural Change). *Chosa Geppo* (Chusho Kigyo Kinyu Koko) (March), 7(4):11–45.

—— 1983. "Jidosha Kogyo ni okeru Shitauke Keiretsu Kozo" (The Changing Structure of Subcontracting in the Automotive Industry.) *Shoko Kinyu* (June), 33(6):3–26.

(Takugin) Chosa Geppo 1983. "Wagakuni Tokei Sangyo no Genjo to Kadai" (Current Status and Issues in the Domestic Timepiece Industry). (Takugin) *Chosa Geppo* (February), no. 371, pp. 8–56.

Tanaka, Minoru. 1981. "Jidosha Yohin no Ryutsu Kozo to Shijo Doko" (The Parts Aftermarket: Distribution System and Market). *Shoko Kinyu* (January), 31(1):28–45.

Tang, Roger Y. W. 1979. *Transfer Pricing Practices in the United States and Japan*. New York: Praeger Publishers.

Taniguchi, Akitake. 1985. "Jigyobu Sei Soshiki no Gendankai: Toshiba no Keisu" (Divisionalization in Japanese Firms: The Case of Toshiba). In Kazuichi Sakamoto, ed., *Gijutsu Kakushin to Kigyo Kozo* (Enterprise Structure and Technological Revolution). Tokyo: Minerva Shobo.

Teece, David J., Henry Ogden Armour and Garth Saloner. 1980. "Vertical Integration and Risk Reduction." Stanford Graduate School of Business Research Paper No. 563.

Telser, Lester. 1987. *A Theory of Efficient Cooperation and Competition*. Cambridge: Cambridge University Press.

Tokyo-to Keizai Kyoku. 1963. *Tokyo-to Jidosha Buhin Kogyo no Jittai Bunseki, Showa 37 Nendo* (Auto Parts Manufacturers in Tokyo. FY 1962 Survey), Chosa Shiryo 37–4.

—— 1964. *Shitauke Kigyo Keiretsu Chosa Hokokusho* (Report on the Survey of Subcontracting Keiretsu).

Tomiyama, Kazuo. 1973. *Nihon no Jidosha Sangyo: Kuruma wa do Kawaru ka* (The Japanese Automotive Industry: How Will Automobiles Change?). Tokyo: Toyo Keizai Shimpo Sha.

Townsend, Robert M. 1982. "Optimal Multiperiod Contracts and the Gain from Enduring Relationships under Private Information." *Journal of Political Economy* (December), 90(6):1166–1186.

Uchihashi, Katsuo. 1978. *Zoku: Takumi no Jidai* (An Age of Heroes: Continued). Tokyo: Sankei Shuppan.

Udagawa, Masaru. 1981. "Jidosha Seizo Jigyoho no Seitei to Gaishikei-gaisha no Taio" (The Passage of the Auto Industry Law and the Response of the Foreign Manufacturers). In Moriaki Tsuchiya and Hidemasa Morikawa, eds., *Kigyosha Katsudo no Shiteki Kenkyu* (Historical Studies of Entrepreneurship). Tokyo: Nihon Keizai Shimbun Sha.

—— 1985. "The Prewar Japanese Automobile Industry and American Manufacturers." *Japanese Yearbook on Business History: 1985*. Tokyo: Japanese Business History Institute.

Ueda, Koshi. 1987. "Jidosha Sangyo in okeru Shitauke Kanri: "A"-sha no

1970–nendai no Hinshitsu, Nonyu, Kakaku Kanri wo chushin ni"
(Supplier Management in the Automotive Industry: Quality, Delivery and Price Controls in the 1970s at Company A). *Shoko Kinyu* (December), pp. 3–23.

Uekusa Masu. 1982. *Sangyo Soshiki Ron* (Industrial Organization Theory). Tokyo: Chikuma Shobo.

Ueno, Hiroya and Hiromichi Muto. 1973. "Jidosha" (Automobiles). In Hisao Kumagai, ed., *Nihon no Sangyo Soshiki* (Industrial Organization in Japan), vol. 1. Tokyo: Chuo Koron Sha.

——— 1974. "The Automobile Industry of Japan." *Japanese Economic Studies* (Fall), 3(1):3–90. (Partial Translation of 1973.)

Umeki, Akira. 1984. *Ashita wo Ikiru Chusho Kigyo: Soi to Kufu wa Keiei no Sasae* (For a Small Business to Survive: Inventiveness and Effort as the Key to Management). Tokyo: Chusho Kigyo Research Sentaa.

UNIDO. 1974. *Subcontracting for Modernizing Economies.* New York: United Nations.

U.S. Congress. Office of Technology Assessment. 1990. *Making Things Better: Competing in Manufacturing.* OTA-ITE-433. Washington, D.C.: GPO.

U.S. International Trade Administration. 1988. *Proceedings of the Conference on Selling Auto Parts to the Japanese.* Indianapolis, Indiana, May 27 and 28, 1987. Washington, D.C: GPO.

U.S. International Trade Commission. 1987. *U.S. Global Competitiveness: The U.S. Automotive Parts Industry.* USITC Publication 2037.

Uyterhoeven, Hugo. 1972. "Timex Corporation." Case Study #373–080. Boston: Harvard Business School Case Services.

Vancil, Richard F. 1979. *Decentralization: Management Ambiguity by Design.* Financial Executives Research Foundation. Homewood, Ill.: Dow Jones—Irwin.

Vogel, Ezra. 1971. *Japan's New Middle Class: The Salary Man and His Family in a Tokyo Suburb.* 2nd ed. Berkeley: University of California Press.

Wada, Junzo. 1976. "A Case History of Guidance and Upgrading of Sub-Contracting Firms." In *Intra-National Transfer of Technology.* Tokyo: Asian Productivity Organization.

Walton, Richard E. 1985. "From Control to Commitment in the Workplace." *Harvard Business Review* (March-April), pp. 77–84.

Watanabe, Susumu. 1970. "Entrepreneurship in Small Enterprises in Japanese Manufacturing." *International Labor Review* (December), 102(6):531–76.

——— 1971. "Subcontracting, Industrialization and Employment Creation." *International Labor Review* (July-August), 104(1–2):51–76.

——— 1974. "Reflections on Current Policies for Promoting Small Enterprises and Subcontracting." *International Labor Review* (November), 110(5):405–22.

———, ed. 1983. *Technology, Marketing and Industrialization: Linkages between Large and Small Enterprises.* For the International Labor Office by Delhi: MacMillan India.

Williamson, Oliver E. 1975. *Markets and Hierarchies: Analysis and Anti-Trust Implications.* New York: Free Press.

——— 1983. "Credible Commitments: Using Hostages to Support Exchange." *American Economic Review* (September), 73(4):519–40.

——— 1985. *The Economic Institutions of Capitalism.* New York: Free Press.

——— 1986. "Vertical Integration." Working Paper Series D, Yale School of Management.

Womack, James P., Daniel T. Jones and Daniel Roos. 1990. *The Machine That Changes the World.* New York: Rawson.

Wood, Robert Chapman. 1980. "Japan's Multitier Wage System." *Forbes* August 18, pp. 53–58.

——— 1982. "Unlimited Partnerships." *Inc.* (November), 4(11):83–88.

——— 1984. *Small Business: Foundation of Japan's Best Known Successes.* Report Prepared for the U.S. Small Business Administration, Washington, DC.

Wright, J. Patrick. 1979. *On a Clear Day You Can See General Motors: John Z. DeLorean's Look Inside the Automotive Giant.* Grosse Pointe, Mich.: Wright Enterprises.

Wright, Gavin. 1987. "The Economic Revolution in the American South." *Journal of Economic Perspectives* (Summer), 1(1):161–178.

Yamamoto, Kiyoshi. 1978. "Jidosha Kogyo ni okeru Chingin Taikei" (Wage Structure in the Automotive Industry). *Shakai Kagaku Kenkyu* 30(1):176–205.

——— 1981. *Jidosha Sangyo no Roshi Kankei* (Labor Relations in the Automotive Industry). Tokyo: Tokyo Daigaku Shuppan Kai.

Yamamoto, Naokazu. 1959. *Nihon no Jidosha: Toyopetto Seicho Shi* (The Japanese Automotive Industry: The Development of the Toyota "Pet"). Tokyo: Sogen Sha.

Yamamoto, Soji 1961. *Nihon Jidosha Kogyo no Seicho to Henbo* (Growth and Change in the Japanese Automotive Industry), Tokyo: Sanei Shobo.

Yamazaki, Mitsuru. 1980. *Japan's Community-Based Industries: A Case Study of Small Industry.* Tokyo: Asian Productivity Organization.

Yano Keizai Kenkyusho (Yano Economic Consultants). 1967. *Nissan Takara Kai No Jittai to Ashita eno Tenbo* (Nissan Takara-kai: Current Structure and Future Changes). Aichi: Yano Keizai Kenkyusho.

Yokokura, Takashi. 1988. "Small Business." In Ryutaro Komiya, Masahiro Okuno and Kotaro Suzumura, eds., *Industrial Policy of Japan.* Tokyo: Academic Press.

Yoshii, Tadaaki. 1980. *Waarudo Kaa no Ohei: Mitsubishi Jidosha Kogyo* (Mitsubishi Motors: Vanguard of the World Car). Tokyo: Asahi Sonorama. Yoshino, Michael and Robert Lifson. 1986. *The Invisible Link: Japan's Sogo Shosha and the Organization of Trade.* Cambridge: MIT Press.

Index

Studies of the East Asian Institute

The Ladder of Success in Imperial China, by Ping-ti Ho. New York: Columbia University Press, 1962.

The Chinese Inflation, 1937–1949, by Shun-hsin Chou. New York: Columbia University Press, 1963.

Reformer in Modern China: Chang Chien, 1853–1926, by Samuel Chu. New York: Columbia University Press, 1965.

Research in Japanese Sources: A Guide, by Herschel Webb with the assistance of Marleigh Ryan. New York: Columbia University Press, 1965.

Society and Education in Japan, by Herbert Passin. New York: Teachers College Press, 1965.

Agricultural Production and Economic Developments in Japan, 1873– 1922, by James I. Nakamura. Princeton: Princeton University Press, 1967.

Japan's First Modern Novel: Ukigumo of Futabatei Shimei, by Marleigh Ryan. New York: Columbia University Press, 1967.

The Korean Communist Movement, 1918–1948, by Dae-Sook Suh. Princeton: Princeton University Press, 1967.

The First Vietnam Crisis, by Melvin Gurtov. New York: Columbia University Press, 1967.

Cadres, Bureaucracy, and Political Power in Communist China, by A. Doak Barnett. New York: Columbia University Press, 1968.

The Japanese Imperial Institution in the Tokugawa Period, by Herschel Webb. New York: Columbia University Press, 1968.

Higher Education and Business Recruitment in Japan, by Koya Azumi. New York: Teachers College Press, 1969.

The Communists and Peasant Rebellions: A Study in the Rewriting of Chinese History, by James P. Harrison, Jr. New York: Atheneum, 1969.

How the Conservatives Rule Japan, by Nathaniel B. Thayer. Princeton: Princeton University Press, 1969.

Aspects of Chinese Education, edited by C. T. Hu. New York: Teachers College Press, 1970.

Documents of Korean Communism, 1918–1948, by Dae-Sook Suh. Princeton: Princeton University Press, 1970.

Japanese Education: A Bibliography of Materials in the English Language, by Herbert Passin. New York: Teachers College Press, 1970.

Economic Development and the Labor Market in Japan, by Koji Taira. New York: Columbia University Press, 1970.

The Japanese Oligarchy and the Russo-Japanese War, by Shumpei Okamoto. New York: Columbia University Press, 1970.

Imperial Restoration in Medieval Japan, by H. Paul Varley. New York: Columbia University Press, 1971.

Japan's Postwar Defense Policy, 1947–1968, by Martin E. Weinstein. New York: Columbia University Press, 1971.

Election Campaigning Japanese Style, by Gerald L. Curtis. New York: Columbia University Press, 1971.

China and Russia: The "Great Game," by O. Edmund Clubb. New York: Columbia University Press, 1971.

Money and Monetary Policy in Communist China, by Katharine Huang Hsiao. New York: Columbia University Press, 1971.

The District Magistrate in Late Imperial China, by John R. Watt. New York: Columbia University Press, 1972.

Law and Policy in China's Foreign Relations: A Study of Attitude and Practice, by James C. Hsiung. New York: Columbia University Press, 1972.

Pearl Harbor as History: Japanese-American Relations, 1931–1941, edited by Dorothy Borg and Shumpei Okamoto, with the assistance of Dale K. A. Finlayson. New York: Columbia University Press, 1973.

Japanese Culture: A Short History, by H. Paul Varley. New York: Praeger, 1973.

Doctors in Politics: The Political Life of the Japan Medical Association, by William E. Steslicke. New York: Praeger, 1973.

The Japan Teachers Union: A Radical Interest Group in Japanese Politics, by Donald Ray Thurston. Princeton: Princton University Press, 1973.

Japan's Foreign Policy, 1868–1941: A Research Guide, edited by James William Morley. New York: Columbia University Press, 1974.

Palace and Politics in Prewar Japan, by David Anson Titus. New York: Columbia University Press, 1974.

The Idea of China: Essays in Geographic Myth and Theory, by Andrew March. Devon, England: David and Charles, 1974.

Origins of the Cultural Revolution, by Roderick MacFarquhar. New York: Columbia University Press, 1974.

Shiba Kōkan: Artist, Innovator, and Pioneer in the Westernization of Japan, by Calvin L. French. Tokyo: Weatherhill, 1974.

Insei: Abdicated Sovereigns in the Politics of Late Heian Japan, by G. Cameron Hurst. New York: Columbia University Press, 1975.

Embassy at War, by Harold Joyce Noble. Edited with an introduction by Frank Baldwin, Jr. Seattle: University of Washington Press, 1975.

Rebels and Bureaucrats: China's December 9ers, by John Israel and Donald W. Klein. Berkeley: University of California Press, 1975.

Deterrent Diplomacy, edited by James William Morley. New York: Columbia University Press, 1976.

House United, House Divided: The Chinese Family in Taiwan, by Myron
L. Cohen. New York: Columbia University Press, 1976.
*Escape from Predicament: Neo-Confucianism and China's Evolving Polit-
ical Culture,* by Thomas A. Metzger. New York: Columbia Univer-
sity Press, 1976.
*Cadres, Commanders, and Commissars: The Training of the Chinese
Communist Leadership, 1920–45,* by Jane L. Price. Boulder, Colo.:
Westview Press, 1976.
Sun Yat-Sen: Frustrated Patriot, by C. Martin Wilbur. New York: Colum-
bia University Press, 1977.
Japanese International Negotiating Style, by Michael Blaker. New York:
Columbia University Press, 1977.
Contemporary Japanese Budget Politics, by John Creighton Campbell.
Berkeley: University of California Press, 1977.
The Medieval Chinese Oligarchy, by David Johnson. Boulder, Colo.: West-
view Press, 1977.
*The Arms of Kiangnan: Modernization in the Chinese Ordnance Industry,
1860–1895,* by Thomas L. Kennedy. Boulder, Colo.: Westview Press,
1978.
Patterns of Japanese Policymaking: Experiences from Higher Education,
by T. J. Pempel. Boulder, Colo.: Westview Press, 1978.
*The Chinese Connection: Roger S. Greene, Thomas W. Lamont, George E.
Sokolsky, and American-East Asian Relations,* by Warren I. Cohen.
New York: Columbia University Press, 1978.
Militarism in Modern China: The Career of Wu P'ei-fu, 1916–1939, by
Odoric Y. K. Wou. Folkestone, England: Dawson, 1978.
A Chinese Pioneer Family: The Lins of Wu-Feng, by Johanna Meskill.
Princeton University Press, 1979.
Perspectives on a Changing China, edited by Joshua A. Fogel and William
T. Rowe. Boulder, Colo.: Westview Press, 1979.
The Memoirs of Li Tsung-Jen, by T. K. Tong and Li Tsung-jen. Boulder,
Colo.: Westview Press, 1979.
*Unwelcome Muse: Chinese Literature in Shanghai and Peking, 1937–
1945,* by Edward Gunn. New York: Columbia University Press,
1979.
*Yenan and the Great Powers: The Origins of Chinese Communist Foreign
Policy,* by James Reardon-Anderson. New York: Columbia Univer-
sity Press, 1980.
Uncertain Years: Chinese-American Relations, 1947–1950, edited by Dor-
othy Borg and Waldo Heinrichs. New York: Columbia University
Press, 1980.
The Fateful Choice: Japan's Advance into Southeast Asia, edited by James
William Morley, New York: Columbia University Press, 1980.

Tanaka Giichi and Japan's China Policy, by William F. Morton. Folke-stone, England: Dawson, 1980; New York: St. Martin's Press, 1980.

The Origins of the Korean War: Liberation and the Emergence of Separate Regimes, 1945–1947, by Bruce Cumings. Princeton University Press, 1981.

Class Conflict in Chinese Socialism, by Richard Curt Kraus. New York: Columbia University Press, 1981.

Education Under Mao: Class and Competition in Canton Schools, by Jonathan Unger. New York: Columbia University Press, 1982.

Private Academies of Tokugawa Japan, by Richard Rubinger. Princeton: Princeton University Press, 1982.

Japan and the San Francisco Peace Settlement, by Michael M. Yoshitsu. New York: Columbia University Press, 1982.

New Frontiers in American-East Asian Relations: Essays Presented to Dorothy Borg, edited by Warren I. Cohen. New York: Columbia University Press, 1983.

The Origins of the Cultural Revolution: II, The Great Leap Forward, 1958–1960, by Roderick MacFarquhar. New York: Columbia University Press, 1983.

The China Quagmire: Japan's Expansion of the Asian Continent, 1933–1941, edited by James William Morley. New York: Columbia University Press, 1983.

Fragments of Rainbows: The Life and Poetry of Saito Mokichi, 1882–1953, by Amy Vladeck Heinrich. New York: Columbia University Press, 1983.

The U.S.-South Korean Alliance: Evolving Patterns of Security Relations, edited by Gerald L. Curtis and Sung-joo Han. Lexington, Mass.: Lexington Books, 1983.

Discovering History in China; American Historical Writing on the Recent Chinese Past, by Paul A. Cohen. New York: Columbia University Press, 1984.

The Foreign Policy of the Republic of Korea, edited by Youngnok Koo and Sungjoo Han. New York: Columbia University Press, 1984.

State and Diplomacy in Early Modern Japan, by Ronald Toby. Princeton: Princeton University Press, 1983.

Japan and the Asian Development Bank, by Dennis Yasutomo. New York: Praeger Publishers, 1983.

Japan Erupts: The London Naval Conference and the Manchurian Incident, edited by James W. Morley. New York: Columbia University Press, 1984.

Japanese Culture, third edition, revised, by Paul Varley. Honolulu: University of Hawaii Press, 1984.

Japan's Modern Myths: Ideology in the Late Meiji Period, by Carol Gluck. Princeton: Princeton University Press, 1985.

Shamans, Housewives, and other Restless Spirits: Women in Korean Ritual Life, by Laurel Kendell. Honolulu: University of Hawaii Press, 1985.

Human Rights in Contemporary China, by R. Randle Edwards, Louis Henkin, and Andrew J. Nathan. New York: Columbia University Press, 1986.

The Pacific Basin: New Challenges for the United States, edited by James W. Morley. New York: Academy of Political Science, 1986.

The Manner of Giving: Strategic Aid and Japanese Foreign Policy, by Dennis T. Yasutomo. Lexington, Mass.: Lexington Books, 1986.

Security Interdependence in the Asia Pacific Region, James W. Morley, Ed., Lexington, MA-DC: Heath and Co, 1986.

China's Political Economy: The Quest for Development Since 1949, by Carl Riskin. Oxford: Oxford University Press, 1987.

Anvil of Victory: The Communist Revolution in Manchuria, by Steven I. Levine. New York: Columbia University Press, 1987.

Single Sparks: China's Rural Revolutions, edited by Kathleen Hartford and Steven M. Goldstein. Armonk, N.Y.: M. E. Sharpe, 1987.

Urban Japanese Housewives: At Home and in the Community, by Anne E. Imamura. Honolulu: University of Hawaii Press, 1987.

China's Satellite Parties, by James D. Seymour. Armonk, N.Y.: M. E. Sharpe, 1987.

The Japanese Way of Politics, by Gerald. L. Curtis. New York: Columbia University Press, 1988.

Border Crossings: Studies in International History, by Christopher Thorne. Oxford & New York: Basil Blackwell, 1988.

The Indochina Tangle: China's Vietnam Policy, 1975–1979, by Robert S. Ross. New York: Columbia University Press, 1988.

Remaking Japan: The American Occupation as New Deal, by Theodore Cohen, Herbert Passin, ed. New York: The Free Press, 1987.

Kim Il Sung: The North Korean Leader, by Dae-Sook Suh. New York: Columbia University Press, 1988.

Japan and the World, 1853–1952: A Bibliographic Guide to Recent Scholarship in Japanese Foreign Relations, by Sadao Asada. New York: Columbia University Press, 1988.

Contending Approaches to the Political Economy of Taiwan, edited by Edwin A. Winckler and Susan Greenhalgh. Armonk, NY: M. E. Sharpe, 1988.

Aftermath of War: Americans and the Remaking of Japan, 1945–1952, by Howard B. Schonberger. Kent: Kent State University Press, 1989.

Suicidal Narrative in Modern Japan: The Case of Dazai Osamu, by Alan Wolfe. Princeton: Princeton University Press, 1990.

Neighborhood Tokyo, by Theodore C. Bestor. Stanford: Stanford University Press, 1989.

Missionaries of the Revolution: Soviet Advisers and Chinese Nationalism, by C. Martin Wilbur Julie Lien-ying How. Cambridge, MA: Harvard University Press, 1989.

Education in Japan, by Richard Rubinger and Beauchamp. Honolulu: University of Hawaii, 1989.

Financial Politics in Contemporary Japan, by Frances Rosenbluth. Ithaca: Cornell University Press, 1989.

Thailand and the United States: Development, Security and Foreign Aid by Robert Muscat. New York: Columbia University Press, 1990.

State Power, Finance and Industrialization of Korea, by Jung-Eun Woo. New York: Columbia University Press, 1990.

Anarchism and Chinese Political Culture, by Peter Zarrow. New York: Columbia University Press, 1990.

Competitive Ties: Subcontracting in the Japanese Automotive Industry, by Michael Smitka. New York: Columbia University Press, 1990.

China's Crisis: Dilemmas of Reform and Prospects for Democracy, by Andrew J. Nathan. Columbia University Press, 1990.

The Study of Change: Chemistry in China 1840–1949, by James Reardon-Anderson. New York: Cambridge University Press, 1991.

Explaining Economic Policy Failure: Japan and the 1969–1971 International Monetary Crisis, by Robert Angel. New York: Columbia University Press, 1991.

Pacific Basin Industries in Distress: Structural Adjustment and Trade Policy in the Nine Industrialized Economies, edited by Hugh T. Patrick with Larry Meissner. New York: Columbia University Press, 1991.

From Bureaucratic Polity to Liberal Corporatism: Business Associations and the New Political Economy of Thailand, by Anek Laothamatas. Boulder: Westview Press, 1991.